Fessenden Nott Otis

Isthmus of Panama. History of the Panama Railroad

And of the Pacific Mail Steamship Company

Fessenden Nott Otis

Isthmus of Panama. History of the Panama Railroad
And of the Pacific Mail Steamship Company

ISBN/EAN: 9783337212650

Printed in Europe, USA, Canada, Australia, Japan

Cover: Foto ©ninafisch / pixelio.de

More available books at **www.hansebooks.com**

ISTHMUS OF PANAMA.

HISTORY

OF

THE PANAMA RAILROAD;

AND OF THE

PACIFIC MAIL STEAMSHIP COMPANY.

TOGETHER WITH A

TRAVELLER'S GUIDE AND BUSINESS MAN'S HAND-BOOK
FOR THE PANAMA RAILROAD,

AND

THE LINES OF STEAMSHIPS CONNECTING IT WITH EUROPE, THE UNITED
STATES, THE NORTH AND SOUTH ATLANTIC AND PACIFIC
COASTS, CHINA, AUSTRALIA, AND JAPAN.

By F. N. OTIS, M.D.

WITH ILLUSTRATIONS BY THE AUTHOR.

NEW YORK:
HARPER & BROTHERS, PUBLISHERS,
FRANKLIN SQUARE.
1867.

Entered, according to Act of Congress, in the year one thousand eight hundred and sixty-seven, by

HARPER & BROTHERS,

In the Clerk's Office of the District Court of the Southern District of New York.

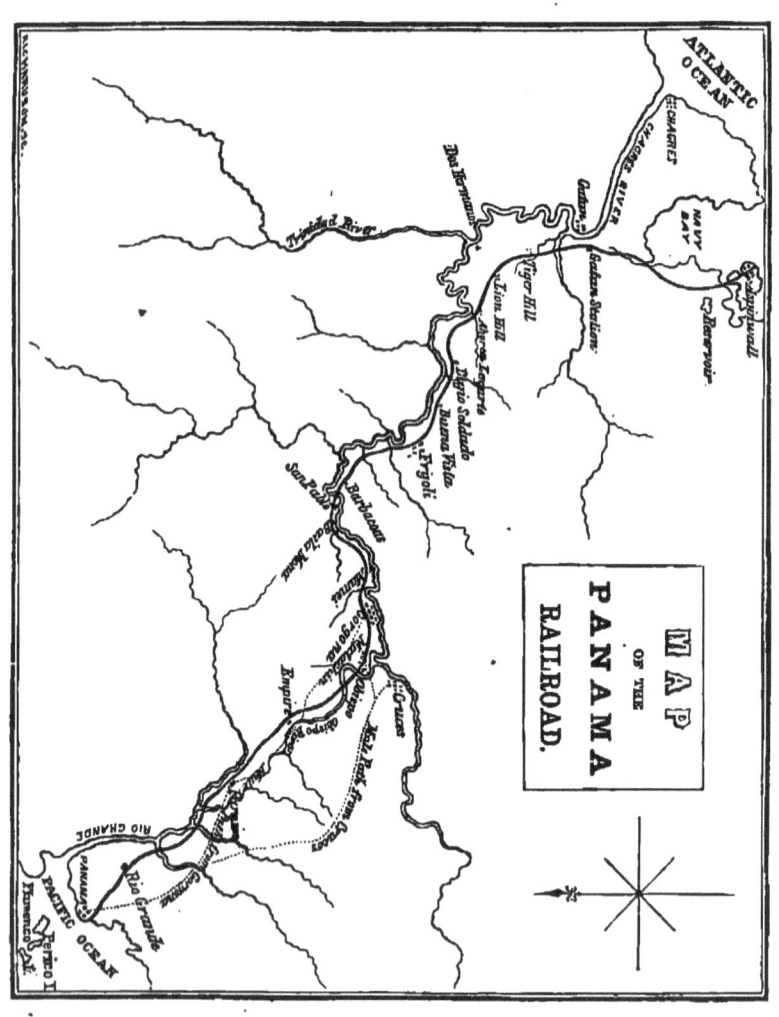

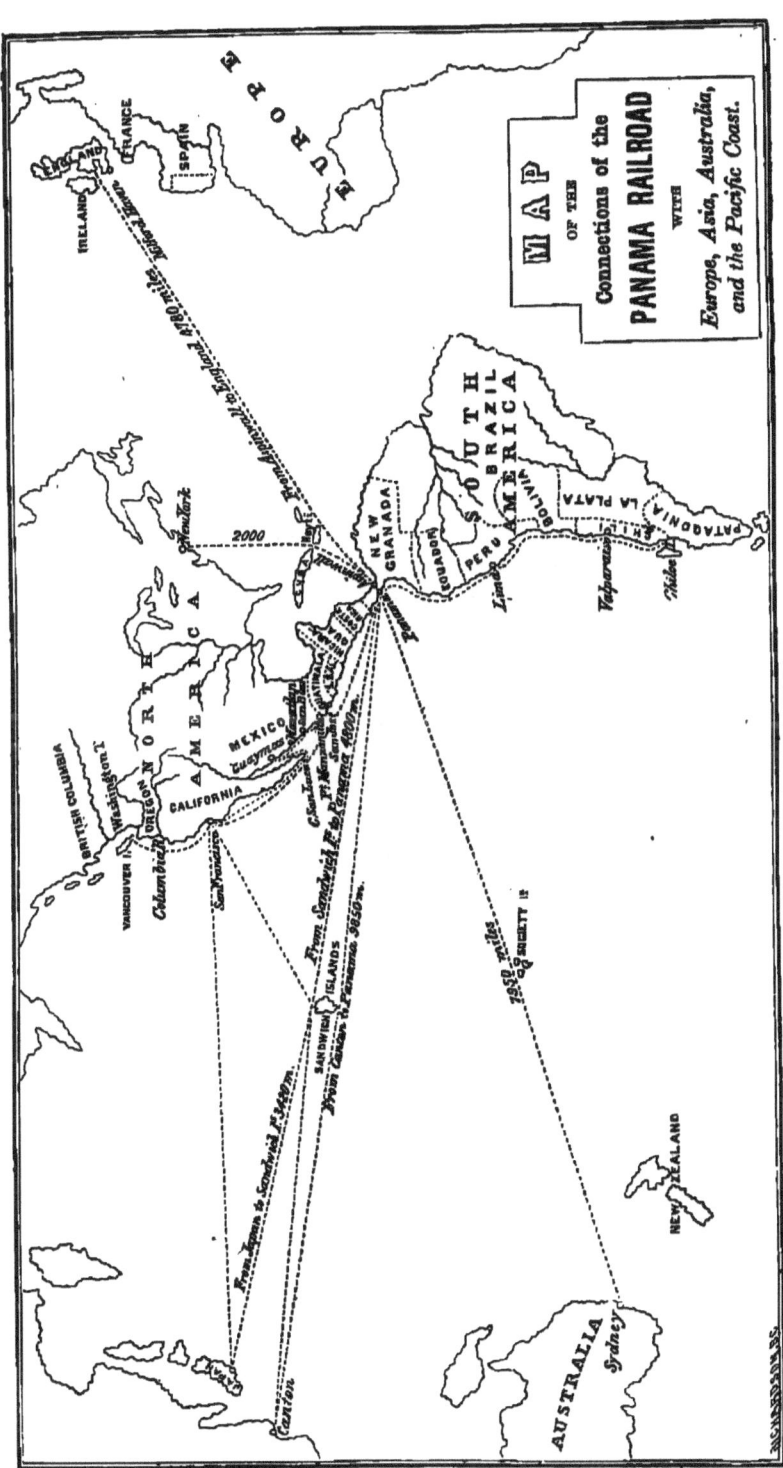

INTRODUCTION.

PURSUANT to a resolution offered by the Hon. Henry Clay, of Kentucky, in the Senate of the United States, in the year 1835, the President, General Andrew Jackson, appointed Mr. Charles Biddle, formerly of Philadelphia, then of Tennessee, as a commissioner to visit the different routes on the Continent of America best adapted for inter-oceanic communication, and to report thereon, with reference to their value to the commercial interests of the United States.

Mr. Biddle, accompanied by Dr. Gibbon, of Philadelphia, sailed from that port for St. Jago de Cuba, to gain preliminary information regarded to be important. Thirty years ago there existed few conveniences for an approach to the Isthmus of Panama. An occasional packet then plied between St. Jago de Cuba and Kingston, in the Island of Jamaica, and from thence some small vessel of the British navy conveyed a monthly mail to Chagres, which there crossed the Isthmus to the city of Panama for distribution on the Pacific coast. Mr. Biddle visited and remained for several months at these different points, in order to approach the objects of his mission with the best information attainable from merchants or travelers who had interests on the proposed routes or knowledge of their peculiarities. After gaining what information he was able at these points, Mr. Biddle proceeded to Chagres, then the only Atlantic port of the Isthmus, and pursued his journey up the Chagres River to Cruces, the head of boat navigation, making careful observations of the country through which he passed, with the view of its possible selection as the proposed railway route. From Cruces the party traveled on muleback to the port and city of Panama, which at this time was in a thoroughly dilapidated condition, maintaining a merely nominal trade with the neighboring Pacific ports, and even this wholly by means of foreign ships. The object of Mr. Biddle's visit being made known to the leading citizens of Panama, every facility was afforded by them for advancing his enterprise. The people of Gorgona cut a new road through the woods to communicate by portage with the head of the Rio Grande, which opens into the Pacific north of Panama. His varied means of information soon persuaded Mr. Biddle of the great importance of this route to the commerce of the United States, as well as to that of the Continents of America on each ocean, and Europe.

After a residence of several months in Panama, he decided to accompany the senators and members of Congress from the two provinces of the Isthmus to the seat of the national government at Bogota. Don José Obaldia, one of the representatives, exerted himself actively in promoting the enterprise, and was efficiently aided by the others. The perfect acquaintance of Señor Obaldia with the English language enabled him to be of much service to Mr. Biddle, which, together with his acknowledged influence among his countrymen, as well as with foreign residents at Bogota, certainly aided greatly in effecting the final arrangements.

Mr. Biddle had decided before he left Panama to offer propositions to the government of New Granada for a decree authorizing a company to construct a railroad across the continent through the Isthmus. A small Peruvian schooner conveyed the travelers to the mouth of the Buenaventura River, some 500 miles south of the Isthmus. Light canoes, manned by Indians, negroes, and boatmen of mixed blood, conveyed the party, with their servants and baggage, to the base of mountains near the Pacific, over which all were obliged to be carried in bamboo chairs on the backs of Indians, over almost perpendicular passages entirely inaccessible to mules. After several weeks of slow movement through a beautiful but thinly-settled country, the travel-worn and weary adventurers reached the city of Bogota. General M'Afee, of Kentucky, then Charge d'Affaires of the United States, promptly received the Americans into his house, and assisted to promote the views of Mr. Biddle, who at once proceeded to frame an application for a railroad privilege across the Isthmus of Panama, and which, without loss of time, was offered to the attention of the Congress by the representatives from the States of Veragua and Panama. After protracted delays, a law or decree finally passed both houses of legislation, making large grants of public lands, and conveying many important privileges to certain citizens of the United States in the event of their establishing a railroad across the Isthmus at Panama. The decree was regarded as sufficiently favorable to incline the capitalists of the United States, Europe, and New Granada to promote the success of the undertaking.

Mr. Biddle left the capital with an official copy of the decree granting the right to build a railroad across the Isthmus of Panama. After descending the Magdalena River to Carthagena, he reached the United States during the eventful year of 1837, at a period when a monetary crisis had deranged every facility or disposition for such an investment. Mr. Biddle considered the advantages of the Panama route to be superior to all other routes between the two oceans. He regarded his success in New Granada sufficient to warrant him in omitting farther investigations. The visit to the Central American and Tehauntepec routes was abandoned, although he was urgently solicited to undertake an inspection of both. Mr. Biddle died soon after his return from the Isthmus, without making any official report to the government.

CONTENTS.

	PAGE
HISTORY OF THE PANAMA RAILROAD	15–56
FINANCIAL STATEMENTS OF THE PANAMA RAILROAD, 1856-1861	59–69
TRAVELERS' GUIDE	70–134
REGULATIONS OF THE PANAMA RAILROAD	139–146
OFFICERS OF THE PANAMA RAILROAD COMPANY	147
STEAM-SHIP LINES CONNECTING WITH THE PANAMA RAILROAD	148
HISTORY OF THE PACIFIC MAIL STEAM-SHIP COMPANY	149–167
OFFICERS OF THE PACIFIC MAIL STEAM-SHIP COMPANY	168
GENERAL TRANSATLANTIC COMPANY	169–179
WEST INDIA AND PACIFIC STEAM-SHIP COMPANY	180–187
ROYAL MAIL STEAM PACKET COMPANY	188–205
PANAMA AND NEW ZEALAND COMPANY	205–215
PACIFIC MAIL STEAM NAVIGATION COMPANY	215–220
CALLAO DOCK COMPANY	221
PANAMA RAILROAD COMPANY'S CENTRAL AMERICAN STEAM-SHIP LINE	222–225
CALIFORNIA, OREGON, AND MEXICO STEAM-SHIP COMPANY	225, 226
PANAMA COMPANY'S LINE OF SAILING VESSELS	226, 227
WELLS, FARGO, AND CO.'S EXPRESS	228, 229
REPUBLICS OF CENTRAL AMERICA	235–260
REPUBLICS OF SOUTH AMERICA	263–302
MEXICO	303–307
CALIFORNIA, OREGON, ETC.	309–317

ILLUSTRATIONS.

ON THE ROAD	*Frontispiece.*
MAP—THE LINE OF THE PANAMA RAILROAD	Page 7
MAP—CONNECTIONS OF THE PANAMA RAILROAD	8
PORTRAIT OF GEORGE M. TOTTEN (*Chief Engineer*)	*To face page* 15
RUNNING THE LINES	19
PARAISO	23
THE FIRST SHANTY	30
ANCIENT BRIDGE, OLD PANAMA	37
THE CABILDO, PANAMA	43
VIEW FROM THE RAMPARTS, PANAMA	47
NORTHEASTERN RAMPART, PANAMA	53
SOUTHEASTERN RAMPART, PANAMA	57
VIEW OF ASPINWALL	72
PROTESTANT EPISCOPAL CHURCH OF ASPINWALL	80
DEPARTURE FOR PANAMA	83
MOUNT HOPE	88
GATUN STATION	94
STEPHENS'S TREE	99
BUJIO SOLDADO	102
STEPHENS'S COTTAGE	105
BREAD-FRUIT, STAR-APPLE, MANGO, AVOCADO PEAR	107
BARBACOAS BRIDGE	111
SAN PABLO STATION	114
NATIVE HUT AT MATACHIN	116
MAMBI STATION	117
MONUMENT HILL	119
BASALTIC CLIFF	123
PARAISO STATION	126
TERMINUS AT PANAMA	129
CITY OF PANAMA	132
CATHEDRAL AT PANAMA	135
RUINS OF CHURCH OF SAN DOMINGO	138
TOWER OF SAN JEROME	233
NATIVE BONGO, PANAMA	245

Eng^d by F. Halpin from a Photo. by Fredricks & Co.

HISTORY

OF

THE PANAMA RAILROAD.

IN ancient or in modern times there has, perhaps, been no one work which in a few brief years has accomplished so much, and which promises for the future so great benefit to the commercial interests of the world, as the present railway thoroughfare between the Atlantic and Pacific Oceans at the Isthmus of Panama. A glance at its geographical position can not fail to discover to the most casual observer that, situated as it is midway between the northern and southern, and alike between the eastern and western hemispheres, it forms a natural culminating point for the great commercial travel of the globe. Wise men in every enlightened nation had seen this for centuries, and had urged the importance of free interoceanic communication at this point; but its lofty and rugged mountain ranges, its deep and pestiferous morasses, seemed almost equally to defy the skill of the engineer and the physical endurance of the laborer. Even the possibility of opening such a communication by the government exercising jurisdiction over that portion of the isthmus through which it should pass had never been seriously entertained; but New Granada had long and earnestly challenged the more powerful nations of the world to break down this barrier to commerce and civilization, and reap the richest benefits which might result therefrom. England had looked toward the project with longing eyes, but quailed before the magnitude of the labor. France had done more—surveyed and entered into a contract to establish it; but too many millions were found necessary for its completion, and it was lost by default.

Events at last occurred which turned the attention of the American people to this transit, viz., the settlement of the northwestern boundary, by which we came into possession of Oregon, and the war with Mexico, which added California to our possessions. But, while the accession of these territories was of the highest importance to us in a national point of view, their distance rendered them almost inaccessible to the class of emigrants who usually settle our new domains, as well as inconvenient to the proper administration of law and government. Still, urged on by that pioneering spirit which seems inherent in the blood of the American, and invited by the prolific soil and genial climate of these distant possessions, and a prospect of a new and enlarged field for commercial pursuits, large numbers of our people migrated thither around Cape Horn. Congress, however, in 1848, in order to render these countries more accessible, authorized contracts to be entered into for the establishment of two mail lines of steam-ships, the one from New York and New Orleans to Chagres, and the other to connect with this by the Isthmus of Panama, from Panama to California and Oregon. The inducements to invest in these projects were not sufficient to attract the favorable attention of capitalists, and the contracts were taken by parties without means, who offered them for sale, and for a long time without success.

Men were at last found bold enough to venture upon the enterprise. Mr. William H. Aspinwall secured the line on the Pacific side, and George Law that on the Atlantic. In the Atlantic contract there was comparatively little risk, and a promise of almost immediate remuneration, as it connected with the cities of Savannah and New Orleans, and terminated at the portals of the Pacific Ocean. But the

Pacific contract was looked upon by the generality of business men as a certain sequestration of a large amount of property for an indefinite time, with a faint prospect of profit; and the wonder seemed to be that so sound a man as Mr. Aspinwall should have engaged in it. But it soon became evident that he expected no great profit from the steam-ship line *per se;* but that, with those enlarged and far-reaching views for which he is so justly noted, this line was only a part of the great plan which he had conceived, the remainder being embraced in the bold design of a railroad across the Isthmus of Panama; and at this time he, with Mr. Henry Chauncey and Mr. John L. Stephens, entered into a contract with the government of New Granada for the construction of that work. Mr. Chauncey, like Mr. Aspinwall, was a large-minded and public-spirited capitalist, whose integrity and straightforwardness were undoubted. Mr. Stephens possessed an experience in the country through which the road was to pass, and a knowledge of its geography and its inhabitants, gained by practical study and observation. These three gentlemen were associated together for the prosecution of this great enterprise, and shortly after, Mr. Stephens, accompanied by Mr. J. L. Baldwin, a skillful and experienced engineer, made an exploration of the route, and decided upon its entire feasibility, dissipating the fears entertained by many that no line could be established without such heavy grades as would interfere materially with the paying character of the undertaking by the discovery of a summit gap no more than three hundred feet above the ocean level.

A formal contract was then entered into with the government of New Granada, on the most favorable terms, for the exclusive privilege of constructing a railroad across the Isthmus of Panama. Among the most important concessions by the terms of this contract was one guaranteeing that all public lands lying on the line of the road were to be used gratuitously by the Company; also a gift of 250,000 acres of land, to be selected by the grantees from any public lands on the Isthmus. Two ports, one on the Atlantic and the other on the Pacific (which were to be the termini of the road), were to be *free* ports; and the privilege was granted of establishing such tolls as the Company might think proper. The contract was to continue in force for forty-nine years, subject to the right of New Granada to take possession of the road at the expiration of twenty years after its completion, on payment of five millions of dollars; at the expiration of thirty years, on payment of four millions; and at the expiration of forty years, on payment of two millions. Three per cent. was to be paid to the New Granadian government upon all dividends declared. The entire work was to be completed within eight years, and a sum of one hundred and twenty thousand dollars was to be deposited at its commencement, as security for the fulfillment of the contract, but to be refunded, with interest, on the completion of the road within the given time.

Up to this period calculations for the ultimate success of the undertaking were based upon the advantages it would afford in shortening, by many thousand miles, not only the route to California and Oregon, but to China, Australia, and the East Indies, and in the development of the rich, but then almost inaccessible countries bordering the whole Pacific coast. At this time, however (the latter part of 1848), the discovery of gold in California, with its accompanying tide of emigration across the Isthmus of Panama, changed the prospects of this projected road; and, from an enterprise which looked far into the future for its rewards, it became one promising immediate returns from the capital and labor invested, and in which the people, as well as the government of the United States, must be immediately and deeply interested. A charter was now granted by the Legislature of the State of New York for the formation of a

RUNNING THE LINES.

stock company, under which one million dollars of stock was taken—the original grantees having previously transferred their contract into the hands of this company. A large and experienced party of engineers, under the command of Colonel G. W. Hughes, of the United States Topographical Corps, were sent down, in the early part of 1849, to survey and locate the line of the road. The result of their work not only confirmed the previous reconnoissance in regard to the entire practicability of the railroad, but another summit gap was discovered by Mr. J. L. Baldwin, thirty-seven feet lower than that previously established by him, and a line was run from ocean to ocean not exceeding fifty miles in length. The Pacific terminus of the road was located at the city of Panama, on Panama Bay, and the Atlantic terminus at Navy Bay, on the Atlantic shore.

The character and geographical position of the country through which the line of the road had been carried was such as might well have made the hardiest projectors shrink from attempting its construction. The first thirteen miles, beginning at Navy Bay, was through a deep morass, covered with the densest jungle, reeking with malaria, and abounding with almost every species of wild beasts, noxious reptiles, and venomous insects known in the tropics. Farther on, though some of the land was so fair and beautiful that the natives called it *Paraiso*, the greater part of the line was through a rugged country, along steep hill-sides, over wild chasms, spanning turbulent rivers and furious mountain torrents, until the summit-ridge was surmounted, when it descended abruptly to the shores of the Pacific Ocean.

Situated between the parallels of 8° and 9° north of the equator, a sultry tropical heat prevailed throughout the year, nearly half of which time the country was deluged with rains that, if they would not seriously damage the works, were certain to impede their progress, and add greatly to the arduous character of the undertaking. The whole isthmus, though covered with the most luxuriant vegetative growth, possessed little or no timber sufficiently durable to be of use in the construction of a permanent work. The native population, composed of a mongrel race of Spaniards, Indians, and Negroes, were too indolent and unaccustomed to labor to be depended on to any great extent. The resources of the country were entirely inadequate for the support of laborers. Men, materials, and provisions were to be transported thousands of miles. And yet, despite all these obstacles, the dim glimpses of which had, at a previous time, caused European capitalists to shrink back with fear, our bold operators at once, and earnestly, pushed forward this stupendous enterprise.

In the early part of 1849 a contract was entered into with Messrs. George M. Totten and John C. Trautwine for the construction of the road. The services of these gentlemen had been solicited by the Company, not only on account of their previously established reputation as skillful and successful engineers, but from having only a short time before been engaged upon a work of considerable magnitude in a neighboring province—the "Canal del Dique," connecting the Magdalena River with the Caribbean Sea at Carthagena: they had, consequently, a large experience in the character and resources of the country, and the conditions necessary to the success of such a project. The contractors at once proceeded to the Isthmus with a large force, and commenced the final location of the road.

Basing their operations upon the reconnoisance of Colonel Hughes and party, a native town called Gorgona, on the Chagres River, about thirty miles from the Atlantic, was selected as a point for the commencement of the work. This place was chosen on account of the facilities it afforded for communication with the Atlantic by the River Chagres (which was supposed to be navigable to this point for vessels of light draught), by which men, materials, and stores

PARAISO.

could be transported to a central point on the proposed road; and, on the completion of the Pacific section, traffic between the two oceans could at once be established, while the Atlantic section might be completed at the leisure or convenience of the Company. To this end, two steam-boats of very light draught were dispatched to Chagres for the navigation of the river. It was soon ascertained, however, that it was impossible to make use of these boats (drawing only from fourteen to eighteen inches of water), and that even the native bongoes and canoes were capable of the service only by great labor and exposure. In addition to this, the rush of California travel, which was then directed through this river as far as Gorgona, had so raised the hire of the native boatmen that the expense of river transportation was enormously increased. It was therefore determined to change the point of beginning to the Atlantic terminus of the road.

Mr. Trautwine, after a careful survey of the whole line of coast from the mouth of the Chagres to the harbor of Porto Bello, had located this terminus at the island of Manzanilla, on the eastern shore of the Bay of Limon, or Navy Bay, where the city of Aspinwall now stands. It was also found that, instead of a secluded and rarely-visited region, where laborers and materials such as the country afforded were comparatively inexpensive, as was the case when the contract was framed, and had been time out of mind, it was now swarming with emigrants from all parts of the globe *en route* for the land of gold. The conditions under which the contract was entered into were changed, the whole *morale* of the country had assumed an entirely different aspect, and it was evidently impossible to continue the work under the arrangement agreed upon. A fair representation of these things being made to the Company by Messrs. Totten and Trautwine, they were released from their obligations as contractors, and retained as engineers, the Company having determined to take charge of the construction themselves.

The plan of commencing at the Atlantic terminus being approved, Colonel Totten left for Carthagena to make arrangements for procuring an increased supply of laborers. Mr. Trautwine, in company with Mr. Baldwin, as chief assistant engineer, then proceeded to Manzanilla Island with a small party, and commenced clearing in the month of May, 1850. This island, cut off from the main land by a narrow frith, contained an area of a little more than one square mile. It was a virgin swamp, covered with a dense growth of the tortuous, water-loving mangrove, and interlaced with huge vines and thorny shrubs, defying entrance even to the wild beasts common to the country. In the black, slimy mud of its surface alligators and other reptiles abounded; while the air was laden with pestilential vapors, and swarming with sand-flies and musquitoes. These last proved so annoying to the laborers that, unless their faces were protected by gauze veils, no work could be done, even at midday. Residence on the island was impossible. The party had their quarters in an old brig which brought down materials for building, tools, provisions, etc., and was anchored in the bay.

Thus situated, with a mere handful of native assistants -most of the original forty or fifty having previously deserted on account of the higher wages and easier life promised them by the Transit—Messrs. Trautwine and Baldwin struck the first blow upon this great work. No imposing ceremony inaugurated the "breaking ground." Two American citizens, leaping, axe in hand, from a native canoe upon a wild and desolate island, their retinue consisting of half a dozen Indians, who clear the path with rude knives, strike their glittering axes into the nearest tree; the rapid blows reverberate from shore to shore, and the stately cocoa crashes upon the beach. Thus unostentatiously was announced the commencement of a railway, which, from the interests and difficulties involved, might well be looked upon as one of the grandest and boldest enterprises ever attempted.

Work upon the island was now fairly commenced. A portion was cleared, and a temporary store-house erected from the materials on board the brig. On the 1st of June Colonel Totten arrived from Carthagena with forty natives of that province as laborers for the work: these were descendants of the old Spanish slaves, a peaceable and industrious race, who, from having been employed on the works in Carthagena for several years, proved a valuable accession to their forces. Mr. T. was accompanied by Mr. John L. Stephens, the president of the Company, who was on his return from Bogotá, where he had been to obtain some important revisions in the contract. With their increased corps the clearing progressed rapidly; but the rainy season soon setting in, the discomforts to which they were subjected were very great. The island was still uninhabitable, and the whole party were forced to live on board the brig, which was crowded to its utmost capacity. Here they were by no means exempt from the causes which deterred them from living on shore, for below decks the vessel was alive with musquitoes and sand-flies, which were a source of such annoyance and suffering that almost all preferred to sleep upon the deck, exposed to the drenching rains, rather than endure their attacks. In addition to this, most of their number were kept nauseated by the ceaseless motion of the vessel. Labor and malarious influences during the day, exposure and unrest at night, soon told upon their health, and in a short time more than half the party were attacked with malarious fevers. Having neither a physician nor any comfortable place of rest, their sufferings were severe. At this time the hull of a condemned steam-boat—the Telegraph —lying at Chagres, was purchased, and sent down as a residence. This proved a vast improvement upon the accommodations afforded by the brig, but still annoyance from the insects was at times almost insupportable.

In the latter part of June Mr. Totten again left for Carthagena to procure more men, and Messrs. Stephens and Trautwine returned to New York to digest farther plans of procedure. The work was left in charge of Mr. Baldwin, who continued the clearing with his crippled forces until the latter part of the following month, when Mr. Totten returned with fifty more laborers. Surveys of the island and adjacent country were now pushed vigorously onward. It was in the depth of the rainy season, and the working parties, in addition to being constantly drenched from above, were forced to wade in from two to four feet of mud and water, over the mangrove stumps and tangled vines of the imperfect openings cut by the natives, who, with their *machetas*, preceded them to clear the way. Then, at night, saturated and exhausted, they dragged themselves back to their quarters in the Telegraph, to toss until morning among the pitiless insects. Numbers were daily taken down with fever; and, notwithstanding that the whole working party was changed weekly, large accessions were constantly needed to keep up the required force. The works were alternately in charge of Messrs. Totten and Baldwin, one attending to the duty while the other recuperated from his last attack of fever. In the month of July Mr. Trautwine returned with a surgeon—Dr. Totten, a brother of the colonel —and several assistant engineers. About fifty Irishmen also arrived soon after from New Orleans.

The line had already been located for two and a half miles, and decided upon for two miles farther. It was so laid out as to strike a range of small hills half a league from the terminus, when it again stretched into the deep morass. The distance now required to be traversed from the work to the terminus was so great, and attended with so much

THE FIRST SHANTY.

fatigue and loss of time, that it was determined to erect a shanty for Mr. Baldwin and party in the swamp. The lumber for this was dragged on the backs of the men for more than three miles. Here was erected the first dwelling-house, built of rude boards, high upon the stumps of trees, to raise it above the waters of the swamp; and in the heart of this dank, howling wilderness our hardy pioneers took up their abode.

Large parties of mechanics and laborers were now constantly arriving from Jamaica, Carthagena, and the United States, so that the quarters on board the hulk were no longer adequate to house them. The insects had greatly diminished in numbers as the clearing progressed, and shanties were erected on the high ground before alluded to for the accommodation of the laborers. In August, 1850, the work of construction was commenced at this place. Another station was also established eight miles distant, opposite to the native town of Gatun, on the bank of the Chagres River, which was navigable to this point; and two of the Company's vessels arriving, laden with machinery, building material, and stores, they were debarked here, and the work of piling and grading was carried on from this station toward the terminus. The number of men now employed on both stations was between three and four hundred, among whom were many mechanics. The construction and surveys for a time progressed with vigor, and comfortable dwellings and hospitals were erected; but sickness, caused by exposure to the incessant rains, working waist-deep in the water, and in an atmosphere saturated with malarious poison, soon made such sad inroads among them that, in a few weeks, more than half their number were on the hospital records, and, either frightened by the fevers or seduced by higher wages offered on the California Transit, so many of the remnant deserted that the work came to a pause. Here the bravest might well have faltered, and even turned back from so dark a prospect as was then presented to the leaders of this forlorn hope; but they were men whom personal perils and privations could not daunt, whose energy and determination toil and suffering could not vanquish. Even in this apparent cessation of labor they were not idle; but, pushing off into the neighboring islands and provinces, they collected recruits in such numbers that but a few weeks had passed before the work was again forced onward. Colonel Totten now assumed the direction of the work, and Mr. Center, the vice-president of the Company, repaired to the Isthmus to co-operate with him in the rapid advancement of the enterprise, so that by December over a thousand laborers were employed. With the commencement of the dry season the sickliness abated, the hospitals were soon cleared, and by April, 1851, a large portion of the road between the terminus and Gatun was completed. The line had been located to Barbacoas, sixteen miles farther on, while Mr. J. C. Campbell, chief assistant engineer, was actively employed in extending the location toward Panama, and work had been commenced at several intervening points.

Docks had been constructed at Navy Bay, and vessels were almost daily arriving from Jamaica and Carthagena with laborers, and from New York with stores, machinery, and materials for the road. On the first day of October, 1851, a train of working cars, drawn by a locomotive, passed over the road as far as Gatun. In the following month two large steam-ships, the Georgia and Philadelphia, arrived at the open roadstead of Chagres with passengers from the United States *en route* for California *via* the Chagres River Transit; but the weather was so tempestuous that, after several lives had been lost in attempting to effect a landing, they were forced to take refuge in the harbor of Navy Bay. It was then proposed that, instead of waiting for fair weather in order to return to Chagres, the passengers should be transported over the railroad to Gatun, from whence they could proceed up the river in bongoes as usual. There was not yet a single passenger car on the road: an accident like the present had never been included in the calculations of the Company. Every objection was, however, soon overruled by the anxious emigrants, over one thousand in number, who were then disembarked and safely transported on a train of working cars to the Rio Chagres at Gatun.

At about this time the affairs of the Company in New York looked very dark and unpromising. The first subscription of one million dollars of stock was expended, and the shares had gone down to a low figure. The directors were obliged to keep the work moving, at an enormous expense, on their own individual credit. Never since the commencement of the undertaking had its supporters been more disheartened; but on the return of the Georgia to New York, carrying news that the California passengers had landed at Navy Bay instead of Chagres, and had traveled over a portion of the Panama Railway, its friends were inspired with renewed hope, the value of its stock was enhanced, and the steadfast upholders of the work were relieved from the doubts and anxieties that had well-nigh overwhelmed them.

Up to this time the settlement around the terminus at Navy Bay had been without a distinctive name: it was now proposed by Mr. Stephens, the president of the Company, that it should commemorate the services of one of the originators and unswerving friends of the road. On the 2d of February, 1852, it was formally inaugurated as a city, and named ASPINWALL. The works during this season progressed with rapidity, for great numbers of laborers were constantly arriving, and the mail-steamers, which now came regularly to Navy Bay, as regularly, on their return, carried away the sick and disabled. By March the road was completed to a station on the Rio Chagres called Bujio Soldado, eight miles beyond Gatun, and passenger trains ran in connection with every steamer; by the 6th of July it was pushed on to Barbacoas, at which point the course of the road was intersected by the Chagres River, making a total distance from the city of Aspinwall of twenty-three miles.

Thus far the work had cost much more than was anticipated. In the hope of constructing the remainder more economically, it was decided by the Board of Directors to complete the road from Barbacoas to Panama by contract. Accordingly, an agreement was entered into with Minor C. Story, as principal, to complete the work. The death of the lamented president of the Company, Mr. John L. Stephens, took place at this time. From the very inception of the original contract he had devoted to the enterprise his active and intelligent mind with a zeal that knew no faltering. Much of his time had been spent amid the dangers and hardships of the wilderness through which it was projected, and his loss was deeply deplored by the Company. Mr. William C. Young was appointed his successor.

The work under the contract for construction had been commenced by the attempted erection of a bridge across the Chagres River at Barbacoas. The river at this point was about three hundred feet in width, flowing through a deep and rocky channel, and subject to sudden and resistless freshets, often rising forty feet in a single night: the bridge was nearly completed when one span was swept away. Work was again commenced upon it, as well as upon several sections of the road between this point and the Pacific terminus. At times there was a force of several hundred men employed; but they were mostly Irish, unable to endure the effects of the climate, and, being also badly cared for, their numbers were soon so thinned by sickness and death that the contractor found himself unable to accomplish any part of the contract for the price agreed upon. The work faltered, and at last stopped almost entirely; so that when a year had expired not only was the bridge still unfinished, but not a tenth part of the work under the contract was completed, and the Company were obliged again to take the enterprise into their own hands, and carry it on by the same system pursued before the unfortunate contract was entered into. Mr. Young now resigned the presidency, and Mr. David Hoadley (the present president) was appointed his successor—a gentleman who deservedly enjoys the respect and confidence not alone of the Company which he represents, but also of the entire commercial community.

Valuable time had been lost from the delay occasioned by the non-fulfillment of the late contract. Not disheartened, however, the Company now redoubled their exertions, determined, if possible, to retrieve the error. Their working force was increased as rapidly as possible, drawing laborers from almost every quarter of the globe. Irishmen were imported from Ireland, Coolies from Hindostan, Chinamen from China. English, French, Germans, and Austrians, amounting in all to more than seven thousand men, were thus gathered in, appropriately as it were, to construct this highway for all nations. It was now anticipated that, with the enormous forces employed, the time required for the completion of the entire work would be in a ratio proportionate to the numerical increase of laborers, all of whom were supposed to be hardy, able-bodied men. But it was soon found that many of these people, from their previous habits and modes of life, were little adapted to the work for which they were engaged. The Chinamen, one thousand in number, had been brought to the Isthmus by the Company, and every possible care taken which could conduce to their health and comfort. Their hill-rice, their tea, and opium, in sufficient quantity to last for several months, had been imported with them—they were carefully housed and attended to—and it was expected that they would prove efficient and valuable men. But they had been engaged upon the work scarcely a month before almost the entire body became affected with a melancholic, suicidal tendency, and scores of them ended their unhappy existence by their own hands. Disease broke out among them, and raged so fiercely that in a few weeks scarcely two hundred remained. The freshly-imported Irishmen and Frenchmen also suffered severely, and there was found no other resource but to reship them as soon as possible, and replenish from the neighboring provinces and Jamaica, the natives of which (with the exception of the Northmen of America) were found best able to resist the influences of the climate. Notwithstanding these discouragements, and many others too numerous to be narrated within the compass of this brief sketch, the work continued to advance, so that by January, 1854, the summit-ridge was reached, distant from the Atlantic terminus thirty-seven miles, and eleven miles from the city of Panama.

Simultaneously with the operations toward the Pacific, a large force was established at Panama, under the superintendence of Mr. J. Young, one of the Company's most efficient and energetic officers, and the road was pushed rapidly onward, over the plains of Panama, through the swamps of Corrisal and Correndeu, and up the valley of the Rio Grande, to meet the advancing work from the Atlantic side; and on the 27th day of January, 1855, at midnight, in darkness and rain, the last rail was laid, and on the following day a locomotive passed from ocean to ocean.

The entire length of the road was 47 miles 3.020 feet, with a maximum grade of sixty feet to the mile. The summit grade was $258\frac{64}{100}$ feet above the assumed grade at the Atlantic, and $242\frac{7}{10}$ above the assumed grade at the Pacific terminus, being $263\frac{9}{100}$ feet above the *mean* tide of the Atlantic Ocean, and the summit-ridge two hundred and eighty-seven feet above the same level. Commencing at the city

ANCIENT BRIDGE AT OLD PANAMA.

of Aspinwall, on Limon or Navy Bay, the Atlantic terminus of the road, latitude 9° 21′ 23″ N. and longitude 79° 53′ 52″ W., the road skirted the western shore of the island of Manzanilla for about three quarters of a mile, then bent to the east, and crossed the channel which separates the island from the main land at a point nearly central of the breadth of the island, thence around the southern and eastern shore of Navy Bay until it reached the small river Mindee, cutting off a bend of this river about one thousand feet from its mouth; then it stretched across the peninsula formed by this bay and the River Chagres up to the mouth of the River Obispo, one of its branches, seldom, however, following the tortuous course of that stream, but cutting across its bends, and touching it only at intervals of two or three miles. The line continued upon the right or easterly bank of the Chagres as far as Barbacoas (twenty-five miles from Aspinwall), where it crossed that river by a wooden bridge six hundred and twenty-five feet in length; from thence it followed the left bank of the Chagres to the mouth of the Obispo River, thirty-one miles from the Atlantic terminus, leaving the native town of Gorgona on the left. After striking the Obispo, the line followed the valley of this stream to its head in the summit-ridge, which it reached $37\frac{3}{4}$ miles from the Atlantic and $10\frac{1}{4}$ miles from the Pacific terminus. The lower part of the valley of the Obispo, being crooked and bound in by precipitous hills, compelled the line to cross the stream twice within the first mile, when it passed the summit-ridge by a cut one fourth of a mile in length and twenty-four feet in depth, and then struck the head waters of the Rio Grande, which flows into the Pacific Ocean. Following the left bank of this stream, and descending by a grade of sixty feet to the mile for the first four miles, the line crossed the rivers Pedro Miguel, Caimitillo, and Cardenas, near their entrance into the Rio Grande; thence it stretched across the savannas of Corrisal and the swamps of Correndeu, and cut through a spur of Mount Ancon, leaving the main elevation to the right, and reached the Pacific Ocean at Playa Prieta, the northern suburb of the city of Panama.

Four tracks were laid at the Atlantic and three at the Pacific terminus, and the line of the road was well supplied with sidings and machinery for reversing locomotives. A machine shop one hundred and fifty feet long by fifty wide, stocked with first class machinery, sufficient to do all the repairs required for the road, was in operation at Aspinwall; also a blacksmith's shop, containing six suitable forges, and a brass foundry, with a small cupola for iron castings. There was also a car-repair shop, one hundred feet long by eighty feet wide, a freight-house and passenger depôt at either terminus, and suitable buildings for the accommodation of the employes of the Company.

A pier of four hundred and fifty feet in length was constructed at the Panama terminus, which gave greatly increased facilities for embarking and landing passengers and freight, and a steam-tug was substituted for the lighters and small boats which had been previously used for transportation between ship and shore, a distance of two and a half miles. The Company owned, by purchase, fourteen acres of land, having a front of five hundred feet on the bay. The Company also obtained by purchase, in connection with the Pacific Mail Steam-ship Company, a group of four islands in the Bay of Panama, about two and a half miles from the city, affording good shelter and anchorage for vessels of the largest class, and well supplied with good springs of water.

But the road at this time, though in *working* order and performing a large and daily-increasing service, was by no means actually completed. Much of the work, especially on the Pacific division, was of a temporary character; streams were crossed on temporary trestles, many of them of timber procured from the adjoining woods, and which it was known would not last more than six or eight months; deep ravines, requiring embankments from twenty to eighty feet in height (which it was found, from the nature of the adjoining soil, as well as from the amount of work involved in filling them, would delay the laying of the track for many months), were crossed on temporary trestle-work, in order to obtain the advantage of immediate communication between the two oceans by rail, thereby saving the thousands of men, women, and children, who were then crossing the Isthmus every month, the thirteen miles of mule-ride over a dangerous path, as well as the almost incredible hardships and perils to which they were subjected.

The difficulty and expense of keeping the road open in this state was very great; but, while this was safely accomplished, the work, under the energetic and skillful management of Messrs. Totten and Center, rapidly assumed a permanent character; firm and thoroughly secured embankments took the place of the trestle-work; for the temporary bridges were substituted heavy iron substantial structures, with abutments of stone.

Some idea of the magnitude of the bridge and culvert work may be obtained when it is known that the waterways on the route were no less than one hundred and seventy in number, viz., one hundred and thirty-four culverts, drains, and bridges ten feet and under, the remaining bridges ranging from twelve to six hundred and twenty-five feet in breadth.

The iron bridge across the Chagres at Barbacoas may be taken, for its great strength and durability, as the type of all like structures on the line of the road. This bridge was composed of six spans of over a hundred feet each, built of boiler iron, with a top and bottom chord two feet in breadth and one inch in thickness, and joined together by a web of boiler iron nine feet in height at the centre and seven feet at the ends. The track was laid on iron floor-girders three feet apart, and the whole structure supported by five piers and two abutments of hewn stone twenty-six feet wide and eight feet in thickness, increasing in the proportion of an inch to the foot down to their foundations, which were constructed of piles and concrete.

The ballasting, which was, however, previously well under way, was carried on and completed throughout the entire line of the road in the most substantial manner, and the rapidly decaying spruce, pine, and native wood ties were removed, and replaced with ties of lignum-vitæ, imported from the province of Carthagena. Additional buildings for the accommodation of freight and passengers were erected at the Pacific terminus, to meet the wants of a greatly increased business, and at the Atlantic terminus new and commodious wharves were built, besides a massive stone warehouse three hundred feet long by eighty wide, the stone taken from quarries along the line of the road. Large and commodious station-houses, for the use of the local superintendents, were erected at intervals of four miles along the entire line, and an electric telegraph was established between the termini for the use of the Company. These, besides many other improvements, in reducing grades* and straightening curves, were accomplished

* TABLE OF THE GRADES FROM ASPINWALL TO PANAMA.

Rate of grade per mile in feet.	Length of grade in feet.	Rate of grade per mile in feet.	Length of grade in feet.
Level.	123,539	24.82	418
2.64	1,000	26.40	13,600
5.28	1,900	30.00	8,868
7.92	1,500	30.25	1,936
8.45	2,500	31.68	1,100
9.24	3,100	34.15	1,400
10.56	13,313	36.00	2,200
12.14	2,600	36.96	2,396
12.41	4,300	37.49	1,916
13.20	6,500	38.54	1,707
15.10	2,100	46.20	3,430
15.84	3,700	47.30	3,250
17.42	200	52.80	6,300
19.01	1,400	58.87	3,355
20.60	4,900	60.00	20,107
21.12	4,595		71,983
23.25	2,052		179,199
	179,199		251,182

THE CABILDO AT PANAMA.

during the two years following the opening of the road in 1855, involving an additional expenditure of nearly two millions of dollars. This great expenditure was not, however, incurred without satisfactory proof that the enterprise would equal, in its pecuniary advantages, all the calculations which had been made in regard to its increase of revenue. Up to the opening of the road in 1855, that is to say, from the running of the first passenger train in 1852, the amount received for the transportation of passengers and freight was $2,125,282 81.

From 1857 the Company were actively engaged in establishing every needful arrangement and improvement which was found necessary to facilitate the perfect working of the road. Side tracks at either terminus were added to meet its increased requirements; the wharves at Aspinwall were improved and covered, and substantial bulk-heads were erected over a considerable portion of the frontage of the port. Much of the low ground on the island was filled in and laid out into streets, and many buildings erected. In addition to this, an immense reservoir was in process of construction on the site of a natural basin some two miles distant, from which water was to be conveyed in iron pipes to Aspinwall for the use of the town and shipping; and a substantial iron light-house, sixty feet in height, and furnished with a Fresnel light, was substituted for the wooden structure at the western side of the entrance to the port. At Panama the wooden pier was replaced by one of iron four hundred and fifty feet in length, and steam-tugs for towage, and several iron launches, each of one hundred tons burthen, were added to the facilities for the transhipment of goods between ship and shore. These were the principal works and improvements up to January, 1859, when the construction account of the road was closed, showing its entire cost up to that date to have been eight millions of dollars.

The *gross earnings* of the road up to that time amounted

to eight millions one hundred and forty-six thousand six hundred and five dollars.

The running expenses, together with depreciation in iron, ties, buildings, etc., amounted to $2,174,876 51, leaving a balance of $5,971,728 66 as the legitimate returns for the money invested in the road in a period of seven years, during the first of which but twelve miles were in operation, the second twenty-three, the third thirty-one: only for the last four years was the road in use throughout its entire extent.

Out of these receipts, the directors of the Company, having paid the regular interest on all mortgage and other bonds, a ten per cent. dividend to stockholders in 1852, one of seven per cent. in each of the years 1853 and '54, and one of twelve per cent. for every succeeding year, showed a balance of $529,041 50, besides a sinking fund of $153,395 83, and no floating debt.

The increase in the receipts from the commencement of the road was as follows:

From December, 1852, 12 miles open,
To " 1853, 23 " " } $73,266 32.
From 1853 to 1854, 31 miles open, $131,143 91.
From 1854 to 1855, opening of the entire road, $645,497 29.
From 1855 to 1858 showed an increase of $416,006 84; and
From 1858 to 1859, an increase above that of $419,477 93.

(For a particular statement of items of expenditure and income, see Appendix B, page 61, et seq.)

HEALTH OF THE ISTHMUS.

It may interest the general reader to know that more than four hundred thousand passengers have been transported over the road during the thirteen years ending in December, 1867, and it is not known that a single case of sickness has occurred in consequence of the transit since the entire opening of the road in 1855. The diseases contracted by persons in transit previous to that time were of a purely ma-

VIEW FROM THE RAMPARTS, LOOKING TOWARD THE SITE OF THE ANCIENT CITY.

larious character, and identical with the intermittent (fever and ague) and bilious fevers of the Western States, always found resulting from great exposure and fatigue, so often unavoidable while the transit was performed upon mules and in open boats, occupying from two to five days, the traveler frequently obliged to live upon the vilest food, and sleep upon the wet ground or in the but little less comfortless huts of the natives; the comfortable railway carriage, and the passage from ocean to ocean reduced to *three hours*, having fully demonstrated a *perfect* immunity to the traveler from all those varieties of sickness long popularly recognized under the head of *Panama Fever*. The sanitary condition not only of Aspinwall, but of the country along the entire line of the road, has also been improved by the filling in and draining of the swamp and low land to such a degree that the congestive forms of fever among the laborers and residents which, during the earlier days of the road, were the chief causes of mortality, are now rarely met with, and the whole line of the transit will, in point of healthiness, compare favorably with many of the equally recent settlements in the Western States.

SAFETY TO PROPERTY.

The amount of specie conveyed over the road from 1855 to 1867 was over seven hundred and fifty millions of dollars, *without the loss of a single dollar;* and during the same period there were sent over the road some 300,000 bags of mail matter (the greater part of which consisted of mails between the Atlantic States and California), not one of which was lost. And of the many thousands of tons of freight which have been transported over the Panama Railroad since it was first opened, the losses in transportation, by damage and otherwise, has been comparatively trifling.

SOURCES OF BUSINESS.

Erroneous impressions in regard to the sources from whence the business of the Panama Railroad is derived prevail extensively even among intelligent business men and members of our national councils, many regarding it as entirely dependent upon our trade with California. The fact seems to be overlooked that while California has a population estimated at only 500,000, the population of Central America is over 2,000,000; and that that portion of South America, whose only means of communicating with the Atlantic is either by the Isthmus of Panama or around Cape Horn, contains nearly 8,000,000, and that regular and direct steam marine communication exists between those countries and the Panama Railroad.

The fact that up to the establishment of the Isthmus Railroad the trade of South and Central America had been carried on almost exclusively with Europe (that between the United States and those countries being estimated at less than ten per cent. of the whole) has prevented its magnitude and importance from being fully appreciated by the American people.

Careful estimates, however, show that the value of the trade of these countries to and from the Atlantic exceeds $60,000,000 per annum. The managers of the Panama Railroad Company, from its earliest existence, were aware of that important circumstance, and looked confidently to the business of those regions already existing, and that which would undoubtedly be developed by the facilities afforded by the railroad, as one of the surest elements in its ultimate and permanent success.

It was not lost sight of that the European trade (as far as European influence extended) would cling tenaciously to its circuitous track around Cape Horn, fully aware that, when the business was turned into the direct route across the Isthmus, a large portion of the trade would be inevitably directed to the nearer markets of the United States; notwithstanding this, the Company rested in the conviction that the shortening of the distance from three thousand to more than four thousand miles for the South American markets, and more than five thousand for the Pacific Central American, besides the avoidance of the well-known perils of Cape Horn, must bring much of the most valuable merchandise across their road so soon as those countries were able to avail themselves of its advantages. The South American states, Chili, Peru, Bolivia, and Ecuador, were put in immediate connection with the road by a British line of steam-ships, which was organized some time previous to the opening of the road, and which, up to that time, had been mainly dependent upon the coastwise trade. The business resulting fully justified the expectations of the Company; but the Central American states had at that time no means of connection with the road. Their Pacific ports had been so long shut out from remunerative commercial relations that they could not at once realize the advantages the Isthmus railroad offered over the tedious and expensive land-route to the Atlantic; they required to be lifted from the ruts along which they had been creeping and groaning for ages, and placed upon this great commercial highway.

This was accomplished in 1856 by the Panama Railroad Company, who at that time organized a line of steam communication with all their ports from Panama to San Jose de Guatemala.

This departure from the legitimate business of the road was not made until the directors had vainly exhausted every available means in their power for the establishment of an independent company. But the development of the Central American trade was so manifestly for the interest of the Isthmus transit, and so certain to follow the establishment of such a line, that they finally decided to identify its interests with those of the road. In the latter part of 1856 the first vessel was dispatched under the command of Capt. J. M. Dow. The returns from the monthly voyages of the "Columbus" soon proved the wisdom of the measure, for in less than two years the cargoes of merchandise brought from those states for transportation over the road often exceeded half a million of dollars, while a large amount of foreign merchandise found its way to those countries by the same channel.

In 1858, the business over the road from the South and Central American states exceeded in value *nine times* the freighting business of California *via* the Isthmus, and by 1860 less than *one fifteenth* of the freighting business of the road was due to the California trade,* the remaining fourteen fifteenths consisting mainly of shipments from the United States, British manufactures and other goods shipped direct from England for South and Central America, and the produce of those countries in return, such as indigo, cochineal, India-rubber, coffee, cocoa, deer-skins and goat-skins, besides orchilla, pearl-shells, tobacco, balsams, Peruvian bark, ores, straw hats, etc., etc.

When it comes to be considered that in the California trade large amounts of goods and merchandise for Oregon and Washington Territory and the British Possessions are included, likewise occasional shipments from China and the Sandwich Islands, and that it is still in its infancy, the importance of the South and Central American trade to the Panama Railroad may be in a measure appreciated. The conveyances by which the business of the Pacific coast finds its way to and from the road are,

1st. By the Pacific Mail Steam-ship Company, plying tri-

---

* The California trade over the Panama Road has increased since 1860 to such an extent, that now (1867) about one third of its business is due to that source.

RAMPARTS ON THE NORTHEASTERN FACE OF PANAMA.

monthly between New York, Panama, Mexico, California, Japan, and China, with a fleet of twenty-five large steam-ships.

2d. The General Transatlantic Company (Compagnie Générale Transatlantique), running between St. Nazaire, France, the West Indies, Mexico, and Aspinwall, with a large fleet of powerful steam-ships.

3d. The West India and Pacific Steam-ship Company, limited—running between Liverpool, England, the West Indies, the western coast of South and Central America, and Aspinwall, with a large and well-appointed fleet of steam-ships.

4th. The Royal Mail Steam Packet Company, running semi-monthly between Southampton, England, the West Indies, the eastern coast of Mexico, South and Central America, and Aspinwall, with a fleet of nineteen large steam-ships.

5th. The Panama, New Zealand, and Australian Royal Mail Company, limited — running between Panama, New Zealand, and Australia.

6th. The British Pacific Steam Navigation Company, running between Panama and the ports of New Granada, Ecuador, Peru, Bolivia, and Chili.

7th. The Panama Railroad Company's Central American line of steam-ships, running between Panama, Nicaragua, Costa Rica, Salvador, and Guatemala.

8th. The California, Oregon, and Mexico Company's line of steam-ships, running between San Francisco, California, and Mexico, and between San Francisco and Portland, Oregon, and the Island of Vancouver.

Besides the steam lines are,

1st. The Bremen and Aspinwall line of sailing vessels, monthly.

2d. The Bordeaux and Aspinwall line of sailing vessels, quarterly.

3d. The Panama Railroad Company's line of sailing vessels from New York to Aspinwall—seven vessels: five barks and four brigs.

4th. Five ships a year from Boston to Aspinwall.

CHARACTER OF THE SERVICE PERFORMED ON THE ROAD.

As early as the year 1855 daily trains were established each way over the road, requiring in its then imperfect state from five to six hours for the transit. As the character of the road improved, a corresponding improvement took place in the time-table, and for the past seven years the passage has been uniformly and safely accomplished in three hours, or even less, when the exigency of the case required it. The rolling stock of the road has always been most ample. Fifteen hundred passengers, with the United States mails, and the freight of three steam-ships, have not unfrequently been transported over the road during a single half day. The engines, some fourteen in number, are of the first class, averaging twenty tons burden; the passenger-cars are large and commodious, and built for convenience and comfort, especially with reference to the climate; the cars for the transportation of the mails and treasure are entirely of iron. The usual freight-cars are built to carry not only the ordinary freight, but the heaviest and coarsest materials—large quantities of gold and silver ore, timber, anchors, and chains of the largest size, cannon shot and shells, iron-work in pieces of twenty-five tons, heavy machinery, guano, whale-oil, etc., more or less of which are daily passing over the road. The arrangements for the loading and unloading of cargoes are unusually perfect; double tracks run from the main road down the different wharves to the very ship's side, and the lading process is so effectively managed that frequently less than two hours pass between the *arrival of the largest ships*, laden with from two to three hundred tons of merchandise, besides the baggage of from four to eight hundred passengers, and the *departure of the trains* for Panama bearing the entire freight.

SOUTH-EASTERN RAMPART.

PANAMA RAILROAD COMPANY.

Financial Statement for the Year ending December 31st, 1852.

Gross receipts to December 31st, 1852		$250,161 81
Amount credited Construction Account for proportion of running expenses	$65,000 00	
Sundry expenses, mule hire for troops, etc.	8,999 32	
Dividend No. 1, 10 per cent. on $1,467,720	146,772 00	
New Granadian government proportion of dividend	4,403 16	225,174 48
Balance to credit of Income Account		$24,987 33

Statement for the Year ending December 31st, 1853.

Balance to credit of Income Account, December 31st, 1852		$24,987 33
Gross receipts to December 31st, 1853		322,428 13
		$347,415 46
Amount charged for running expenses	$118,949 99	
Dividend No. 2, 5 per cent. on $2,194,062	109,703 10	
New Granadian government proportion of dividend	3,291 09	226,944 18
Balance to Income Account, December 31st, 1853		$120,471 28
Dividend No. 3, 3¼ per cent. on $2,716,572	$95,080 02	
New Granadian government proportion of dividend	2,852 40	97,932 42
Balance to credit of Income Account		$22,538 86

PANAMA RAILROAD.

Statement for the Year ending December 31st, 1854.

Balance to credit of Income Account, December 31st, 1853			$22,588 86
Gross receipts to December 31st, 1854			453,572 04
			$476,110 90
Amount charged for running expenses		$116,542 37	
Dividend No. 4, July, 3¼ per cent. on $2,832,000		99,120 00	
Interest on bonds, due July 1st, on $2,168,000, at 3½ per cent.		75,880 00	
" on bonds, due January 1st, on $2,125,000, at 3½ per cent.		74,375 00	
New Granadian government proportion of dividend		2,543 63	368,461 00
			$107,649 90
Dividend No. 5, January, 3½ per cent. on $2,875,000		$100,625 00	
New Granadian government proportion of dividend		3,018 75	103,643 75
Balance to credit of Income Account			$4,006 15

Statement for the Year ending December 31st, 1855.

Balance to credit of Income Account, December 31st, 1854			$4,006 15
Gross receipts to December 31st, 1855			1,099,069 33
			$1,103,075 48
Amount charged for running expenses		$284,156 00	
Dividend No. 6, July, 6 per cent. on $3,743,000		224,580 00	
New Granadian government proportion of dividend		6,737 40	
Interest on bonds due July 1st, $1,257,000, at 3½ per cent.		43,995 00	
" on sterling mortgage bonds, with commission and exchange		53,466 78	
" on bonds due January 1st, $468,000, at 3½ per cent.		16,380 00	
" on sterling mortgage bonds, with commission and exchange		77,770 00	
Office expenses to January 1st		8,918 00	
Interest on bonds converted		8,210 00	724,213 18
			$378,862 30
Dividend No. 7, January, 6 per cent. on $4,532,000		$271,920 00	
New Granadian government proportion of dividend		8,157 60	280,077 60
Balance to credit of Income Account			$98,784 70

PANAMA RAILROAD.

Statement for the Year ending December 31st, 1856.

Balance to credit of Income Account, December 31st, 1855			$98,784
Amount of earnings received to credit same, to December 31st, 1856			1,284,639
United States Post-office Department—mail-service for quarter ending December 30			42,204
Earnings in December, for which returns have not been received, and uncollected freight on the Isthmus			27,500
Royal Mail Steam Packet Company—freight on foreign treasure not yet adjusted			6,398
			$1,459,525
Deduct interest on sterling bonds (£450,000), including exchange and commission		$155,540	
" on convertible bonds, 1st July, $283,000—3½ per cent	$9,905		
" " " 1st Jan., 250,000 " "	8,750	18,655	
Running expenses, per returns of chief engineer and superintendent		323,788	
Office expenses		22,266	
New Granadian government proportion of mail receipts		10,000	
		$530,249	
Dividend No. 8, paid July 1st	$283,020		
New Granadian government proportion, 3 per cent	8,490	291,510	
			821,759
Balance to credit of Income Account, December 31st, 1856			$637,766
Dividend No. 9, declared January 5th, on $4,750,000, at 6 per cent	$285,000		
New Granadian government proportion, 3 per cent	8,550		293,550
Balance to credit of Income Account after dividends			$344,216

PANAMA RAILROAD.

Statement for the Year ending December 31st, 1857.

Balance to credit of Income Account, after dividend, January 5, 1857.............				$878,894 42
Receipts from December 31st, 1856, to December 31st, 1857, viz.:				
From passengers.............			$698,250 18	
" freight.............			354,487 78	
" do.—treasure.............			122,076 60	
" mails.............			112,058 12	
" baggage.............			16,591 03	
" miscellaneous.............			2,405 89	$1,305,819 60
				$1,684,214 02
Deduct interest on first mortgage sterling bonds (£450,000), with exchange and commission.............			$155,540 90	
" second " " (£56,250), for 6 mos. " "			9,720 00	
" convertible bonds, 1st July....$223,000, at 3½ per cent. " "	$7,805			
" " " 1st Jan.....$160,000, " " " "	5,500		13,405 00	
Running expenses.............			848,387 00	
Estimated depreciation in iron, ties, etc.............			40,000 00	
Loss on steamers Columbus and Panama.............			50,000 00	
Office expenses.............			22,250 00	
New Granadian government proportion of mail receipts.............			10,000 00	
			$649,302 00	
Dividend No. 10, July 6th, on $4,770,000, 6 per cent.............	$286,620 00			
New Granadian government proportion do., 3 per cent.............	8,596 60		295,218 60	$944,520 60
				$739,693 42
Balance to credit of Income Account, December 31st, 1857.				
Dividend No. 11, January 4th, on $4,840,000, 6 per cent.............	$290,400	$299,112		
New Granadian government proportion do., 3 per cent.............	8,712			
Amount appropriated to Sinking Fund.............		50,000		349,112 00
Balance to credit of Income Account after dividends.............				$390,581 42

Statement for the Year ending December 31st, 1858.

Balance to credit of Income Account, after dividend, January 4th, 1858			$392,855 91
Receipts from December 31st, 1857, to December 31st, 1858:			
From passengers	$743,573 27		
" freight—merchandise	432,455 73		
" " treasure	147,853 78		
" mail transportation	100,000 00		
" baggage	18,509 76		
" miscellaneous, wharfage, light money, etc.	3,683 73		
Earnings in December, for which returns have not been received, estimated	60,000 00		$1,506,076 27
			$1,898,932 18
Deduct interest on first mortgage bonds (£450,000), with exchange and commission	$153,860 88		
" " second " " (£129,375), " " "	28,470 28		
" " convertible bonds, July 1st, $77,000, at 3½ per cent.	$2,695 }		
" " " " Jan. 1st, $33,000, " " "	1,155 }	3,850 00	
Running expenses	386,234 39		
Equipment Account	13,523 13		
Depreciation in iron, ties, etc.	40,000 00		
Office expenses	22,750 00		
New Granadian government proportion of mail receipts	10,000 00		
	$658,688 68		
Dividend No. 12, June 30th, on $4,923,000, at 6 per cent.	$295,380 00		
New Granadian government proportion, 3 per cent.	8,861 40		
Appropriated to Sinking Fund, June 30th	50,000 00	354,241 40	$1,012,930 08
Balance to credit of Income Account, December 31st, 1858			$886,002 10
Dividend No. 13, Jan. 3d, 1859, on $4,967,000, at 6 per cent.	$298,020 00		
New Granadian government proportion, 3 per cent.	8,940 60		
Appropriated to Sinking Fund, Jan. 3d, 1859	50,000 00		$356,960 60
Balance to credit of Income Account after dividends			$529,041 50

Statement for the Year ending December 31st, 1858—continued.

The Construction Account, now closed, amounts to			$8,000,000 00
Which is represented by			
Capital stock		$4,967,000 00	
Convertible bonds		33,000 00	
First mortgage sterling bonds; due Dec. 1st, 1859	$ 750,000		
" " " " April 10th, 1865	1,250,000	2,000,000 00	
Second mortgage sterling bonds, due Feb. 20th, 1872		1,000,000 00	
			$8,000,000 00

Of the latter, 425 bonds, equal at par to $425,000, are still in the hands of the Company unissued. The Sinking Fund invested now amounts to $158,395 83. The Company has no floating debt.

Statement for the Year ending December 31st, 1859.

Balance to credit of Income Account, after dividend, January 6th, 1859, per statement		$529,041 50	
Add excess of receipts over estimate for portion of December, 1858		6,068 13	$535,109 63
Receipts from December 31st, 1858, to December 31st, 1859:			
For passengers		$1,068,882 17	
" freight—merchandise		587,689 01	
" " treasure		158,876 98	
" mail transportation		100,000 00	
" baggage		18,951 65	
" miscellaneous, wharfage, light money, etc		6,094 76	
Earnings for the latter part of December, not yet received, estimated at		40,000 00	1,925,444 57
			$2,460,554 20
Deduct, interest on first mortgage bonds (£450,000), with exchange and commission		$150,694 37	
" " second " " (£225,000), " " "		77,770 00	
" " convertible bonds, July 1st, $33,000, at 3½ per cent	$1,155 00		
" " " " Jan. 1st, $27,000, " " "	945 00	2,100 00	
Running expenses		416,818 76	
Premium of exchange on remittances to meet bonds, paid in London, December 1st		73,157 78	
Office expenses		25,207 43	

Appropriated to cover depreciation in iron, ties, buildings, etc.	40,000 00	
New Granadian government proportion of mail receipts	10,000 00	795,748 34
		$1,664,805 86
Dividend No. 14, paid July 1st, on $4,967,000, 6 per cent	$298,020 00	
" 15, payable January 3d, 1860, on $4,973,000, 6 per cent	298,380 00	
New Granadian government proportion, 3 per cent, on ditto	17,892 00	
Appropriated to Sinking Fund	100,000 00	714,292 00
Surplus income after dividend, January 3d, 1860		$950,513 86
Balance as above		$950,513 86
Sinking Fund and accumulations		260,962 21
		$1,211,476 07

Out of which the Company have paid during 1859,

For stock in North Atlantic Steam-ship Company	$500,000 00	
" steamer Guatemala	150,000 00	
On account of bonds, due December 1st	550,000 00	
	$1,200,000 00	

All the Company's interest in steamers is covered by marine insurance excepting the Columbus, valued at $25,000.

The cost of the road, per Construction Account, closed January, 1859, is.................. $8,000,000 00

Against which there are,

Capital stock	$4,973,000 00	
Convertible bonds	27,000 00	
Sterling bonds, due 1865	1,250,000 00	
" " 1872	1,150,000 00	
	$7,400,000 00	

Statement for the Year ending December 31st, 1860.

Balance to credit of Income Account, after dividend, January 3d, 1860, per statement		$960,513 86
Add excess of receipts over estimate for portion of December		10,227 55
		$960,741 41
Deduct payment for portion of sterling bonds retired in December, 1859, the balance having been paid from the Sinking Fund		442,830 13
		$517,911 28
Receipts from December 31st, 1859, to December 31st, 1860:		
Surplus after dividends of 1859		
For passengers	$688,378 74	
" freight, merchandise (including baggage)	618,578 04	
" treasure	128,946 38	
" mail transportation	50,000 00	
" miscellaneous, wharfage, light money, interest, etc.	14,972 66	
" earnings uncollected, or for which returns have not been received, estimated	50,000 00	$1,550,875 82
		$2,068,792 10
Deduct interest on sterling bonds (£540,000), with exchange and commission	$186,468 45	
" " convertible bonds, $24,000, at 7 per cent.	1,680 00	
Running expenses, including materials, repairs, subsistences, labor, etc.	406,050 55	
Equipment Account, new cars, etc.	$17,019 32	
Permanent improvements (paid for out of Income Account, Construction being closed):		
New wharves	20,072 13	
Water-works	15,204 16	
Dredging machine	18,489 96	
Stone-breakers and engines	5,000 00 — 75,785 57	
Office expenses	22,904 73	
New Granadian government proportion of mail receipts	10,000 00	$702,889 30
		$1,365,897 80
Dividend No. 16, paid July 2d, 1860, on $4,976,000, 6 per cent.	$298,560 00	
" 17, payable January 2d, 1861, on $4,976,000, 6 per cent.	298,560 00	
New Granadian government proportion of do., 3 per cent.	17,973 60	

PANAMA RAILROAD.   67

Paid trustees of Sinking Fund, July, 1860........... 50,000 00 } 100,000 00
Appropriated to   "   "   December, 1860........ 50,000 00 } $715,093 60
                              Surplus after dividends of 1860.............................$650,804 20

GENERAL STATEMENT.

Assets: Construction Account..$8,000,000 00
  Cash in bank..204,920 52
  Loans on demand..127,455 75
  Amounts due from agents and others..93,088 52
  Cavan Brothers & Co., London..49,557 31
  Sinking Fund..50,369 06
  Real estate on the Isthmus and islands in the Bay of Panama.......................69,431 97
  Stock in North Atlantic Steam-ship Co..500,000 00
  Steamer Guatemala (cost $155,000), valued at.....................................130,000 00
  "   Columbus (cost $50,500),   "   "..25,000 00
  Steam-tugs and launches in the Bay of Panama (cost $50,500), valued at............28,000 00
  Interest in sailing vessels (cost $41,000), valued at............................
                                                                                  $9,302,823 13

Liabilities: Capital stock...$4,976,000 00
  Sterling bonds, with exchange.. 2,466,237 78
  Convertible bonds..   24,000 00
  Book accounts..   44,900 60
  Dividend declared and payable Jan. 2d, with New Granadian government proportion..   307,546 80
  Trustees of Sinking Fund, appropriation not invested.............................   50,000 00
  Undivided earnings from road......................................$650,804 20
    "   "   of steamers, sailing vessels, tugs, and launches (after
                    deducting depreciation)..........................183,333 75
    "   "   bonds redeemed....................................... 600,000 00—1,434,142 95
                                                                                  $9,302,823 13

Jos. F. Joy, *Secretary.*

PANAMA RAILROAD.

Statement for the Year ending December 31st, 1861.

Balance to credit of Income Account, after dividend, January 2d, 1861, as per statement		$650,809 20
Add excess of receipts over estimate for part of December		35,615 31
		$686,424 51
Less amount carried to credit undivided earnings account		650,809 20
		$35,615 31
Receipts from December 31st, 1860, to December 31st, 1861:		
For passengers	$694,414 36	
" freight, merchandise	630,996 32	
" " treasure	134,144 26	
" mails	11,515 47	
" interest, wharfage, light money, etc	23,789 28	
" earnings for a portion of December, estimated	45,000 00	$1,539,859 69
		$1,575,475 00
Deduct interest on sterling bonds, £540,000 with exchange and commission	$180,951 08	
" " convertible bonds	1,505 00	
Working expenses, including materials, repairs, subsistence, labor, and salaries, etc	396,192 14	
Office expenses	23,014 89	
New Granadian government proportion of mail receipts	10,000 00	611,663 11
Net earnings for the year		$963,811 89
Dividend No. 18, paid July 2d, on $4,976,000, 6 per cent	$298,560 00	
" " 19, payable January 2d, on $4,981,000, 6 per cent	298,860 00	
New Granadian government proportion of do., 3 per cent	17,922 60	
Paid trustees of Sinking Fund, July, 1861	$50,000	
Appropriated to " December, 1861	50,000	100,000 00	$715,342 60
Surplus after dividends of 1861, to credit undivided earnings account		$248,469 29

GENERAL STATEMENT.

Assets: Construction Account		$8,000,000 00
" Cash in bank		250,966 77
" Loans on demand		261,942 10
" Cavan, Lubbock & Co., London		102,774 14
" Investment in United States 7.30 per cent. Treasury notes		100,580 00
" " Company's sterling bonds, 1865		34,369 15
" North Atlantic Steam-ship Company, representing five ninths steamers Baltic and Atlantic		277,777 78
" Sinking Fund, invested		150,369 86
" Amounts due from agents and others		72,981 08
" Steamers (valued) Guatemala, $115,000; Columbus, $20,000		135,000 00
" New steamer Salvador, payments on account		80,580 54
" Interest in sailing vessels, valued at		24,000 00
" Steam-tug and launches in the Bay of Panama, valued at		35,000 00
" Real estate on the Isthmus and islands in the Bay of Panama, cost		68,446 99
" Coal Account, amount on hand		8,742 02
		$9,603,530 43
Liabilities: Capital stock	$4,981,000 00	
Convertible bonds still out	19,000 00	$5,000,000 00
Sterling bonds, amount originally issued for construction	3,000,000 00	
Loss amount matured in 1859, paid and held by the Company	600,000 00	
	2,400,000 00	
Exchange	66,237 78	$2,466,237 78
Book Accounts		60,054 40
Dividend declared, payable Jan. 2d, 1862, with New Granadian government proportion		307,825 80
Appropriation to Sinking Fund, December 24, 1861		50,000 00
Bonds redeemed and held by the Company, as above		600,000 00
Undivided earnings from road	$899,278 49	
" " from sailing vessels, steamers, tugs, launches, etc.	220,133 96	$1,119,412 45 — $9,603,530 43

Jos. F. Joy, *Secretary.*

The early history and present condition of the road, at least so much of it as has been thought would prove interesting and serviceable to the general reader, has been presented. The sources of its present business have been shown, and some idea of its probable increase from these; but a large and important field within the legitimate scope of the enterprise demands a little attention from its bearings on the future business of the road. A glance at the geographical situation of the Isthmus of Panama, in its relation with Australia, China, Japan, and the Sandwich Islands, will discover the capacity of the transit to shorten the distances from those countries to the markets of the United States by so many thousands of miles as must make it an eventual necessity for the trade, at least a large portion of it, to seek this, the only direct route between the Atlantic and Pacific Oceans.*

TRAVELER'S GUIDE.

As the traveler enters the harbor of Navy Bay he can not fail to observe the beauty of the scene spread out before him. On the right and in front of the harbor, which sweeps around a semicircle of some three miles in extent, the primeval forest of the tropics, with its dense vinous un-

---

* The distance from New York to Sydney, Australia, via Cape Horn, is... 12,870 miles.
" " " " " " via Panama 9,950
In favor of Panama.................................... 2,720
The distance from New York to Honolulu, Sandwich Isl., via Cape Horn.. 13,560
" " " " " " via Panama 6,800
In favor of Panama.................................... 6,760
The distance from New York to Hong Kong, via Cape Horn............. 17,420
" " " " " via Panama................ 11,850
In favor of Panama.................................... 5,570
The distance from New York to Jeddo, Japan, via Cape Horn............. 16,710
" " " " " " via Panama................ 10,220
In favor of Panama.................................... 6,490
The distance from England to Sydney, Australia, via Cape of Good Hope.. 12,828
" " " " " via Panama 12,730
In favor of Panama.................................... 98
The distance from San Francisco to Yokohama, Japan.. 4900 miles.
" " Yokohama to Shanghai, China....... 900 "
" " Yokohama to Hong Kong .... 1700 "
" " Shanghai to Nagasaki................ 450 "
" " Nagasaki to Yokohama.............. 450 "

dergrowth and its towering cocoa and palm trees, meets his view; on the left, from the iron light-house on the extreme seaward point, the brightly-painted Americo-Spanish town of Aspinwall extends, its long covered wharves filled with the shipping of many nations. A verandaed street skirts the shore, and a dense equatorial forest rising up behind is relieved by the faint and misty mountain range, which forms the *back-bone* of the Isthmus, and connects the great *Cordillera* of the northern and southern continents—the Rocky Mountains and the Andes. This harbor (said to have been discovered by Columbus during his third voyage, and by him named "Navy Bay") is three miles in length by two in breadth, with an average depth of seven fathoms, affording good anchorage ground in every part. Since the establishment of the Panama Railroad it has been a rendezvous for the United States Atlantic squadron, and one or more frigates of the first class may usually be seen at anchor; also a United States store-ship, which has its permanent station here.

The city of Aspinwall, which has grown up from the necessity of its position as the Atlantic terminus of the railroad, while answering its purpose as a receiving and transhipping depôt, has but little, architecturally, to recommend it to notice, the dwellings, some two hundred in number, being of wood, and built in a style midway between the New England house and the verandaed structures usual in the tropics. They are built on land leased from the Company by private individuals.

The voyager coming to Aspinwall by the United States mail steam-ships will be landed at the end of an immense wharf belonging to the Company, and will find it worth his while to take a walk about the town ere making the transit of the Isthmus. First, it may not be amiss to notice the wharf itself, which extends from the shore out upon a coral reef, nearly a thousand feet, to where a depth of wa-

D

ter exists sufficient to float the largest ships. It is forty feet in breadth, and covered by a lofty metallic roof; the piles upon which it stands are coppered to protect them from the *teredo*, a boring worm which infests these waters, and rapidly destroys every kind of timber unless thus protected. At the upper end of the wharf a grove of cocoanut-trees shoots up through the flooring, and at any and every season of the year the cocoanut, in the bud, the blossom, and full grown, may here be seen. Several large iron tanks are situated at the head of the wharf, each of a capacity of several thousand gallons. The whole island of Manzanilla, upon which Aspinwall is situated, a mile in length by three quarters in width, being a low coral foundation, has no springs of water, and that obtained by digging is so brackish that rain-water is used instead; these tanks, filled by the rains which prevail for more than half the year, before the establishment of the great reservoir, furnished the supply of water for the shipping during the dry season. At the head of the wharf you reach the quadruple track of the railway. Proceeding toward its Atlantic terminus, you pass, on your left, the line of stores, shops, and hotels which were visible from the entrance of the harbor. The shops, perhaps half a dozen in number, usually display a very respectable assortment of goods, principally ready-made clothing, fancy articles, and groceries. Among them are several quite extensive importing houses of French, English, and American merchandise, and Havana cigars for the South American market and the shipping visiting the port.

The hotels,* of which there are, great and small, at least a dozen, have, for this country, very fair accommodation for all classes of travelers, at from one to four dollars per day;

---

* Probably the best accommodation will be found at the Howard, City, and Aspinwall Hotels. Usual charge for first class passengers $3 per day. Second class passengers are accommodated at the other houses at considerably lower rates. It is well to have the terms well understood beforehand.

but little business, however, is done among them except on the arrival of the passenger steamers of the California line. In 1852, when these hotels were erected, travelers were often detained here for several days, when the landlords drove a brisk trade; but now the ship-loads of passengers are seldom detained here more than two or three hours, and, although a brisk business is done for the time, the publican finds his opportunity too brief to realize much profit.

At the end of the row stands the Panama Railroad Company's office, a respectable fire-proof two-story brick building, into the upper windows of which the wires of the Isthmus Telegraph converge. The poles, or, more properly, the pillars, which serve to support the wires of this telegraph line, from their symmetry, strength, and novel construction, are worthy of particular notice. They are apparently of *hewn stone.* Some two years since, after much trouble and expense had resulted in consequence of the rapid decay of the wooden poles formerly used, Colonel Totten conceived the idea of moulding a support of concrete. A small straight stick of the necessary height was placed upright, and surrounded by a jointed wooden mould, fifteen inches in diameter at the base, tapering to about eight inches at the top, and sunk into the earth sufficiently for firm support; this was filled with *concrete,* and allowed to stand for several days. When the mould was removed, it was found firm and strong, and apparently every way adapted to the purpose. This fact once settled, the entire line was supplied with these quasi stone columns, but little exceeding the unsightly wooden poles in expense, and perfectly weather and insect proof. It is now nearly two years since their establishment, and they bid fair, extraordinary occurrences excepted, to last for a century.

Farther along the track, on your right, you pass the main railroad wharf, at which any day in the year several vessels, sail or steam, may be seen actively discharging cargoes for shipment across the road. A couple of hundred yards brings you to a massive stone structure three hundred feet long by eighty wide, through whose broad-arched entrances a triple track is laid. This is the freight depôt of the Panama Railroad Company, and the following description by a recent visitor will give the traveler an idea of its usual internal appearance:

"Bales of quina bark from the interior were piled many tiers deep, and reached to the iron triangular-braced roof of the edifice. Ceroons of indigo and cochineal from San Salvador and Guatemala; coffee from Costa Rica, and cacao from Ecuador; sarsaparilla from Nicaragua, and ivory-nuts from Porto Bello; copper ore from Bolivia; silver bars from Chili; boxes of hard dollars from Mexico, and gold ore from California; hides from the whole range of the North and South Pacific coast; hundreds of bushels of glistening pearl-oyster shells from the fisheries of Panama lay heaped along the floor, flanked by no end of North American beef, pork, flour, bread, and cheese, for the provisioning of the Pacific coast, and English and French goods for the same markets; while in a train of cattle-cars that stood on one of the tracks were huddled about a hundred meek-looking lamas from Peru, on their way to the island of Cuba, among whose mountains they are used for beasts of burden as well as for their wool."

Its situation is on the direct line of the road, its seaward side opening by great doors out upon the waters of the bay, so as to allow vessels of light tonnage to discharge cargo directly into the depôt, while for the heavier a covered wharf extends from the centre into six fathom water. On emerging from the farther extremity of the freight-house, a hundred paces brings you to the *Mingillo*, or native market-place. A few lusty half-naked negroes, descended from the African slaves of the old Spanish dominion (who form a large proportion of the littoral population of the Isthmus) are generally seen supplying their customers with fish, cassava, bananas, plantains, and many other fruits and vegetables of the country, from out the bongoes which lay alongside the wharf, or, grouped on the shore over smoking kettles of *sancoche*, ladling out this favorite compound to their native patrons. Large quantities of the vegetable ivory-nut are also brought here by the natives for barter and sale. Sometimes a few aboriginal Indians from the region of San Blas (some sixty miles down the coast) may be seen here. Rather under the medium stature, they are broad-shouldered and muscular, with the straight black hair and high cheek-bones of the North American tribes. They have a peculiar interest from the fact that they belong to a tribe never subjugated by the *Conquistadores*, but who have maintained an unwavering hostility to the Spaniard since the first discovery of the country, and have cherished such a jealousy of their independence that, to the present day, no white man has been permitted to land upon their shores. Their usual dress consists of a simple fold of cloth tied about the loins, though they are not unfrequently seen clad after the manner of the Spanish natives, in a loose shirt and loose cotton or hempen trowsers. Though apparently apathetic and uncommunicative, there is a considerable degree of intelligence in their expression, and a conscious independence in their bearing, that gives one a fair idea of the races which Columbus and his followers found here in the days of old. They have recently allowed one or two small trading schooners twice or thrice a year to anchor near their shores and traffic with them, receiving calicoes, beads, and other ornaments, machetas, etc., in exchange for tortoise-shell, ivory-nuts, and gold dust; but every attempt to explore their country has been uniformly resisted. Their chief weapon is the bow and arrow (the arrow armed with fish-bones), in the use of which they are said to be very skillful, and to be in the habit of using it effectively not only upon land, but in their waters; with barbed palm-wood arrows some four feet in length, they have the reputation of being able to transfix large fish at a distance of two or three feet beneath the surface.

Along the opposite side of the railway from the *Mingillo* lies a broad lagoon covering a couple of acres, and connected with the waters of the harbor by a narrow opening under the road. This lagoon is crossed at about the centre by a recently-made street, and will soon be still farther reduced in extent by others. A line of low tenements, principally occupied by the native population, a few stores, and a large hotel, the Aspinwall House, bound its opposite shore, beyond which a dense swamp-forest shuts off the view. Proceeding a little farther, you pass "Johnson's Ice-house," or, rather, if you have an eye to creature comfort, you will not pass it, for it is a depôt for ice and such things for the inner man as may be preserved in it of northern product. Five ships a year come consigned to this establishment from the Boston Ice Company, and Johnson, "the Ice-man of the Isthmus," is decidedly a man whose acquaintance is worth cultivating in this climate. Turning now to the left, toward the sea-beach, which forms a semicircle around this end of the island, the driving surf of centuries has washed up along its whole extent a wide barrier of shells and coral. Upon this you will first observe the hospitals of the Railroad Company, a couple of large, airy buildings, surrounded by generous tiers of piazzas, about which a general air of tidiness and comfort prevails. Although built for the exclusive use of the Company, strangers requiring medical aid are permitted to avail themselves of their advantages. A little to the left is a long wooden building, which contains the lecture-room, library, and club-room of the employes of the Company. A well-selected library of several hundred volumes, and the standard periodicals and journals, may be seen here; there are also materials for a snug

To the eastward of the "Mess-house," and distant about 200 yards, stands a beautiful Gothic edifice, built of hewn stone. It is the Protestant Episcopal Church of Aspinwall, and the only Protestant church in this country. It was erected by private subscription, aided by the Panama Railroad Company, in 1864, from plans executed by Mr. James Renwick, Architect, of New York, and is capable of seating about 300 people. It was consecrated by the late Rt. Rev. Bishop Alonzo Potter, of Pennsylvania, in the month of June, 1865, and was one of the last acts of his professional life. Its pastor, the Rev. Richard Temple, was commissioned for this field of labor by the Protestant Episcopal Missionary Society of New York, and is maintained here by the Company.

game of billiards, backgammon, or chess. Three or four neat little cottages come next along the line of the beach, the residences of the principal officers of the Company, with little garden-plats in the rear, and an occasional cocoa-tree throwing pleasant shadows over them. A little farther on is a fine corrugated iron dwelling, the residence of the Royal Mail Steam Packet Company's agent; next to this is seen the general domestic rendezvous of the Railroad Company's officials (usually known as the "Mess-house"), imbedded in a grove of cocoa and banana trees. Within fifty yards of the rolling surf, the sea-breeze ever playing through its surrounding foliage, it would be difficult to find a more desirable tropical residence.

Still farther on to the right are the buildings of the terminus, car repositories, etc., and machine-shops, whose tall chimneys send up steady columns of smoke, while the ring of many hammers breaks cheerily upon the ear. Along the beach a nicely-graded road has been constructed, which extends the entire circumference of the island, and for more than two thirds of its course it passes along or through the dense and luxuriant tropical forest with which nearly one half the island is still covered. The "Paseo Coral," as this beautiful walk or drive is called, was built by the citizens of Aspinwall, every facility and aid being rendered by the Railroad Company; and morning and evening, especially on Sundays and holidays, it is a favorite resort of the inhabitants of all classes, a few on horseback or in light wagons, but the great majority on foot. Any lover of the beautiful in nature will find it worth his while to make a tour of this "Paseo;" on one side charming glimpses of the ocean and of the "Archipelago" (which cuts off the island of Manzanilla from the main land) meet the eye at every turn, and at almost any point the conchologist may step out upon the coral reef and find sea-shells, fans, and coral to an indefinite extent; on the other, a great variety of tropical vegetation invites the lover of botany to cull from its varied and luxuriant growth; here and there narrow paths lead from it to little native plantations of banana, papaya, and yam, imbedded in which the native hut, with its severely simple furnishing, may be seen, and will convey to the traveler an idea of the habits and character of the native inhabitant of this country. The land in and about Aspinwall, though highly productive, has not yet been brought under proper cultivation to any extent, though several promising plantations have been recently established by foreign residents; fowls, yams, and tropical fruits are, however, found in plenty, and native beef is abundant; the harbor also abounds in excellent fish, and the neighboring islands afford an unlimited supply of the finest green turtle, the usual market-price of which is five cents per pound. Aspinwall, though belonging to New Granada, has a separate civic government, the control of which is possessed chiefly by residents from the United States, most of whom are connected with the Panama Railroad Company.

JOURNEY OVER THE ROAD.

While the principal portion of the route of the Panama Railroad affords to the traveler but little of historic interest apart from its own construction, passing as it does through the heart of a primeval tropical forest for many miles of its extent, and among the wildest and most picturesque mountain scenery, along beautiful rivers, fertile plains, and luxuriant lowlands, for the remainder it affords the observant traveler an opportunity of an easy enjoyment and acquaintance with intertropical nature unsurpassed in any part of the world. Though in point of climate a perpetual summer reigns, the summer and winter are represented by the dry and wet seasons, which produce in the appearance of the vegetation a constant succession of changes in color and form ever new and beautiful. From May until October

DEPARTURE FOR PANAMA.

the rains fall almost daily for several hours; there are usually also several hours each day of bright sunshine. Occasionally throughout the wet season the rain falls for several days without cessation, and in violence and amount seldom if ever seen in northern latitudes. During this season the forests are clothed in brilliant and varied greens, and many of the large forest-trees are covered with blossoms of white, scarlet, or yellow, which, together with the myriads of parasites, epiphytes, and flowering vines, often produce the most gorgeous effects. During the dry season, which occupies the rest of the year, while showers are not uncommon, it is usual to see two, and even three months pass without rain, and the vegetation is scarcely less beautiful than in the wet, though toward the latter part many of the larger trees are destitute of foliage, and the browns and yellows of dying leaves are seen on every side; yet the rich greens still preponderate sufficiently to give a decided summer character to the whole; and the evergreen palms, from which hang numberless clusters of ripe palm-nuts of the richest scarlet; the lowland trees, that blossom at every season; and the passifloras, and many other beautiful flowers, that develop only in the dry season, make it difficult to say which of the two seasons will afford the rarest botanical and floral treat to the traveler; at any and every season the vegetation is varied, luxuriant, and gorgeous beyond comparison. There are, besides, at almost every step, objects novel and interesting among the riches of the animal kingdom, and also in the varied geological formations displayed along the line of the road; in fact, few locations in the world present a more promising field of research for the botanist, the geologist, or the student of natural history. Eminent scientific men from the United States, England, and Germany have already spent considerable time and labor in explorations here, but the results of their researches have not as yet been given to the public. As, however, few travelers over the road have any opportunity other than that afforded by the rapid railway transit to examine the objects of interest on its course, a brief account of the more prominent and readily recognized will perhaps be deemed sufficient for the general reader.

In making the journey over the railroad to the Pacific terminus, starting at the depôt at Aspinwall, a third of a mile brings you to that part of the island shore where the railway leaves it, and crosses over the frith to the swamps of the main land. At this point, which is crossed by an artificial isthmus (built originally of piles and crib-work, but since replaced by solid stone and earth), the channel is about two hundred yards in width, broadening rapidly to the eastward into a miniature archipelago, with a dozen little islands overgrown with mangrove bushes, and lying upon its glassy surface like emeralds upon a mirror. To the westward it again expands into a wide, placid basin, only separated by a narrow belt of foliage from the waters of the bay. The shores on every hand are skirted with a dense growth of mangrove bushes, which droop deep into the water, while directly in front, through the vista opened by the railway, an apparently interminable forest meets the eye. These waters abound in the beautiful varieties of fish known among the natives as "flores del mar," or "the flowers of the sea:" in shape and size they resemble the sun-fish of our Northern lakes, and are remarkable for their varied and brilliant colors.

The mangrove bushes are not unlike the banyan-tree in the manner of their growth. Their branches, shooting downward, frequently enter the soil, take root, and, interlacing again and again, form a barrier requiring a stout hatchet or machete to overcome. Many of the branches which dip into the water are loaded with a variety of the Crustaceæ, almost, if not quite, identical with our Northern oysters, varying in size from a dime to a dollar: several pounds often

MOUNT HOPE.

depend from a single bough. Submerged by every tide, they are well nourished and exceedingly palatable, and, although so small, well worth the trouble of opening. English snipe, plover, teal, heron, and pelican are abundant about here at certain seasons.

About a mile farther on, to the left of a spur of high land, through which the railway passes by a deep long cut, is seen the tall forest of Mount Hope, upon which is located the general cemetery of Aspinwall. A pleasant winding path through the thick undergrowth soon brings you upon the spot. Dense foliage surrounds it on every side. This place was selected for a burial-ground shortly after the commencement of the road, and many victims to the hardships of the work and the virulence of the climate were then buried here; but those days of trial have passed, and the long grass waving over their graves tells of the years since then. A few are recent, and marked by simple monuments; among them will be noticed several of the officers of the United States Home Squadron. The lamented Strain (whose suffering and heroism as the leader of the ill-fated Darien expedition are still fresh in the memory of his countrymen) lies buried here. The surrounding woods, especially toward evening and in the early morning, are vocal with the notes of numerous birds. The sweet and sonorous whistle of the *turpiale* and the cooing of the turtle-dove mingle with the harsh cries of the parrot tribe and the still harsher note of the toucan. Frequent opportunities occur of procuring these different varieties of birds from the natives, as they are more or less numerous along the entire line of the road, and become domesticated with little trouble. The turpiale, which is about the size of a robin, with deep black and bright yellow plumage, is quite equal to the magpie in intelligence and cunning, and is one of the finest whistlers known. The toucan, a dark scarlet-breasted bird, about the size of a pigeon, with a heavy serrated bill six or seven inches in length, is one of the ornithological curiosities of this region; picking up its food on the point of its huge beak, by a sudden jerk it tosses it up half a yard, and as it falls catches it deep in its throat; it also makes extraordinary motions over the water when attempting to drink. The habits of the toucan in this respect were noticed by the early Spanish-American priests, who, averring that this bird, in drinking, made the sign of the cross over the water, called it "Dios te de" (God gives it thee). Considerable land in the vicinity of Mount Hope has been cleared, and cultivated with success and profit. Proceeding along the track beyond Mount Hope, you begin to bring more fully into view the wondrous wealth of the Isthmian forest. For a space of fifty feet on either side of the solid track embankment the original growth has been swept away and replaced by a rich display of aquatic plants, through whose broad shining leaves myriads of callas and long, slim-petaled pond-lilies struggle out to fill the air with their delicious perfume. This low and recent vegetation is walled in by a primeval growth of a variety and luxuriance that almost defies description. Palm-trees, slender and tall, from under whose crowns hang long scarlet and yellow tassels; palms, low and huge, with trunks scarce lifted above the slimy ooze, sending out graceful pinnate leaves half a dozen yards in length; great cedro and espabe trees, towering up like giants for a hundred feet, then sending out strong arms that almost clasp each other across the clearing, their trunks covered with thick vines and parasites. These and many other varieties are so closely set and interwoven together that the eye fails to penetrate into the depths of the forest. The great number and variety of parasitic growths can not fail to attract constant attention. Almost every tree and shrub supports more or less of these treacherous leeches, in form and size ranging from the simple tuft of grass to the enormous growths whose branches equal in magnitude those of the largest trees, and frequently exceed those of the poor victim from which their strength is drawn. Some are seen which had originally taken root upon the trunks of large and thrifty trees, which, under their exhausting demands and vice-like embrace, have died and rotted out, leaving the well-conditioned leech, though a mere shell, upright, and so like the original tree that, except for occasional apertures which discloses the hollowness within, their villainy might at a little distance escape detection. Many bear beautiful and fragrant flowers. A curious and exceedingly common variety springs from seeds deposited in the ordure of birds upon the highest trees, sending long fibrous tendrils, without a single branching twig, down to the earth, when it again takes root, and increases in size until it frequently attains a diameter of five or six inches. Often trees, so decayed that otherwise they must have fallen, are by these supports retained in their upright position for many years. The smaller ones, combining pliability with great strength, are much used as cordage by the natives. Trailing vines and blossoming creepers are on every side in great profusion and luxuriance, enwrapping the trees and hanging in variegated festoons from the branches. As you proceed, every moment new, and, if possible, richer varieties of vegetation pass in quick review, until you are almost lost in wonder and admiration. At about three miles from the terminus a bend is cut off in the small sluggish stream, called the Mindee, whose waters are half concealed by the overhanging verdure; along its banks the tall and graceful bamboo, that giant of the grasses, adds a new beauty to the scene. The waters of the Mindee, which empties into Navy Bay about a mile and a half from Aspinwall, abound with alligators, often of great size, which afford plenty of exciting sport to parties from the city, who make occasional incursions upon them, and to the natives, who value them greatly for their oil, which is used for medication, and their teeth, which are worn as potent charms. Not unfrequently these ugly beasts crawl out into the pools along the railway track, where they may be seen basking in the sun, scarcely deigning to lift their unwieldy heads as the train thunders by.

In the immediate vicinity of the Mindee some of the lands are dry enough to be susceptible of tillage. Native huts may here and there be seen near the road surrounded by patches of plantains, bananas, Indian-corn, and sugar-cane. Beyond this the forest vegetation is varied and enriched by a species of the palm, from the fruit of which the palm-oil of commerce is extracted. It differs little in form from the tasseled variety which has been previously noticed, except that it attains a greater size, and, instead of the gaudy tassel, bears immense clusters of scarlet nuts about as large as a lime; the clusters, shooting out from the trunk of the tree just underneath its foliage, hang by a single stem, and are often two or three feet in length, contrasting vividly with the surrounding verdure. The palm-tree, that prince of the vegetable kingdom, which is so characteristic of tropical vegetation, is nowhere more abundant in variety and beauty than upon the Isthmus, no less than twenty-one varieties having already been found and classified here. Conspicuous among them for their practical use to the natives of the country are the "wine palm," from the sap of which is distilled a sweet and intoxicating beverage; the "motombo," or sago palm, which furnishes the sago; the "ivory palm," producing the vegetable ivory-nut of commerce; the "glove palm," which furnishes, by the covering of its spatha, ready-made bags, capable of holding grain, etc., to the amount of nearly half a bushel; the "cabbage palm," the tender shoots upon the summit of which resemble in appearance and nutritiousness the ordinary cabbage; others also there are from which they manufacture flax, sugar, various domestic utensils, weapons, and

GATUN STATION.

food; besides this, the habitations of the people are framed of their trunks and roofed with their leaves.

Passing the seventh mile-post, you emerge from the swamp, and come to the Gatun Station, located upon the eastern bank of the Rio Chagres, which is at this point about fifty yards in width, and here makes a great bend, opening beautiful vistas through the dense forests up and down its course. This bank of the river is formed by a ridge of low hills, across the foot of which the railway runs. A few yards from the road, on the high ground to the left, are the buildings of the station. A large, two-story framed building, about forty feet in length by thirty in breadth, surrounded by piazzas and balustrades, is the residence of the local superintendent and the foreign workmen employed on this section. Suitable out-buildings are situated in the rear, and a little garden in front, where the roses and peonies, the pinks and pansies of our northern clime, challenge comparison with the orchids, fuchsias, and passifloras of the tropics; and there are radishes, cucumbers, and lettuce contrasting curiously with the native products of the place. With a few unimportant exceptions, this establishment is similar to that of all the stations, which are situated about four miles distant from each other along the entire length of the road. The duty of the local superintendent is not only to keep the track along his section in perfect repair, but to give his personal attention to all matters which can in any way impede the safety or dispatch of the regular trains; and to this ample service, in a great measure, is due the immunity from accident which has characterized the running of the Panama Railroad from its first establishment to the present day. On the opposite shore of the river stands the ancient native town of *Gatun*, which is composed of forty or fifty huts of cane and palm, and situated on the edge of a broad savanna that extends back to a range of hills a mile or two distant. This place is worthy of mention as a point where, in the days by-gone, the bongo-loads of California travelers used to stop for refreshment on their way up the river; where "eggs were then sold four for a dollar, and the rent for a hammock was two dollars a night."

From Gatun the course of the road lies along the base of an irregular line of high lands that rise up from the eastern side of the valley of the Rio Chagres, and a few hundred yards brings you to the Rio Gatun, a tributary of the Chagres, which is crossed by an iron truss-girder bridge of ninety-seven feet span. The dense swamp-growth looms up on either side like a wall, while rising out of it, close on the left, are two fine conical peaks, called "Lion" and "Tiger" hills, which attract attention by the regularity of their outlines and the dense and gorgeous forests with which they are covered. These hills received their titles from the immense numbers of howling monkeys which inhabited this district previous to and during the construction of the road, and whose frequent roaring made the night-hideous, and were often mistaken by the uninitiated for the formidable animals which their cries closely resembled. These, as well as several smaller varieties, still abound in the neighborhood, and their howlings at nightfall are frequently heard, but the progress of improvement has driven them from the immediate vicinity of the road. .

Passing the Lion Hill Station, which has a fine cultivated clearing on the high ground behind it, the vegetation becomes less dense, and more decidedly aquatic in its character; large patches of cane-brake, huge tree-ferns, low palms in great variety, and scrubby mangroves, rise out of the dark pools in the swamps by the road-side. Along this section is found that rare variety of the Orchid family, the *Peristera elata*, known as the "Espiritu Santo." Its blossom, of alabaster whiteness, approaches the tulip in form, and gives forth a powerful perfume not unlike that of the magnolia; but it is neither for its beauty of shape, its purity of color, nor its fragrance that it is chiefly esteemed. Resting within the cup of the flower, so marvelously formed that no human skill, be it never so cunning, could excel the resemblance, lies the prone image of *a dove*. Its exquisitely moulded pinions hang lifeless from its sides, the head bends gently forward, the tiny bill, tipped with a delicate carmine, almost touches its snow-white breast, while the expression of the entire image (and it requires no stretch of the imagination to *see* the expression) seems the very incarnation of meekness and ethereal innocence. No one who has seen it can wonder that the early Spanish Catholic, ever on the alert for some phenomenon upon which to fasten the idea of a miraculous origin, should have bowed down before this matchless flower, and named it "Flor del Espiritu Santo," or "the Flower of the Holy Ghost," nor that the still more superstitious Indian should have accepted the imposing title, and ever after have gazed upon it with awe and devotional reverence, ascribing a peculiar sanctity even to the ground upon which it blossoms, and to the very air which it ladens with its delicious fragrance. It is found most frequently in low and marshy grounds, springing from decayed logs and crevices in the rocks. Some of the most vigorous plants attain a height of six or seven feet; the leaf-stalks are jointed, and throw out broad lanceolate leaves by pairs; the flower-stalks spring from the bulb, and are wholly destitute of leaves, often bearing a cluster of not less than a dozen or fifteen flowers. It is an annual, blooming in July, August, and September, and has in several instances been successfully cultivated in the conservatories of foreign lands. In former times bulbs of the plant could rarely be obtained, and then only with much labor and difficulty; but since their localities have become familiar to the less reverential Anglo-Saxon, great numbers

E

have been gathered and distributed throughout different parts of the world, though their habits and necessities have been so little appreciated that efforts to bring them to flower usually prove ineffectual; if, however, they are procured in May or June, *after the flower-stalk has started*, when sufficient appropriate nutriment resides in the bulb to develop the perfect flowers, they can be safely transplanted, and will flower under the ordinary treatment adapted to the bulbous plants of colder climates. The bulbs, dried or growing, may be procured either at Aspinwall or Panama at from two to five dollars per dozen.

The next station is called "Ahorca Lagarto," "to hang the lizard," deriving its name from a landing-place on the Chagres near by; this, again, named from having, years back, been pitched upon as an encampment by a body of government troops, who suspended from a tree their banner, on which was a lizard, the insignia of the Order of Santiago. The land around this station, though low and level, is covered with a noble forest-growth, among which is found the huge cedro-tree, from which the native hollows out his canoe, sometimes of fifteen or twenty tons burthen; its broad, plane-shaped roots extend out on every side like buttresses, and its trunk towers up, without a branch, for a hundred feet, supporting a canopy of foliage often fifty yards in diameter. A short distance from the station, close to the left side of the track, is one called "Stephens's Tree," not less than five or six yards in diameter at its base. A luxuriant growth of vines decorates its trunk, and, winding out upon its branches, hangs down like a thickly-woven curtain to the lesser growth beneath. Its trunk is studded with parasites, and usually fine specimens of the Orchidaceæ may be seen blooming among its foliage. Several varieties of mahogany are also found here, and occasionally the lignum-vitæ-tree; the most of the trees, however, are only known by local names, which can convey

STEPHENS'S TREE.

RUSTIC SOLITUDE.

to the traveler but little idea of their character. Along the track may be seen the sensitive plant, with its feathery pink blossoms growing in wild profusion. The wild pine-apple, a species of *Agave*, is also abundant. This plant is similar in form and growth to the cultivated pine-apple, except that the leaves are often eight or ten feet in length, and afford a vegetable fibre which makes excellent cloth; the fruit, which is edible and not unpleasant, is of the most brilliant scarlet, and forms a beautiful contrast with the surrounding foliage. A mile or so farther on the forest becomes less lofty, and the traveler soon passes what may easily be mistaken for the overgrown ruins of some ancient city: walls, watch-towers, tall columns, and Gothic arches are on either hand, and it will be difficult to realize that Nature alone, with a lavish and fantastic hand, has shaped this curious scene out of myriads of *convolvuli*; whole clumps of trees are covered in by them, so that they appear like the remains of huge fortifications; tall stumps of palm look like broken columns overgrown with verdure; and when they lean together, as in several instances is the case, great Gothic arches are formed. So dense is this enshrouding web of creepers that scarce a tree or branch can be recognized through it over a space of several acres, and the whole of this wondrous display is, at certain seasons, decorated with bright blue trumpet-shaped flowers.

Leaving behind this city of verdure, a chain of high and densely-wooded hills on the left is brought into view, and, winding along its base, another station, called "Bujio Soldado," or "Buyo Soldado" ("*the Soldier's Home*"), is passed. Here opens, on the right, a fine view up the Rio Chagres. A mile farther on is an excellent quarry of freestone alongside the track, from which large quantities of building and ballasting material have been quarried by the Company. A little farther on, upon the edge of the steep river bank, is the site of a cottage, notable as having been the favorite residence of the late J. L. Stephens, the celebrated author and traveler, who spent much of his later life in developing this great railway enterprise; but little now remains except its ruins, and the stately palm that long ago threw its shadow over his once beautiful garden. From this point beautiful views up and down the river are visible, while across, the high opposing bank stretches back in a broad plateau, covered with low foliage, from among which occasional tall trees shoot up, until it meets a range of distant hills. Continuing your course, with an occasional view of the river, which winds like a great serpent along this tortuous valley, you soon come to the native town of "Bueno Vistita" ("beautiful little view"). This is a collection of thirty or forty rude palm huts, skirting the track, and occupied by the families of native laborers along the road. A few native women, bareheaded, in long, heavily-flounced muslin dresses, off at the shoulder, and usually a naked "picaninny" astride the hip, forms the chief feature of the population, while the balance is made up of dogs, pigs, chickens, and children, in a charming state of affiliation. Very few of the aborigines of the country are found on this portion of the Isthmus, the inhabitants being, for the most part, a mixture of Spaniard and Indian. There are, however, many Africans and half-breeds, descended from the old Spanish slaves of this province, or imported from Carthagena and Jamaica. The former, usually peaceable and industrious, cultivate little patches of land, and occasionally raise a few cattle; but the latter are a restless, turbulent set, requiring a strong hand to keep them in subjection; being, however, hardy and athletic, they have been much employed as laborers on the road. A glance into the huts of these people and at their surroundings will give an idea of the manner of living of the greatest portion of the native inhabitants of the country. The body of the dwelling is composed of bamboo; the roof is thatched with leaves of the

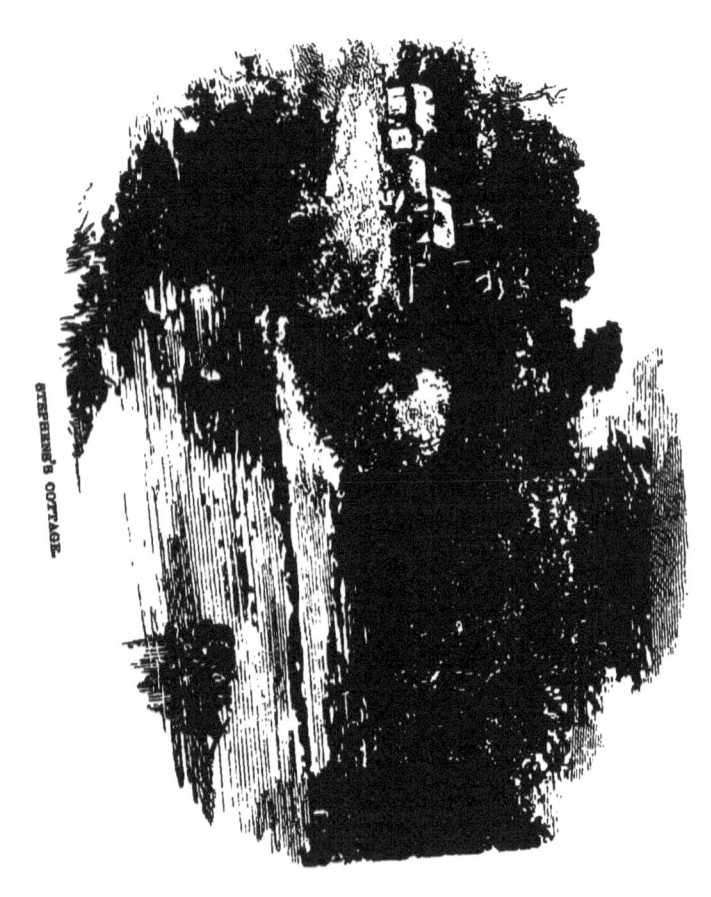

STEPHENS'S COTTAGE.

palm; the floor is the bare earth; occasionally there is a loft, which is reached by an upright post, with deep notches cut on either side answering for stairs. Hammocks of vegetable fibre or cotton cloth are the usual beds, which also constitute the favorite lounging-place during the day. Besides these, a rude bench or two, a kettle, half a dozen earthen platters and water-jars, and a few gourds for water, complete the furniture of the native hut. Sun-dried and fresh beef, and pork, eggs, and fowls, are cheap and plenty. Their food, however, is mostly vegetable, the yam and plantain holding the chief place. The *bread-fruit* is plentiful, and grows spontaneously. Rice is raised, and consumed to a considerable extent; and a large variety of tropical fruits

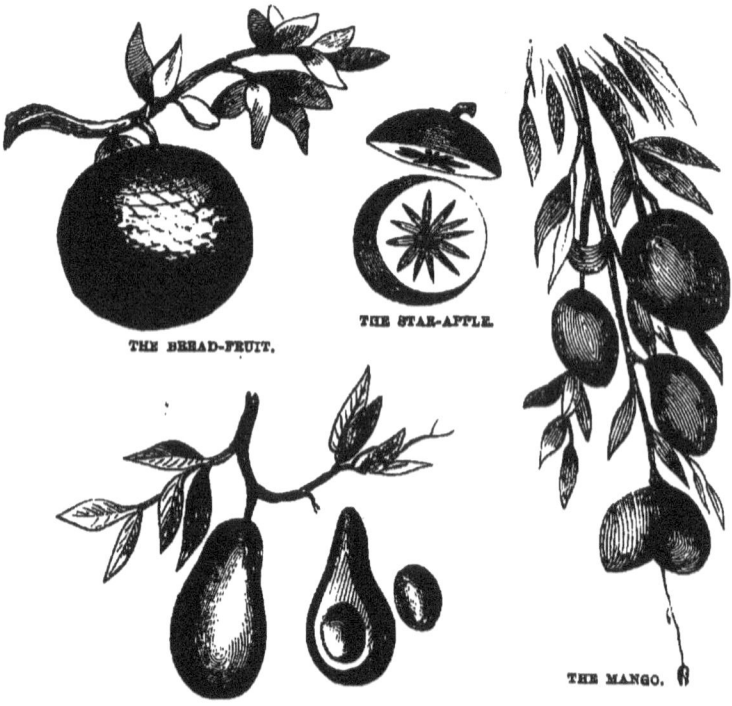

THE BREAD-FRUIT.

THE STAR-APPLE.

THE AVOCADO PEAR.

THE MANGO.

are abundant. Besides the pine-apple, orange, lemon, lime, and banana, which arrive at great perfection here, there are many kinds of fruit seldom seen out of the tropics, which are delicious and wholesome; the bread-fruit, the avocado or alligator pear, the papaya, the Mamei and star-apples, the chirimoya, the mango, the zapote, the granadilla (fruit of the passion-vine), and many others, growing spontaneously or with the most careless cultivation.

The Spanish language is universally spoken by the natives, greatly corrupted, however, by provincialisms. In disposition the native is usually peaceable and inoffensive. The Roman Catholic religion is universally professed, but their ideas of it, beyond a superstitious appreciation of the power and influence of the priests, and the efficacy of holy relics and tokens, are exceedingly limited.

Squatter sovereignty obtains here on a very liberal scale, each citizen being entitled to claim, occupy, and hold "all that lot, piece, or parcel of land" that can be distinctly seen from any given point thereon, of the unoccupied lands of the government. The Spaniard and half-breed frequently avail themselves of this privilege, carrying on cattle-raising to a considerable extent, besides occasionally producing a little sugar, rice, etc., for market. The general class of natives, however, are gregariously inclined, and seldom covet more than enough for a little hut and garden-patch which supplies the necessities of life.

Passing a couple of miles more of forest, intersected by one or two small tributaries of the Chagres River, you arrive at the Frijoli Station; here, during the dry season, may be seen the gorgeous scarlet passion-flower, as well as the purple variety, in great abundance. Occasionally small gangs of natives are seen engaged in clearing away the recent growths along the track with their machetas. The machete is a sort of hiltless broadsword, from two to three feet in length, heavy, straight, and pointed, with a handle of wood or bone, and is the universal companion of the native of this country; with it he cuts his path through the tangled forest, clears his little plantation, builds his hut; with it, too, he plants his crops and reaps them; it is usually his only weapon of offense and defense; and from the half-grown boy to the gray-headed patriarch, you seldom find one, waking or sleeping, without his cherished machete. This section is rich in its variety of the birds, beasts, reptiles, and insects peculiar to intertropical America. Here are found frequent colonies of the oriole, or hanging-bird, whose beautifully-woven nests, often two or three feet long, may be seen depending by scores from the trees. Several richly-colored varieties of parrots and toucans, trogons, tangers, humming-birds, etc., abound. Grouse and the crested wild turkey are found on the higher grounds of the interior. The tapir is occasionally found in the river and marshy grounds adjoining. Monkeys in variety, the opossum, the ant-eater, the peccary, or wild hog, the sloth, the deer, bear, cougar, and two or three varieties of the tiger-cat, are native here. Among the many varieties of the lizard tribe which abound is the iguana, which grows to a large size, viz., from three to six feet in length, and is eagerly sought for by the natives for its flesh, which is tender and delicate as a chicken, and also for its eggs. Females of this species are sometimes captured, cut open, the eggs removed, the animal permitted to escape, and the natives aver that after this barbarous proceeding they uniformly recover. The eggs are about the size of a marble, yellow and shriveled, and may be seen hanging in bunches for sale in any native market, and are by no means unpalatable. Land-crabs abound in great numbers, and are esteemed a delicate article of food. The most common variety is of a pale blue color, and as large as half a cocoanut. Stories are told of their rapacity and carnivorous tastes that almost surpass belief. It is said that the largest animals, dead or wounded past resistance, are frequently reduced by them to whitened skeletons in a single night. There are several other smaller varieties, some of which are beautifully colored. Among the venomous insects, the tarantula, the centipede, and the scorpion are frequently met. Among the troublesome insects are white, red, and black ants, musquitoes, sand-flies, fleas, garapatos, or wood-ticks, and the chigoe, or jigger, which last not only bites, but burrows under the skin, and there deposits its eggs, which, if not speedily removed, will hatch out a troublesome nest of minute worms, producing great inflammatory disturbance in the part. As, however, they are at first very superficial, and inclosed in a little membranous sac, this is easily removed entire with a needle, and no farther trouble ensues; they are fortunately not common here, and seldom annoy any but the barefooted native. Venomous snakes, though occasionally seen, are not common. The boa constrictor is native here, and sometimes is found from twelve to eighteen feet in length; it is, however, exceedingly rare to hear of any serious injury having been done by any of them. The alligator, which is found more or less plentifully in all parts of the Chagres and its tributaries, and the adjacent streams and swamps, frequently attacks and destroys dogs and cattle, and occasional instances have occurred where the natives, imprudently venturing into the waters infested with them, have fallen a prey to their rapacity.

Leaving Frijoli, fine fields of Indian-corn may be seen here and there nestled under the hills; dense groves of palms and superb displays of convolvuli are also found along this section for a couple of miles, when you approach the lofty banks of the Chagres at Barbacoas, and cross the river by a huge wrought-iron bridge six hundred and twenty-five feet in length, eighteen in breadth, and standing forty feet above the surface of the water, and said to be one of the longest and finest iron bridges in the world. After crossing the Chagres at this point, instead of low grounds and virgin forests, a beautiful stretch of meadow-

BRIDGE ACROSS THE RIVER CRACKING AT BARACOAS.

SAN PABLO STATION.

lands, bounded by high precipitous hills, meets the view; while the river, broad and swift, curves around like a horseshoe through its deep channel on the left and behind, displaying along its banks groups of a gigantic species of branchless ceiba, that breaks the outline of dense palm and cocoa groves.

The cultivation of the lands at this point is said to date back for more than two centuries, and to have been worked originally by the Jesuits. At about half a mile from the bridge the San Pablo Station is passed, and a little farther on a fine quarry of recent volcanic rock; from thence, through occasional cleared and cultivated lands, you pass to the station at Mamei and the native town of Gorgona, noted in the earlier days of Chagres River travel as a place where the wet and jaded traveler was accustomed to worry out the night on a raw hide, exposed to the insects and the rain, and in the morning, if he was fortunate, regale himself on jerked beef and plantains. The road now, leaving the course of the river, passes on through deep clay banks and rocky cuts, presenting little novelty beyond the magnitude of the labor expended upon them in establishing the railway, until, sweeping around a hill, the beautiful meadow-lands of Matachin open to the view. Here, rising in their stateliness, the classic sheaves of the royal palm shed an air of Eastern beauty over the landscape. A native village dots the foreground; on the left the waters of the Chagres, broadened at this point by the Rio Obispo (its greatest tributary), is seen through the ceiba groves that skirt its banks, while on the right and in front the scene is bounded by a group of conical hills covered with short grass and studded with palms. The completion of the Panama Railroad in 1855 was here celebrated with great ceremony and rejoicing, and the corner-stone of a monument to its originators and constructors was erected upon the crest of the highest and most beautiful of these hills.

The railway has several side branches at Matachin, and is the usual point of meeting for the trains from either terminus. As there is usually a little delay on such occasions, the natives take advantage of it to traffic with the passengers. Almost every hut displays something for sale:

NATIVE HUT AT MATACHIN.

cakes, "dulces," or native candy, and the various fruits of the region. Here the oranges are unusually fine. There is also a saloon, kept by a native, where very good English beer, French claret, crackers and cheese, etc., may be obtained. From Matachin, passing along the base of "*Monument Hill*," the narrow valley of the Rio Obispo is entered, and its waters are crossed by stout iron bridges twice within the distance of a mile; then you pass the Obispo Station, and continue along the course of the Obispo River, over a fine rolling and luxuriant woodland, where the delicious wild mango, the zapote, the nispero, and the guava are fre-

MAIN STATION.

MONUMENT HILL.—MATACHIN.

quently seen; also occasional native huts, surrounded by cultivated fields. From the station at Obispo the grade is ascending, with a maximum of sixty feet to the mile. Continuing to rise for about three miles, you pass the "Empire Station," and reach the "Summit," or highest elevation of the railway above the mean level of the Atlantic and Pacific Oceans. Here is a little native settlement called "Culebra" ("the Snake"), noted as having been the terminus of the road in 1854. Then, passengers arriving at this place by the cars from the Atlantic shore were compelled to mount upon mules, and flounder on through heavy sloughs and rapid streams, along the borders of deep ravines and over precipitous mountains, exposed to drenching rains in the wet season, and a broiling sun in the dry, not unfrequently attacked and plundered by banditti, with which the road was then infested, until, after a whole day's labor and peril, they arrived at Panama, only twelve miles distant. "Culebra" at that time was a thrifty place, boasting of two or three hotels, imported ready-made from the United States, into which often more than a thousand men, women, and children were promiscuously stowed for a night. There were also twenty or thirty native huts, about twelve feet square, each of which was considered of ample dimensions to house a dozen wayworn travelers, only too thankful to find a spot of dry ground upon which to spread their blankets; but its glory has departed, and scarce a vestige remains to tell of its former estate. From Culebra the road passes through a deep clay cutting from twenty to forty feet in depth, and nearly a third of a mile in length. At this point commences the Pacific slope of the road, with a descending grade of sixty feet to the mile.

The surrounding scenery now becomes bold and picturesque in the highest degree. Lofty conical mountains rise on every side from among the irregular ridges that form the upper boundaries of the Rio Grande. The course of the road now lies across steep rocky spurs and deep ravines between them and along their precipitous sides. High embankments and heavy cuttings are frequent. Here, also, the vegetation is profuse and gorgeous; tall forests cover the whole landscape as far as the eye can reach. At about a mile from the summit the road passes along the side of a huge basaltic cliff, whose great crystals, nearly a foot in diameter, and from eight to twelve feet in length, lie at an angle of about forty degrees. In the earlier days of the road this cliff presented a lofty, broken, and jagged appearance, that seemed almost to overhang and threaten the safety of those passing along the track below. These great crystals of basalt, firm and compact, but easily dislodged, have been so extensively used in the ballasting of the road, etc., along this section, that the once grand and picturesque appearance of the cliff is almost entirely destroyed; enough, however, remains to strike the beholder with admiring wonder, on contemplating this curious formation, at the still visible regularity and beauty of its crystallization, and with awe when he reflects upon the gigantic internal forces that have resulted in its upheaval. It is one of the few known examples in the world where the natural perpendicular which basaltic formations always assume (so beautifully seen in the Fingal's Cave at Staffa, and along the "Palisades" of the Hudson) has been so rent and displaced. But this whole region gives unmistakable evidence that great and comparatively recent volcanic forces have been instrumental in its formation. There is no continuity of the mountain ranges; conical peaks rise up on every side; perfect marine shells and coral are found on their very summits, and the strata of the rocks exposed by the cuttings of the railroad are all volcanic. The Rio Grande at this point is a narrow and noisy torrent, winding along through the dense forests far below the track; the caoba, the cedro, and the malvicino trees rise up like lords of the land over the end-

BASALTIC CLIFF.

PARAISO STATION.

less growths of palm and the innumerable varieties of other tropical woods that interweave below them. After nearly three miles of this, the beautiful undulating valley of "Paraiso," or "Paradise," is reached, surrounded by high conical hills, where Nature, in wild profusion, seems to have expended her choicest wealth. From Paraiso the road continues on over ravines, and curves around the base of frequent conical mountains, gradually descending until the low lands and swamps of the valley of the Rio Grande are passed, when looming up in the distance is seen the high, bald head of Mount Ancon, whose southern foot is washed by the waters of the Pacific Ocean. On the left rises "*Cerro de los Buccaneros*" ("the Hill of the Buccaneers"), from whose summit the pirate Morgan, on his marauding march across the Isthmus in 1670, had his first view of ancient Panama, and where he encamped on the night previous to his attack and pillage of that renowned city. Crossing by bridges of iron the San Pedro Miguel and the Caimitillo (narrow tide-water tributaries of the Rio Grande), the Rio Grande Station is passed. From thence, through alternate swamp and cultivated savanna, the muddy bed of the Rio Cardenas is crossed; when, leaving the Rio Grande to the eastward, a fine stretch of undulating country around the base of Mount Ancon is brought into view, enlivened by native huts and cultivated fields. About a mile farther on may be seen the long metallic roofs of the railroad buildings of the Pacific terminus peeping out from a grove of cocoa-trees, and a little beyond them, and to the right, the Cathedral towers, the high-tiled roofs and dilapidated fortifications of the city of Panama, while through the intervening foliage occasional glimpses of the "ever peaceful ocean" assure the traveler that the transit of the Isthmus is nearly accomplished, and a few minutes more brings him safely into the spacious passenger depôt of the Railroad Company at Panama.

Passing through the depôt, and from thence directly onward to the sandy beach of the Bay of Panama, about fifty yards distant, a beautiful panorama opens upon the view. On the left are the commodious warehouses and the long, covered, iron-piled wharf of the Railroad Company, alongside of which the small steamers and tugs lie to take on or discharge passengers and freight for the larger vessels anchored in the bay. Beyond the wharf a white sandy beach sweeps around a quarter circle of a couple of miles, skirted by tangled masses of foliage interspersed with groups of cocoa-trees. A ridge of high and broken, but heavily wooded land rises up behind, sloping down to the eastward toward the peaceful ocean, that stretches out to the horizon before you. On the right, the city, high-walled and turreted, stands boldly out into the ocean, like Balboa of old, as if still claiming dominion over the limitless expanse; no longer bristling with defiant cannon or decked with the flaunting colors of the Conquistador, but deserted, crumbling, and grass-grown, "mellowed into harmony by time." Within the walls a mass of high-tiled roofs, with here and there a dilapidated tower or pearl-shelled spire, combine to present a scene more beautiful than is often beheld. The city of Panama is peculiarly rich in historical associations connected with the early days of the Spanish rule in this country, and is full of the decayed monuments of its ancient splendor.

Panama is situated in lat. 8° 56' N., and long. 79° 31' 2" W., upon a rocky peninsula that stretches out from the base of the high volcanic hill *Ancon*, and projects a quarter of a mile into the sea. It has at present a population of about 10,000 souls. Its roadstead is one of the finest in the world. At about two and a half miles northwest of the city are situated the beautiful islands of Perico, Flamenco, and Islñao, the joint property of the Panama Railroad and the Pacific Mail Steam-ship Companies, and are occu-

TERMINUS AT PANAMA.

CITY OF PANAMA.

pied by them as the rendezvous of the California and Central American lines of steam-ships. These islands are well wooded, and abound in fine springs of water. Flamenco, the largest of the three (about half a mile in length by a third in breadth), has on its southern side a fine beach, which, as the tides here rise and fall from twelve to twenty-one feet, gives admirable facilities for the repairs of the shipping. Excellent and capacious anchorage exists here. The city of Panama previously to 1744 (when the trade between Europe and Western America first began to be carried on around Cape Horn) was the principal entrepôt of trade on the Pacific coast. From that period, however, with the decline in the Spanish possessions in America, it became reduced in commercial importance almost to a nonentity, and so remained until the past few years. The establishment of the South Coast, the California, the Central American steam-ship lines, and that by which all the business of these lines is carried on, the Panama Railroad, have combined to render it again a place of considerable importance. At Panama there is a first-rate hotel, the Aspinwall House, probably the best on the Isthmus—charge three dollars per day.

The site of the "City of Panama the Ancient" (which was destroyed by the buccaneer Sir Henry Morgan in 1661) is located about six miles southeast of the present city, and is easily reached by water or land. If time permits, the traveler should by all means visit this spot. The ruins of its ancient fortifications, towers, churches, and public buildings are worthy of the attention of all interested in the early history of Central America, and will amply repay the antiquarian or the lover of the picturesque and beautiful the trouble of a visit to this most interesting of all the remains of Spanish greatness in this region. In the Appendices following will be found, first, all information appertaining to the regulations of the trains on the Panama Railroad, the rates of passage and of the transportation of every kind of freight, and all general information in regard to the regulations of the road which will be likely to be of service to the traveler or the man of business. Also an account of all its connections by sail and steam in the Atlantic and Pacific Oceans, their business regulations, and such information in regard to them and the countries and the places they connect with the road, as shall furnish a reliable source of reference to all interested, displaying, as far as is practicable in a small compass, the resources of each country and place, and affording a means of ascertaining the expenses attendant upon either a visit to those regions, or of doing business with them in the most economical and intelligent manner.

THE CATHEDRAL AT PANAMA.

RUINS OF CHURCH OF SAN DOMINGO, PANAMA.

REGULATIONS OF THE PANAMA RAILROAD.

THE regular trains are dispatched daily, Sundays excepted, from Aspinwall to Panama and from Panama to Aspinwall, as per time-table annexed:

TO PANAMA.			STATIONS.	TO ASPINWALL.		
Passenger.	Freight.	Miles.		Miles.	Passenger.	Freight.
Leave.	Leave.	-			Arrive.	Arrive.
8.15 A.M.	2.00 P.M.	....	Aspinwall	47½	1.00 P.M.	5.30 P.M.
8.50 "	2.35 "	7¼	Gatun......	40¼	12.25 "	4.55 "
9.38 "	3.20 "	16	Bujio	31½	11.45 "	4.15 "
10.00 "	3.45 "	22½	Barbacoas	25	11.15 A.M.	3.45 "
10.40 "	4.25 "	30	Matachin .	17½	10.40 "	3.10 "
11.20 "	5.05 "	37	Summit...	10½	10.00 "	2.30 "
Arrive.	Arrive.				Leave.	Leave.
12.15 P.M.	6.00 "	47½	Panama...	....	9.00 "	1.30 "

Besides these regular trains, special trains are always employed whenever the service can not be adequately performed by the regular trains. There are often as many as five and six in number daily for weeks together.

STEAMER TRAINS.—On the arrival of passenger steam-ships at ASPINWALL, special trains are dispatched at any hour, so soon as the passengers are landed, provided that the state of the tide at Panama is such that they can be embarked for the connecting steam-ship immediately on the arrival of the trains. This arrangement has been made solely with a view of affording to the passenger the greatest degree of comfort and convenience consistent with dispatch. To those unacquainted with the cause, it may sometimes appear that time is unnecessarily lost: the Company only consults the interest of the passenger in this respect, and no detention is allowed beyond what is absolutely necessary. On the arrival of passenger steam-ships at PANAMA, the trains are dispatched for Aspinwall immediately on the landing of the passengers, who here step from the steamer directly into the cars without detention.

TARIFF OF RATES FOR PASSAGE AND FREIGHT.

Price of passage through, $25. Children under 12 years, half price; under 6 years, quarter do.

Special Rates of Freight.

Acids—Muriatic, Sulphuric, and Nitric.................................5 cts. per lb.
Agricultural Implements.......................................25 cts. per foot.
Baggage—passengers' (50 lbs. free)..................................10 cts. per lb.
Bees.. $1 50 per foot.
Carriages...20 cts. per cubic foot.
Cartridges, with balls, ordinary trains..............................3 cts. per lb.
Cattle, at owners' risk, ordinary trains, over eight......................$5 each.
    "   "   "   under eight....................$7 each.
  " steamer trains, owners' risk, special agreement...............$70 each.
Coal...$5 per ton of 2240 lbs.
Cocoanuts..$1 per hundred.
Coke..$7 per ton of 2240 lbs.
Copper Ore in bags..¾ths of one cent per lb.
Demijohns (empty)..25 cts. per foot.
Dye-woods..$7 per ton of 2240 lbs.

Express freight, by steamer trains..................................$1 50 per cubic foot.
Furniture, such as tables, chairs, bureaus, bedsteads, etc..25 cts. per cubic foot.
Gold, in dust, coined, or manufactured......................¼ per cent. on value.
Gunpowder, separate cars.......................................5 cts. per lb.
Hides...15 cts. each.
Horses, at owners' risk, special agreement, including feed, stalls, and loading by steamer trains..$100 each.
Jewelry...¼ per cent. on value.
Lumber—White Pine..$10 per M.
"   Yellow Pine..$12 per M.
"   Oak...$15 per M.
"   Cedar and Mahogany...................................$15 per M.
Mules, at owners' risk, special agreement, including feed, stalls, and loading by steamer trains..$100.
Oil, Whale and Palm, toward the Atlantic....................4 cts. per gallon.
Patent Fuel..$5 per ton of 2240 lbs.
Pitch, Rosin, and Tar....................................$1 each per barrel.
Platina..¾ per cent. on value.
Poultry..$1 50 per cubic foot.
Precious Stones...¾ per cent. on value.
Sheep, at owners' risk, by passenger trains......................$18.
Shingles...$3 per M.
Silver, in bars, coined or manufactured.........................¾ per cent. on value.
Silver Ore..½ per cent. on value.
Swine, at owners' risk..$6 to $10 each.
Tin Ores..¾ of one cent per lb.
Quicksilver..50 cts. per iron flask.

Classification of Freight.

First class freight, comprising merchandise, in boxes
    and bales, not otherwise enumerated....................50 cts. per cubic foot.
Second class freight, as per description annexed ....1¼ cts. per lb.
Third   "   "   "   "   "   ....1 ct. per lb.
Fourth   "   "   "   "   "   ....¾ of a ct. per lb.
Fifth   "   "   "   "   "   ....½ a ct. per lb.
Sixth   "   "   "   "   "   ....¼ of a ct. per lb.

All articles not specially named to be assimilated.

FIRST CLASS—50 CENTS PER CUBIC FOOT.

Bonnets, Books, Boots.
Caps, Cards (playing), Cassia lignea, Cigars, Cinnamon, Clothing.
Drugs, Dry Goods, not elsewhere enumerated.
Eau de Cologne, Essences, Essential Oils.
Feathers, Fire-works, Flannel; Furs, not otherwise enumerated.
Glass Shades and Looking-glasses, at owners' risk; Glassware, fine, stained, and plate, at owners' risk; Gloves.
Harness; Hats, fur or felt, and of Guayaquil or Panama straw; Hosiery.
Light goods, not elsewhere specified.
Matches, Medicines, Millinery, Musical Instruments.
Oil-cloth, Organs.
Paintings and Engravings, Paper Hangings, Paper, writing and printing; Peltry, not elsewhere specified; Percussion Caps, Perfumery, Pianos, Porcelain and China-ware, fine.
Saddlery, Shoes, Silks, Stationery; Statuary, at owners' risk.
Toys and Fancy Goods.

PANAMA RAILROAD. 141

SECOND CLASS—1½ CENTS PER POUND.

Almonds, Anchovies, Aniseed.
Balsams, Baskets, Beeswax, Britannia-ware.
Carpeting; Chandeliers, at owners' risk; Chocolate, Clocks, Cochineal, Confectionery, Corks and Corkwood.
Eggs.
Fire-arms, Fruits (dried).
German Silver-ware, Gin, Groceries, not elsewhere specified.
Indigo.
Lamps (ornamental).
Mattresses.
Nuts, not elsewhere specified.
Picture-frames, Plated Goods, Platform Scales, Preserved Meats and Fruits.
Sardines, Soap (fancy), Straw for manufacturing.
Tea, Tobacco (manufac'd), Tortoise-shell, Treenails, Trees and Plants in mats.
Varnish, in tins; Veneers.
Wooden-ware.

THIRD CLASS—1 CENT PER POUND.

Balsam of Copaivi, Bark, Blankets, Brooms, Brushes.
Candles, Cutlery.
Domestics, unbleached, of cotton, in bales.
Gravestones.
Hay in compressed bales.
Leather, dressed.
Liquors.
Nails, copper and brass.
Oils (toward Pacific), Ornaments of Stone, Clay, Marble, Alabaster.
Paints, dry and in oil.
Sarsaparilla, Spirits of Turpentine.
Tacks, Tin-ware; Tobacco, manufactured; Tubing, copper and brass; Type.
Whalebone; Wines in boxes or baskets; Wire, copper and brass; Wool of alpaca or vicuna.

FOURTH CLASS—¾ CENT PER POUND.

Ale.
Bacon in casks; Beef, Blacking, Borax, Bottles (empty), Bread, Butter.
Castings of copper, brass, or bronze; Cheese, Cider, Copper Sheathing and Spikes, Copperas; Cotton in compressed bales; Cotton Waste, Crackers; Crockery, not elsewhere specified; Common Wine in wood.
Deer-skins in bales.
Earthen-ware in casks or crates.
Felt (for sheathing), Fish, Flour.
Grindstones, Glassware (coarse), Window-glass, etc.; Goat-skins in bales.
Hams in casks; Hardware; Hats, coarse country straw or palm leaf; Hemp, unmanufactured; Herrings, Hollow-ware (iron), Hoops of wood or iron.
India-rubber.
Lard.
Manufactures of Hemp, such as Canvas, Osnaburgs, Burlaps, and Bagging.
Machetas, Machinery, Mats, Matting, Meal, Millstones, Molasses.
Oakum, Oats, Orchilla Weed.
Pickles, Pork (salt), Porter, Potatoes.
Rice, Rope.
Safes (iron), Sago, Salt, Screws, Seeds, Sheep-skins in bales, Shot (in bags), Shovels, Sirups, Soap (common), Soda-water, Spades, Steel in bars and bundles, Stoves, Sugar-mills, -moulds, and -pans.

Tallow; Tea (toward Atlantic); Tool-handles, Twine.
Vegetables, Vices (iron), Vinegar.
Window Glass, Wire (brass and copper), Wool of sheep.
Yarn (of cotton).
Zinc in sheets.

FIFTH CLASS—½ CENT PER POUND.

Anchors, Anvils.
Bananas, Beans.
Cables (iron), Cannon, Cannon Balls and Shot (iron), Cocoa, Coffee, Copper in bars, Corn (Indian), Crowbars.
Fruits of the Isthmus not otherwise enumerated.
Hollow Shot, Hoop Iron.
Ice, in quantity; Iron (old), Iron Bars and Pipes, Iron Boiler-plates, Iron Cables, Iron Castings (not machinery), Iron Tubing, Iron in bars.
Lead in pigs, sheet, and pipes, Lemons, Limes.
Nails (iron).
Old Junk (rope), Oranges.
Pearl-shells in sacks; Peas, Plantains.
Sheet Iron, Spikes (iron).
Zinc, ingots.

SIXTH CLASS—¼ CENT PER POUND.

Borate of Lime, Brick. Cement.
Guano in bags. Iron in pigs. Lime.
Marble for building purposes, including flooring tiles and paving.
Nitrate of Soda in bags.
Stone for building purposes, including paving-stones.

Special Conditions.

Freight to be charged on the gross weight of packages, and to be paid in advance or before delivery of goods.

All claims for loss or damage to be presented within five days, otherwise they will not be paid.

The Company will not be responsible for articles of extra value, beyond $100 per package, unless declared and way-billed accordingly.

No package, however small, will be transported for less than one dollar.

The Company will not be responsible for the breakage or loss of contents of any demijohn or jug.

Storage will be charged on all goods remaining in the Company's storehouses, after twenty-four hours, unless by special agreement.

JOSEPH F. JOY, Secretary.

N.B.—Goods shipped for California under through bills of lading must be corded and sealed at the New York Custom-house, or they will be liable to the payment of duties in San Francisco.

RATES OF COINAGE TO BE RECEIVED AND PAID OUT BY THE PANAMA RAILROAD COMPANY.

Gold Coin.

Spanish doubloons	$16 00	Mexican doubloons		$15 50
Peruvian "	15 50	Ecnadorian "		15 50
Bolivian "	15 50	New Granadian doubloons, new coinage		14 00
Chilian "	15 50			
New Granadian ditto. (old)	15 50	Costa Rican and Central American doubloons		13 60
Columbian doubloons	15 50			

Fractional parts in proportion.

Gold 20 franc pieces	$3 80	Ten-guilder pieces	$3 80
Gold 10 franc pieces	1 90	Condors, New Granadian	8 50
English sovereigns	4 85	Condors, Chilian	8 00
English half sovereigns	2 42½		

Fractional parts in proportion.

United States gold and silver at par.

Silver Coin.

Spanish dollars, $1 00; half dollars, 40 cents; quarter dollars, 20 cents.
Mexican dollars, $1 00; half dollars, 40 cents; quarter dollars, 20 cents.

Fractional parts in proportion.

New Granadian dollars of 5 franc value	$0 95
French 5 franc pieces	0 95

Fractional parts as heretofore.

Peruvian and Chilian dollars (new coinage)	0 90
Bolivian dollars (old coinage)	1 00

Bolivian half dollars and quarters not received.

N.B.—Smooth coin not received.

WHARFAGE, LIGHTERAGE, AND HARBOR REGULATIONS.

A pier, 450 feet in length, has been built in the Bay of Panama, to the end of which freight cars are run, to receive cargoes from lighters or vessels lying alongside, and deliver the same on board of vessels at Aspinwall. Vessels of from 200 to 300 tons can lie alongside the pier with safety, grounding in the mud at low water.

Iron launches of the capacity of 100 tons each have been built by the Company to load and discharge vessels whose draught of water prevents them from coming to the pier. These launches are towed to and from the pier by a powerful steam-tug. *The charge for lighterage is one and a half dollars per ton.*

At Aspinwall vessels load and discharge at the wharves. A fire-proof stone warehouse, 300 feet long by 85 feet wide, has been built for the use of the Company.

Regulations in regard to Freight.

1. All freight intended for the morning train must be delivered at the freight-houses of the Company before 5 P.M. on the day previous. The hours for receiving and delivering freight are from 7 to 9 A.M., from 10 A.M. until 2 P.M., and from 3 until 5 P.M.

2. No article will be transported over the road unless it is legibly and properly directed. Packages in bad order may be declined by the freight agent until properly repaired; or, if received in bad order, it will be so noted on the receipt given by the freight agent.

3. Goods will not be received for transportation without a freighting order from the shipper unless by special agreement. Shippers will deliver with their goods a bill of items, signed by themselves or agents, forms for which can be obtained on application to the freight agents. The freighting orders will be compared with the goods by the freight agent, and if found correct, a receipt will be given by him for the same, subject to the rules of the Company.

4. Freight deposited outside, or under the Company's sheds, remains at owners' risk until delivered into cars or freight-house, unless otherwise expressly agreed to; and freight agents will not receipt for goods unless so delivered.

5. Goods for transportation over the road will be received in their turn,

according to priority of delivery, and will remain at owners' risk until examined, compared, and receipted for. Goods for the Company's vessels will also be shipped in order of priority, heavy goods excepted, a sufficient quantity of which may first be put on board to make proper stowage.

6. No article will be delivered from the Company's freight-houses without a receipt or order from the consignee or owner. Draymen and porters calling for goods must be furnished with an order by the consignee, upon whom their receipts will be binding.

7. The Company will not be responsible for articles of extra value beyond $100 per package, unless declared and way-billed accordingly.

8. Freight will be charged on the gross weight of packages; and no package, however small, will be transported over the road for less than one dollar.

9. The Company will not be responsible for breakage or leakage of any description, the decay of any fruits or vegetables, the wastage of ice, or death of poultry or animals, from delay or detention on the road.

10. All payments for transportation will be made at the freight offices in United States currency or its equivalent, at the rates established by the Company (see pages 142, 143).

11. The terms for transportation over the road are prepayment, or cash on delivery of the goods, which may be detained by the freight agent until payment is made.

12. Storage will be charged on all goods remaining in the Company's store-houses for a longer period than twenty-four hours, except under special arrangements, or when they are under through bills of lading authorized by the Company.

Rates of Storage.

The following are the rates of storage per week:

Barrels...............10 cts. each.	Boxes............10 cts. per bbl. bulk.
Half do............... 5 " "	Hides............. 1 ct. each.
Tobacco...............10 " per bale.	Corn.............. 5 cts. per sack.
Hats..................20 " " "	Demijohns.......20 " each.

All articles not above enumerated to be assimilated and charged in proportion.

13. Claims for loss or damage must be made within five days thereafter, and will be settled by the superintendent on application to him through the freight agents. A bill of the cost of articles lost will be required.

14. When goods are forwarded from Panama to Aspinwall for shipment in other than the lines of vessels above named, the service of the Railroad Company ceases with their delivery at the freight-house in Aspinwall, as in the case of local traffic.

The same principles apply also to the shipment of goods to ports on the Pacific, passing over the road from Aspinwall to Panama.

15. When goods are forwarded from Pacific ports for shipment at Aspinwall by vessels not running in connection with the road, it is necessary for shippers to make arrangements for the payment of freight, transportation, and shipping expenses.

16. Cargo arriving by the Central American steamers, unless under *through bills of lading*, must be received by the consignees on the wharf immediately after arrival; otherwise it will be left there at owners' risk; or, if deposited in the Company's store-houses, it will be at their risk and expense. Cargo for the Central American steamers must be delivered at the freight-house for shipment, otherwise the Company will not be responsible for damage from rain or other cause.

17. Consignees of goods at Aspinwall by the Company's line of sailing vessels will please attend and receive them when discharged, with as little de-

lay as possible, the Company not being liable for any loss or damage after delivery from ship's tackles.

18. When the goods of residents or agents at Panama arrive at Aspinwall from abroad for transportation over the road, and are consigned to them at Aspinwall, they must be delivered to the Company at their freight-house in the same manner and form as is usual with local traffic. This also applies to goods consigned to the Railroad Company at Aspinwall not shipped under through bills of lading.

RATES OF WHARFAGE AND LIGHT MONEY.

Wharfage.

Vessels under 50 tons ....$0 75 per day.
"   over   50 " and under 100 .... 1 50 "
"   "   100 "   "   150 .... 2 25 "
"   "   150 "   "   200 .... 2 50 "
"   "   200 "   "   250 .... 3 00 "
"   "   250 "   "   300 .... 3 25 "
"   "   300 "   "   350 .... 3 50 "
"   "   350 "   "   400 .... 3 75 "

And 25 cents per day for each additional 50 tons.

Light Money.

Vessels under 100 tons ....$1 each.
"   over 100 "   and under 200................................ 3 "
"   "   200 "   "   300................................ 5 "
"   "   300 "   .... 7 "

The above rates are calculated upon tonnage by American measurement, and payable in American currency or its equivalent.

HARBOR REGULATIONS OF THE PORT OF ASPINWALL, N. G., ESTABLISHED BY THE PANAMA RAILROAD COMPANY.

1. All vessels entering the harbor of Aspinwall will be charged light fees, and all vessels coming to wharf will be charged wharfage, in proportion to tonnage, as per printed rates of the Panama Railroad Company annexed.

2. Vessels using the donkey engines or mules of the Company (which can be had when not otherwise employed) will be charged as follows :

Use of engine for cargo, per day..$10 00
"   "   "   coal,   " ton... 15
"   mule   "   "   " " 15

3. No vessel will be allowed to hang at the outer buoys, as they are to be used solely for convenience in hauling in and out and making sail.

4. Vessels entering the harbor will anchor outside of the line of buoys, where they will be visited by the harbor-master, who will assign them their berths. Regular lines of steamers or sailing vessels which have specified berths are exempt from the above rule. All vessels, after discharging, will also anchor outside the buoys.

5. No iron chains are allowed to be used in making fast to the wharves, unless by express permission from the harbor-master, and vessels will be held liable for any damage done to the wharves by unnecessary chafing, neglect, etc.

6. No coal-ashes, offal, or rubbish are to be thrown overboard by vessels at anchor in the harbor or at the wharves.

7. Masters of vessels will be governed by the directions of the harbor-master in changing berths, hauling to buoys, anchoring in any part of the harbor, etc., and are requested to notify him when wishing to haul, and also to give him at least six hours' notice before leaving port.

GEO. M. TOTTEN, *Chief Engineer.*

Through bills of lading are issued for merchandise from Europe and the Atlantic United States to Panama, San Francisco, Oregon, Washington Territory, etc., and also to the principal ports of South and Central America.

Parties in Europe desiring to ship goods to Panama or ports on the Pacific, under through bills of lading, will please apply to John Hamilton, at No. 6 Castle Street, Liverpool; in the United States to Mr. Joseph F. Joy, office of the Panama Railroad, 88 Wall Street, New York; Wheatley, Starr, and Company, 156 Cheapside, London.

All freight to be prepaid.

No bill of lading signed for less than five dollars.

A Commercial and Shipping Agency has been established by the Company at Panama, under the management of Mr. Wm. Nelson, who will receive and forward merchandise or produce consigned to the Company for transportation over the road and shipment at Aspinwall or Panama, in accordance with shippers' instructions, for which services no commissions will be charged, and only such expenses as may actually be paid, thus obviating the necessity of appointing agents on the Isthmus.

Merchandise and produce consigned to the Company for transportation and shipment should be addressed to the superintendent of the road, or to the commercial agent of the Company at Panama, Mr. William Nelson. Goods so consigned will be promptly dispatched.

The average freight from New York to Liverpool by sailing vessels is twenty-five shillings sterling per ton; the average passage about twenty days. By screw steamers the freight is higher, but the passage only fifteen days.

Besides the steamers of the Royal Mail Steam Packet Company, which make regular semi-monthly trips between Southampton and Aspinwall, a screw steam-ship line has commenced running between the latter port and Liverpool. Lines of sailing vessels have also been established to run from London, Liverpool and Bordeaux to Aspinwall. These several lines furnish frequent and reliable opportunities to the merchants of the Southwest coast and Central America to obtain their supplies of European manufactured and other goods.

Goods sent by the Company's line of sailing vessels, and consigned to the secretary in New York for reshipment to Europe or elsewhere, will be forwarded free of commissions or other charges than those actually paid.

Farther information in regard to the number and character of the vessels of the various lines connecting with the Panama Railroad, agencies, ports of entry, prices of passage and freight, dates of sailing, etc.; etc., will be found in the following Appendix.

NEW YORK TO ACAPULCO AND MANZANILLA.

The Panama Railroad Company issue through Bills of Lading (by sailing vessels to Aspinwall) for merchandise to the above ports, at the following rates: Dry-goods and first class, $58 per ton of 40 feet; unbleached domestics and coarse goods assimilating, $52 per ton of 40 feet; machinery, $52 per ton of 40 feet or 2000 lbs.; hardware, $50 per ton of 2000 lbs.—with primage 5 per cent.

Freight payable in American gold. Consignees to pay all light-house fees and port charges.

ACAPULCO AND MANZANILLA TO NEW YORK.

The Pacific Mail Steam-ship Company issue through Bills of Lading from the above ports to New York (by sailing vessels from Aspinwall) at the following rates: Hides, dry, 68 cents each; cotton, press-packed, 3 cents per lb.; treasure, $2\frac{3}{4}$ per cent.—with primage 5 per cent.

Officers and Directors of the Panama Railroad.

DAVID HOADLEY, President.
JOSEPH F. JOY, Secretary.
GEORGE M. TOTTEN, Chief Engineer.
HENRY SMITH, Treasurer.
WM. PARKER, General Superintendent.

DIRECTORS.

WILLIAM H. ASPINWALL,	HENRY CHAUNCEY,
EDWIN BARTLETT,	HOWARD POTTER,
GOUVERNEUR KEMBLE,	SAMUEL W. COMSTOCK,
WILLIAM WHITEWRIGHT Jr.,	AUGUST BELMONT,
EDWARD CUNARD,	JOSEPH W. ALSOP,
THEODORE W. RILEY,	FREDERICK G. FOSTER,

DAVID HOADLEY.

STEAM-SHIP LINES CONNECTING WITH THE PANAMA RAILROAD.

1st. The Pacific Mail Steam-ship Company, running between New York, the Isthmus of Panama, California, Japan, and China (page 149).

2d. The General Transatlantic Company (Compagnie Générale Transatlantique), running between St. Nazaire, France, the West Indies, Mexico, and Aspinwall (page 169).

3d. The West India and Pacific Steam-ship Company (limited), running between Liverpool, England, the West Indies, the Western Coast of South and Central America, and Aspinwall (page 180).

4th. The Royal Mail Steam Packet Company, running twice a month from Southampton (England) to and from the West-India Islands, British Guiana, Vera Cruz, Tampico, Greytown, Santa Martha, Carthagena, and Aspinwall; and there, by means of the Panama Railroad, connecting with lines of steamers from Panama to Ports on the West Coast of South America as far as Porto Montt, in Chili, to Acapulco, Manzanillo, San Francisco, Oregon, Vancouver's Island, and British Columbia, to Central American (Pacific) Ports, and once a month to New Zealand and Australia (page 188).

5th. The Panama, New Zealand, and Australian Royal Mail Company, limited (page 205).

6th. The British Pacific Steam Navigation Company, running between Panama and the Ports of New Granada, Ecuador, Peru, Bolivia, and Chili (page 215).

7th. The Panama Railroad Company's Central American Line of Steamships, running between Panama, Nicaragua, Costa Rica, Salvador, and Guatemala (page 222).

8th. The California, Oregon, and Mexico Company's Line of Steam-ships, running between San Francisco, California, and Mexico, and between San Francisco and Portland, Oregon, and the Island of Vancouver (page 225).

LINES OF SAILING VESSELS.

1st. The Bremen and Aspinwall Line, between Bremen and Aspinwall.

2d. The Bordeaux and Aspinwall Line, between Bordeaux and Aspinwall.

3d. The Panama Railroad Company's Line between Liverpool and Aspinwall.

4th. The Panama Railroad Company's Line between New York and Aspinwall.

PACIFIC MAIL STEAM-SHIP COMPANY.

HISTORY.

THE Pacific Mail Steam-ship Company, which now exercises undivided control of the great mail steam-ship route, more than 12,000 miles in length, between New York and Hong Kong, in China, *viâ* the Isthmus of Panama and San Francisco, California, with a branch line between China and Japan, was organized in the year 1847, for the purpose of establishing a line of mail steam-ships between Panama and Oregon.

The treaty of the United States with Great Britain, which had previously adjusted the vexed question of the northwestern boundary-line, had turned public attention to the great agricultural resources of that region, and thousands of settlers were seeking a permanent home in the rich valleys of Oregon by wild and difficult paths across the Plains and the Rocky Mountains. It was with the view of facilitating the intercourse between the Atlantic States and the possessions of the United States on the Pacific that Congress, on the 3d of March, 1847, authorized the Secretary of the Navy to contract for a mail steam-ship service once every two months, or oftener, during ten years, from New York, *viâ* Charleston, Savannah, and Havana, to Chagres, across the Isthmus of Panama, and thence to Astoria or the mouth of the Columbia River, touching at Monterey, San Diego, and San Francisco, in California, thus substituting for the long and perilous journey overland, and the more tedious and hazardous voyage around Cape Horn, a new route and mode of travel that would bring settlers within thirty days' journey of the Eastern States.

A contract for a monthly mail-service on the Pacific Ocean, at a compensation of $199,000 per annum, was awarded in 1847 to Mr. Arnold Harris, who, from pecuniary inability to fulfill its requirements, assigned it to Mr. William H. Aspinwall, on behalf of himself and his associates, on the 30th of November of the same year.

Mr. Aspinwall, in conjunction with Messrs. Alsop and Chauncey, Messrs. G. G. and S. S. Howland, and Mr. Edwin Bartlett, merchants of the city of New York, assignees of Mr. Harris's contract, proceeded to take the necessary measures for carrying out the undertaking, and became personally responsible for the sum of $400,000 to be used for this purpose, being the estimated cost of the ships for the proposed service. Their joint property was placed in the hands of Messrs. G. G. and S. S. Howland and Mr. Henry Chauncey as trustees, and Mr. William H. Aspinwall was made the active manager, the other owners agreeing to pay to the trustees and manager for their services a commission of two and a half per cent. on the gross receipts of the enterprise. These receipts, it was then estimated, would probably reach the annual sum of $400,000.

On the 2d of February, 1848, the treaty of peace with Mexico was signed, in the following May ratifications were exchanged, and in July it was publicly proclaimed, and California became the property of the United States, thus rendering even more imperative the necessity of immediate and improved means of communication with the Pacific coast.

On the 13th of April, 1848, a charter was procured from the Legislature of the State of New York, to continue in force for twenty years from that date, under the title of the "Pacific Mail Steam-ship Company," with a capital stock of $400,000.

It was now found that the three steamers which had been building for this service [viz., the California, which was launched on the 19th of May, 1848; the Panama, soon after; and the Oregon, on the 5th of August of the same year] would cost, with their necessary outfits, nearly $600,000, instead of the $400,000 as originally estimated. Upon representation of this fact to the United States government, Congress granted an advance of $199,000 (being the amount of one year's mail pay, according to the terms of the original contract), provided the Company's steamers should touch at certain ports in California on their voyages. This arrangement enabled the Company to proceed without delay to consummate their plans. On the 30th of September, 1848, the Pacific Mail Steam-ship Company was formally organized, $400,000 of the stock having been paid in according to the terms of their charter.

On the 5th of October, 1848, their pioneer steam-ship, the California, went to sea, and was followed, at short intervals, by the Panama and the Oregon. Thus far the Company had looked for success in their enterprise only to the great agricultural resources of the countries with which their connection was to be established, as, up to that time, no knowledge existed of the rich mineral deposits of those regions. Vague rumors had, it is true, occasionally found currency that great mineral wealth lay hidden among the sierras of California and Oregon, and it is even claimed that a geologist acompanying the famous Wilkes' Expedition had reported numerous collateral evidences of the existence of gold in California, but was unable to confirm his impressions by absolute contact with the precious metal. It was while the Pacific Mail Company's steamers were *en route* for the Pacific on their first voyage that tidings reached this country of an event which marks an era in the history of our country and the world, namely, the discovery of the rich deposits of gold in California — first discovered on Mormon Island, Sacramento, California, in January, 1848, and at Sutter's Mill, on the American fork of the Sacramento River, in the month of February following. In August of that year, Governor Mason, of California, reported 4000 men engaged in digging for gold, with a daily product of from $30,000 to $50,000 in value. So difficult and tedious were the then means of communication with that country that it was nearly a year from the date of the discovery of the precious metal before the authentic news of it was received in New York. Very soon after the first accounts of this discovery appeared in this country the wildest and most exaggerated reports gained circulation and credence, and what was then known as the "California fever" set in, infecting multitudes of people of every business and station. Thousands of adventurers of all classes and nationalities now started from every part of the country for the Golden Land. The shortest route to it was across the Isthmus of Panama, and by the Pacific Mail Company's steamers from that point to California. It soon became known that their ships, which had left New York some time previously, would touch at Panama on their way up the Pacific coast, and immediately the Company's offices in South Street were besieged by eager throngs clamoring for passage-tickets to be issued to them on any terms, so only that they might be assured of precedence over their competitors in the headlong rush for the gold mines of California.

In consequence of these circumstances, and contrary to all anticipation when she left New York, the Company's steamer California found an anxious multitude of gold-seekers, who had crossed the Isthmus from Chagres to meet her, and she soon proceeded thence on her voyage, crowded to her fullest carrying capacity. Her consorts met with a similar crowd on their later arrival; and the prospects of the Company, which had opened with what was considered by many as the too sanguine anticipation of $400,000 per annum from the gross receipts of their trade, now reasonably counted on millions. Ships of increased tonnage were added to the service of the Company. Dépôts were established at Panama and at Benicia, California; and at the latter place machine-shops were erected, with a capacity sufficient for the manufacture and repair of the heaviest machinery. In 1850 the capital stock of the Company was increased from $400,000 to $2,000,000. From this time up to the year 1856 the history of the Company was one of great prosperity, occasionally checkered by reverses from disasters, opposition, and the like, to which all steam-ship property is more or less liable. In 1856, Mr. William H. Aspinwall, the founder of the Company, its first managing director, and its president up to this time, retired from the executive chair, after formally waiving all the rights which he had acquired under the original agreement and terms of subscription to the capital stock of the Company. The resignation of Mr. Aspinwall, whose possession of the entire confidence of the stockholders, a large personal influence in the commercial world, and a long and intimate experience in the affairs of the Company, had enabled him successfully to direct its operations, was received with reluctance and accepted with regret.

Mr. William H. Davidge, their former secretary, was appointed to the presidency. For a long time familiar with the policy and management of the Company as its secretary, Mr. Davidge brought to the responsible labor of its guidance a character of strictest integrity, unwearied industry, and an entire devotion to its interests. During his administration the capital was increased from two to four millions of dollars. But little variation of its previous prosperous career took place until the year 1858, when the mail contract with the United States government expired, as did also the contract with the United States Mail Steam-ship Company, which had hitherto performed the service between New York and the Isthmus of Panama. Inimical interests, represented by some of the keenest and most vigorous business minds of the country, now waged a desperate war against the Company, and with variable success. In 1859 a through service was deemed necessary to answer the requirements of the trade and the interests of the Company. The steam-ships Adriatic, Atlantic, and Baltic, formerly belonging to the Collins line, were purchased jointly by the Pacific Mail Steam-ship Company and the Panama Railroad Company, from the firm of Brown Brothers and Company, bankers, of New York, and payment made to them for the ships in the capital stock of the Company. With these steam-ships a line was established to run between New York and the Isthmus, in connection with the Pacific Company's service. This transaction proved to be one of great importance, aside from the addition to the Company's fleet of these large and valuable steam-ships. It interested in their success one of the heaviest and most reliable banking-houses in the United States—one with a character established throughout the world for the soundest integrity, and a wise conservatism in business enterprises; and the addition to the Company of such a power, with the control of so large a portion of its capital stock, proved of invaluable assistance, moral as well as material, to the Board of Direction in aiding their plans for the furtherance of the present as well as the future interests of their enterprise. In consequence, however, of a determined opposition through to California by the United States Mail Steam-ship Company on the Atlantic, and the veteran steam-ship commodore, Cornelius Vanderbilt, on the Pacific, the Atlantic and Baltic, after a few months' trial, were withdrawn, and the arrangement, which promised, and (as far as the experiment had progressed) had given complete fulfillment of the public requirement, was broken up, and the service was again performed as before by independent companies.

The failure of the health of Mr. Davidge, the President of the Company, began at this time, and in 1860 compelled him to resign the executive chair.

It was then that the present President of the Company was selected as a candidate for this now more than ever responsible office. From his intimate practical acquaintance with the Company's interests throughout the whole extent of their route, he having entered service from the United States Navy in 1849 as a mate of their pioneer steam-ship the California, and from his thorough knowledge of all the actual necessities of the steam-ship service, besides a full appreciation of the hostile elements with which the executive officer of the Company must inevitably be brought in conflict, he was believed by the majority of the stockholders to be well calculated to assume the guidance of their interests, and in November, 1860, Mr. Allan McLane was called from the agency at Panama to fill the executive chair. At once, but gradually and quietly, a new influence began to be felt in renovating the Company's affairs, and re-establishing them on a broader and firmer basis. The *personnel* of the service was thoroughly reorganized in all its departments. Old steamers, as they became worn out, or were outgrown by the necessities of the trade, were laid up, and new ones of increased size and power, and of greatly improved model and appointments, were substituted. In all branches of the business of the Company trade was steadily fostered and encouraged, and the wants of passengers were met by increased accommodations and care for their safety and comfort. The requirements of shippers of merchandise and treasure were recognized and accommodated by increased tonnage and enlarged facilities, while rates were reduced; and stockholders, not less than the traveling and commercial public, derived increased safety and security from the rigid *discipline* which was caused to be enforced on the Company's steamers, and the adoption and use of the most modern and approved appliances and means for the prevention and remedy of disaster. The broad purpose of developing our national commerce was constantly manifested in encouraging the establishment of subsidiary lines, connecting with or collateral to its own, by the sale at low rates of vessels which had been outgrown by its own requirements. These tributary lines, such as those on the routes between San Francisco and Oregon, the Mexican coast, or the Sandwich Islands, and between Panama and Central American ports, requiring less capital, afforded so many fields for profitable employment to individuals and corporations, which became, in effect, the feeders of the Pacific Company. As a legitimate result of this wise and generous policy, public confidence in the value of the capital stock was restored; and, besides paying regularly about 20 per cent. per annum to its holders, it soon more than doubled its nominal value in the market, and was again eagerly taken by capitalists as a permanent investment.

From the unavoidable inconvenience and discomfort attendant upon the possession of the steam-ship service between New York and California by two separate companies, under a widely different management, the traveling and commercial public had long and urgently demanded of the Pacific Company a through line, and, after deliberate consideration of the matter, it was determined that such an extension of the service was advisable. In June, 1866, by an act of the Legislature of New York, the capital stock of the Company was increased from $4,000,000 to $10,000,000. The Board of Management recognized the rights of the Atlantic Mail Steam-ship Company, which they had acquired by preoccupation and transfer from the parties to the original charter of 1848; and although, with their influence and enormous increase of financial power, the Pacific Company could doubtless have successfully carried out the plan of a through service independent of any arrangement with the Atlantic Company — notwithstanding this, a fair and liberal proposal was made to that Company, which absorbed its privileges, and its entire equipment of vessels, and tendered in payment therefor a certain generous proportion of the capital stock of the Pacific Mail Company. This proposal was accepted, the transaction was ratified, and on November 1st, 1865, the Pacific Company took possession of the entire service, and at once placed the line on both oceans upon an equal and complete footing as to their equipment and control. Thus was successfully completed part of a plan for the legitimate development of the Company's resources which had for a long time received grave consideration from the Board of Management. The remaining part of that plan was one of infinitely greater magnitude, and which utterly refuted (if such refutation was ever necessary) the charge sometimes made by its enemies that its aim was to establish a monopoly.

The Board of Direction had contemplated the future of the Company with no narrow spirit of speculation such as would lead them to block the wheels of trade for their own personal aggrandizement. They fully appreciated the necessity of a more direct and intimate commercial connection between the United States and its Pacific possessions; and the project of establishing such a connection by means of the Pacific Railroad, antagonistic as this might appear to more contracted minds, met with its hearty approbation and support; looking with the faith of men who believe in the great commercial destiny of their country, they counted confidently on the fullest success of that grand undertaking. Looking also with a clear foresight upon the inevitable deflection of an important share of the Pacific trade into the new and more direct channel, they saw also the necessity of another and more extended field for their own enterprise. The vast empire of Eastern Asia and the islands of Japan, distant about 5000 miles from their Pacific terminus, had heretofore merely a nominal connection with the United States. England and France had thus far virtually monopolized the foreign trade of those regions. The English and French war with the Chinese, which was concluded in 1858, had resulted in treaties which promised rapid development for the great Chinese Empire in its intercourse with the outer world of civilization and commerce. In the ratification of these treaties, the United States had not only gained all the privileges granted to the other foreign powers, but, besides this, had retained the good will of the Chinese people. Japan had also opened its ports, and guaranteed to the United States unexpected facilities for trade with that country. The already known resources of those countries, representing together the industry of nearly 500,000,000 of people — the peculiarly favorable position of the already existing route of the Pacific Mail Steam-ship Company, occupying 5000 miles of the shortest and most eligible route between those countries and Europe as well as the United States, at once pointed to this grand field as the proper and legitimate one in which to throw their surplus energies. A deliberate and exhaustive canvass of the matter decided the Company to attempt the establishment of a line of steam-ships worthy of the national credit, and equal to the magnitude of such an enterprise. In 1865 a contract for a monthly mail service between San Francisco and Hong Kong, *via* the Sandwich Islands and Japan, was awarded to the Pacific Company by the government of the United States, with an annual subsidy of $500,000 per annum; and, more recently, the government has released the stoppage at Honolulu on condition of the establishment of a branch between Japan and Shanghai. In anticipation of this contract, the Company had some months previously commenced building the ships destined for the China trade, each of which was estimated to cost over $1,000,000. In this year, also, the capital stock of the Company was by act of the New York Legislature increased from $10,000,000 to $20,000,000. This increase was effected in such a manner that the Company issued and sold $5,000,000 of stock for about $10,000,000, and the remaining $5,000,000, completing the $10,000,000 allowed by the amended charter, were distributed among their stockholders. By this means the Company gained the ability to carry out their projected China enterprise without encroaching upon their previously-established business.

It is scarcely too much to say that such a magnificent financial success as that above shown in providing the means for developing and extending trade is unique in the history of commerce, and may be taken as a true measure of the public confidence in the wealth, in the resources, and in the management of this Company.

The capital stock of the Pacific Mail Steam-ship Company, originally $400,000, in 1850 was increased to $2,000,000, in 1860 to $4,000,000, in 1865 to $10,000,000, and in 1866 to $20,000,000; while it is stated on reliable authority that the property of the Company in steam-ships, real estate, coal, stores, and cash, is worth at the present time (February, 1867), at a low estimate, such as might be realized at a public sale, fully $30,000,000.

Should the future realize the present promise of success to this powerful corporation, the time will not be far distant when the commerce of those Eastern countries, which it is the ambition of its managers to develop and bring to our shores, will, as it accumulates in our sea-ports, suggest, if not necessitate a still farther expansion of their field of action; and it seems almost a natural sequence that they should eventually establish the long-looked-for desideratum of a line of steam-ships plying between this country and Europe which shall be equal to the requirements of the service and a credit to the nation.

SERVICE OF THE PACIFIC MAIL STEAM-SHIP COMPANY.

The service now performed by the steam-ships of the Pacific Mail Steam-ship Company is as follows:

1. *The Atlantic Line*, tri-monthly, between New York and Aspinwall, New Granada, there connecting by the Panama Railroad with

2. *The Pacific Line*, also tri-monthly, between Panama and San Francisco, touching at Acapulco, and once a month each way at Manzanillo.

3. *The China Line*, monthly, between San Francisco and Hong Kong, touching at Yokohama (Kanagawa), in Japan.

4. *The Shanghai Branch*, monthly, between Yokohama and Shanghai, *via* Nagasaki, in close connection with the preceding.

The departures, arrivals, and connections of these several lines are as follows:

OUTWARD.

A steamer leaves the Company's dock, Pier No. 42 North River, New York, at noon on the 1st, 11th, and 21st days of every month, save when either date falls on Sunday, and then on the preceding Saturday. Arriving at the wharf at Aspinwall on the morning of the 9th, 19th, and 29th, the passengers, mails, and "fast" freight are immediately transferred by the railroad to the connecting steamer at Panama, which sails the same afternoon or evening for San Francisco, where she is due on the 22d, the 1st or 2d, or the 11th or 12th of the month, as the case may be.

The steamer leaving Panama on the 9th, in connection with the departure from New York of the 1st, touches at Manzanillo. As before remarked, all the steamers touch at Acapulco.

The steamer leaving New York on the 11th, makes a close connection with the steamer of the China Line, sailing from San Francisco on the 3d of the month for Yokohama and Hong Kong, connecting at Yokohama with the branch steamer for Shanghai, *viâ* Nagasaki. Passengers, mails, and "fast" freight by this means reach Yokohama in forty-two days, Shanghai in forty-seven days, and Hong Kong in fifty days from New York, counting all detentions.

Connections are also made on the Isthmus with the steamers of other companies, as follows:

For the West Coast of South America, by the steamers from New York on the 1st and 21st, with the fine steamers of the Pacific Steam Navigation Company, calling at the chief ports of Peru and Chili.

For Central American ports, by steamers from New York on the 1st and 11th of every month, with the Panama Railroad Company's steamers "Salvador," 1200 tons, and

"Guatemala," 1021 tons; leaving Panama on 10th and the 25th of the month for Punta Arenas, Realejo, La Union, La Libertad, Acajutla, and San José de Guatemala.

For Australasia, by the steamer of the 11th, with the Panama, New Zealand, and Australian Royal Mail Steam Packet Company's steamers, leaving Panama on the 24th for Wellington, in New Zealand, and Sydney and Melbourne, Australia; connecting by inter-colonial branches with the chief ports of both colonies. Passengers, mails, and freight reach Wellington in forty-one days, and Sydney in forty-six days after leaving New York.

HOMEWARD.

A steamer leaves the Company's new wharf at the foot of Townsend Street, San Francisco, for Panama, *viâ* Acapulco, at eleven o'clock on the morning of the 10th, 18th or 19th, and 30th day of the month, except when those dates fall on Sunday, in which case on the preceding Saturday. The steamer of the 18th or 19th sails on the *former* date only when the month contains *less than thirty-one days.*

Arriving at the anchorage at Panama on the morning of the 1st, 12th or 13th, and 23d of the month, passengers, mails, and fast freight are at once conveyed by the trains of the Panama Railroad Company to Aspinwall, and are there transferred to the connecting steamer, which sails the same afternoon or evening for New York, where she is due on the 10th, 20th or 21st, and 31st or 1st, according to circumstances.

The steamer of the 10th from San Francisco touches at Manzanillo to land and receive passengers, mails, and freight.

Passengers, mails, and fast freight leaving Hong Kong on the 20th, Shanghai on the 23d, and Yokohama on the

28th of the month, arrive in San Francisco on the 16th or 17th of the following month in season to connect with the steamers of the 18th or 19th for Panama, and are landed in New York on the 10th, thus making the through voyage in fifty days from Hong Kong, forty-seven from Shanghai, and forty-two from Yokohama.

Homeward connections are also made on the Isthmus with the steamers of other companies, as follows:

From Central America, the Panama Railroad Company's steamers from San José de Guatemala and intermediate ports arrive at Panama on the 15th and 30th, and connect with the Pacific Mail Steam-ship Company's steamers from Aspinwall for New York the 23d and 1st.

From the West Coast of South America, the steamers from Aspinwall of the 23d and 1st receive the passengers, mails, and freight destined for New York of the Pacific Steam Navigation Company's steamers, leaving Valparaiso on the 2d and 17th, and due at Panama on the 16th and 31st.

From Australia and Sydney, the Panama, New Zealand, and Australian Royal Mail Company's steamer, leaving Sydney on the 31st or 1st, and Wellington on the 8th, is due at Panama on the 4th or 5th of the following month, and connects with the steamer from Aspinwall of the 12th or 13th.

TO AND FROM EUROPE,

connections are made as follows, giving passengers and shippers the choice at all times of two routes across the Atlantic, namely, the direct route between Aspinwall and Europe, or that by way of New York. By the former one transfer or trans-shipment is avoided; but the latter, passing as it does through a great variety of climate, and through temperate regions, and affording the traveler an opportunity of visiting New York without adding to the duration or expense of his journey, presents attractions so strong that it is rapidly becoming the favorite with men of business as well as with tourists for pleasure.

Viâ New York.

Through tickets are issued, and through bills of lading are in contemplation, in connection with the principal Transatlantic steam-ship lines, viz. :

The Cunard Line, leaving New York and Boston on alternate Wednesdays, and Liverpool every Saturday, for Boston and New York alternately, and making the passage ordinarily within ten days. This line includes the steamers "Scotia," "Persia," "Java," "China," "Asia," "Cuba," "Africa," "Australasian," etc., carrying cabin passengers only.

The Inman Line, sailing from New York every Saturday, and Liverpool every Wednesday, touching at Queenstown, carries first-cabin and steerage passengers. Its fleet consists of the fine steamers "City of Paris," "City of New York," "City of London," "City of Boston," "City of Cork," "City of Washington," "City of Edinburg," etc. Their time is usually about twelve days, though the run is often made in less, and has been accomplished by the "City of Paris" in a few hours over eight days.

The National Line, sailing between the same ports, and on the same days as the Inman steamers, carrying first-cabin and steerage passengers, embraces the steamers "Erin," "The Queen," "Denmark," "Virginia," etc.

The General Transatlantic Company's fortnightly line, leaving New York on alternate Saturdays for Havre, calling at Brest; returning, leave Havre every other Wednesday. This line comprises the fine steamers "Pereire," "Europe," "Ville de Paris," "Napoleon III.," "St. Laurent," etc. It carries only first and second cabin passengers. The time of these steamers is about the same as that of the Cunarders.

The *"Fulton"* and *"Arago"* sail from New York every twenty-eight days for Havre, *via* Falmouth.

The *North-German Lloyd*, fortnightly, for Bremen, *via* Southampton, sailing every other Thursday from either terminus, runs the steamers "Deutschland," "America," "Hansa," "Bremen," "New York," "Hermann," "Union," and "Weser." Carries all classes of passengers.

The *Hamburg American* Packet Company's Line for Hamburg, by way of Southampton, every other Saturday. Its steamers are the "Allemannia," "Bavaria," "Borussia," "Cimbria," "Germania," "Hammonia," "Saxonia," "Teutonia." This line carries all classes of passengers.

The *New York and Bremen* Company run the "Atlantic," "Baltic," and "Western Metropolis" between New York and Bremen, *via* Cowes, leaving either terminus on alternate Saturdays, and carrying all classes of passengers.

Direct.

Through tickets and through bills of lading are granted for the direct route between Aspinwall and Europe, in connection with the following companies:

The Royal Mail Steam Packet Company. Leave Aspinwall for Southampton, *via* St. Thomas, on the 8th or 9th, and 24th of the month, connecting with the steamers which left San Francisco on the 18th or 19th, and 10th, and arrived at Panama on the 1st, and 22d or 23d, arrive at Southampton on the 29th and 14th respectively. Leave Southampton on the 2d and 17th of each month, reaching Aspinwall on the 22d and 7th, and there connecting with the steamers from Panama of the 29th and 9th respectively, for San Francisco. It will be observed that the connections are close by the steamers from Southampton on the

17th, and San Francisco on the 10th; the through time by these departures being thirty-four to thirty-five days.

The West India and Pacific Steam Navigation Company (limited). Leave Liverpool on the 10th and 25th of every month, arriving at Aspinwall on the 6th and 21st, and connecting with the steamers from Panama of the 9th and 29th, arrive at San Francisco on the 22d, and 11th or 12th. A steamer also leaves Liverpool on the 29th of each month, arriving at Aspinwall on the 30th of the following month. Leave San Francisco on the 10th, and 18th or 19th, and 29th, connecting with steamers from Aspinwall of the 1st, 8th, and 10th, arrive at Liverpool on the 25th, 9th, and 13th of the following month, making the through time between Liverpool and San Francisco outward forty-two days, and thirty-eight days homeward by the more favorable connections, namely, the departures from Liverpool on the 10th, and San Francisco on the 18th.

La Compagnie Générale Transatlantique (the General Transatlantic Company). Leave St. Nazaire, France, on the 8th of every month, touching at Santa Martha and Martinique, arrive at Aspinwall on the 28th or 29th; leave Panama the 29th, and arrive in San Francisco on the 11th or 12th. Returning, leave Southampton on the 18th or 19th, arrive at Panama on the 1st; leave Aspinwall on the same or the following day, and reach St. Nazaire on the 23d. The through time between San Francisco and St. Nazaire is, it will be seen, thirty-four days.

THE FLEET

of the Pacific Mail Steam-ship Company is now composed of the following named steamers, the general character of which we have already described:

The Atlantic Line.

	Register Tonnage.		Register Tonnage.
Henry Chauncey	2657	*Spare Steamers.*	
Arizona	2793	Northern Light	2057
New York	2217	Ariel	1700
Ocean Queen	2700	Champion	1450
Rising Star	2727	*Tug.*	
		Clara Clarita	250
			20,468

The Pacific Line.

	Register Tonnage.		Register Tonnage.
Constitution	3675	California	1057
Golden City	3590	Sonora	1616
Sacramento	2683	*Tugs.*	
Montana	2677	Taboga	189
Golden Age	1870	—— (building.)	
Spare Steamers.			
St. Louis	1621		18,978

The China Line.

	Register Tonnage.		Register Tonnage.
Colorado	3728	Nipon (building)	4100
Great Republic	4100	*Spare Steamer.*	
Celestial Empire	4000	Hermann	2000
America (building)	4100		
			22,028

The Shanghai Branch.

Costa Rica........................ 1917 register tonnage.

Making a total of twenty-five steam-ships, having a combined capacity of 61,474 tons.

Officers, Directors, and Agents of the Pacific Mail Steamship Company.

ALLAN McLANE, President.
FRANCIS W. G. BELLOWS, Vice-President.
THEODORE T. JOHNSON, Secretary.
CHARLES S. ABERCROMBIE, Treasurer.
RICHARD B. IRWIN, China Secretary.
SAMUEL K. HOLMAN, Purveyor General.

DIRECTORS.

ALLAN McLANE,	HOWARD POTTER,
FRANCIS SKIDDY,	WILLIAM DENNISTOUN,
JAMES M. BROWN,	MOSES H. GRINNELL,
ELISHA RIGGS,	LOUIS McLANE,

AGENTS.

FRANK R. BABY, New York.	OLIVER ELDRIDGE, San Francisco.
GEORGE B. GIBBONS, Aspinwall.	S. LEDYARD PHELPS, Hong Kong.
DAVID M. CORWINE, Panama.	JAMES H. PHINNEY, Yokohama.
GEORGE F. BOWMAN, Acapulco.	——————, Nagasaki.

RUSSELL & CO., Shanghai.

GENERAL TRANSATLANTIC COMPANY,
8 Place Vendôme, Paris.

FRENCH MAIL STEAM-SHIPS.

By a French law of July 3d, 1861, the General Transatlantic Company received a charter to carry the mails between France, North America, West Indies, and the Isthmus of Panama.

These services are organized as follows:

1st. A line from St. Nazaire to Vera Cruz (Mexico), calling at St. Thomas and Havana.

Additional service from St. Thomas to Fort de France (Martinique), calling at La Pointe-à-Pitre and La Basse-terre (Guadaloupe), and St. Pierre.

Additional service from St. Thomas to Kingston (Jamaica), calling at Porto Rico, Cape Haïtien, and Santiago de Cuba.

Additional service from Vera Cruz to New Orleans, touching at Tampico and Matamoros.

Steamers leave St. Nazaire the 16th of each Month.

OUTWARD.		HOMEWARD.	
Leaving St. Nazaire	the 16th,	Leaving St. Thomas	the 13th,
arriving at Vera Cruz	" 30th.	arriving at St. Thomas	" 16th.
Leaving Havana	" 1st,	Leaving Havana	" 18th,
arriving at Havana	" 5th.	arriving at Havana	" 22d.
Leaving St. Thomas	" 7th,	Leaving Vera Cruz	" 23d,
arriving at St. Thomas	" 10th.	arriving at St. Nazaire	" 8th.

2d. A line from St. Nazaire to Colon (Isthmus of Panama), calling at Fort de France (Martinique) and Santa Martha (Colombia).

Additional service from Fort de France (Martinique) to La Pointe-à-Pitre (Guadaloupe).

Additional service from Fort de France to Cayenne (French Guiana), touching at Ste. Lucie, St. Vincent, La Granada, La Trinidad, Demerara (English Guiana), and Surinam (Dutch Guiana).

Additional service from Fort de France to Guiana and Porto Cabello.

These steamers connect at the Isthmus of Panama with the steam-ships of the North and South Pacific and Central American Steam-ship Companies.

Steamers leave St. Nazaire the 8th of each Month.

OUTWARD.		HOMEWARD.	
Leaving St. Nazaire	the 8th,	Leaving Colon	the 1st,
arriving at Fort de France	" 22d.	arriving at Santa Martha	" 3d.
Leaving Fort de France	" 23d,	Leaving Santa Martha	" 3d,
arriving at Santa Martha	" 27th.	arriving at Fort de France	" 7th.
Leaving Santa Martha	" 27th,	Leaving Fort de France	" 9th,
arriving at Colon	" 29th.	arriving at St. Nazaire	" 23d.

H

Rates of Passages.

From St. Nazaire, and vice versâ.	One Berth in Cabins with one or two Berths.	One Berth in Cabins with more than two Berths.	Steerage.
	Francs.	Francs.	Francs.
St. Thomas............................	965	825	500
Havana	1100	965	500
Vera Cruz.............................	1240	1100	600
Tampico	1240	1100	600
Matamoros............................	1240	1100	500
Porto Rico	1000	875	500
Cape Haïtien.........................	1000	875	500
Santiago de Cuba..................	1050	925	500
Jamaica	1050	925	500
La Guadaloupe	965	825	500
La Martinique	965	825	500
Santa Martha	1100	965	500
Colon...................................	1100	965	500
Ste. Lucie	965	825	500
St. Vincent...........................	965	825	500
La Granada...........................	965	825	500
La Trinidad	965	825	500
Demerara	965	825	500
Surinam	1000	875	500
Cayenne, Guiana, P'rto Cabello.	1000	875	500

The difference in the rates of cabin passage is caused merely by the choice of cabins; in all other respects passengers of first class will have the same advantages.

A cabin of two berths kept for the exclusive use of one passenger will be charged for at the rate of a fare and a half.

The cabin passage includes living, attendance, and table wine.

Bedding is also furnished by the Company.

Passengers are provided with superior wines, cordials, and cool drinks at moderate prices.

The fare of steerage passengers will be the same as that of the subordinate officers of the ship.

Children.—Passengers' children under three years old are admitted gratuitously; those from three to eight years shall pay a quarter fare; those from eight to twelve a half fare, and those above twelve an entire fare.

Passengers' Servants will be charged at the same rate as the steerage passengers, and will take their meals with the ship's attendants.

Return Tickets will be furnished to cabin passengers for the transatlantic voyage at a discount of 25 per cent. of the double rate. These tickets will be paid for when delivered, and are not transferable. They will be good for six months after delivery, but no allowance will be made to ticket-holders if they do not return by the steam-ships of the Company.

Baggage.—150 kilogrammes (half a cubic metre) are allowed to each cabin passenger for his baggage.

75 kilog., or 250 cubic decimetres, to children paying half price.

40 kilog., or 150 cubic decimetres, to those paying quarter fare.

75 kilog., or 250 cubic decimetres, to steerage passengers.

The surplus or excess of baggage shall be taxed according to merchandise tariff.

GENERAL TRANSATLANTIC COMPANY. 171

Notice.—Passage shall not be considered as positively engaged until after payment of fare and delivery of the ticket.

Passengers having, when necessary, their regular passports, countersigned by competent authorities, must present themselves at the office of the port of embarkation at least six hours before departure.

They can bring with them only small packages. Baggage must be on board the day before departure.

Passengers are requested to write their names and destination on their baggage legibly.

CONNECTIONS AT THE ISTHMUS OF PANAMA.
SERVICES ON THE PACIFIC OCEAN.

1st. With the steamers of the Pacific Steam Navigation Company, calling at the ports between Panama and Valparaiso (Ecuador, Peru, Chili)—leaving Panama the 2d of each month.

2d. With the *Panama* Railroad Company, calling at the ports of *Central America (Guatemala,* Honduras, San Salvador, Costa Rica)—leaving Panama the 10th and 25th of each month.

3d. With the steamers of the Pacific Mail Steam-ship Company, going to Acapulco (Mexico), Mansanillo, and San Francisco (California)—leaving Panama every month the 9th, 19th, and 29th.

By agreement with the aforesaid companies, through tickets are delivered by the General Transatlantic Company for all ports where their steamers stop.

Rates of passage from St. Nazaire to the different ports of the Pacific coasts, to which the steamers of the before-mentioned companies run, are as follows:

1st. Special Connection with the Steamers of the Pacific Steam Navigation Company (Southern Coast).

From St. Nazaire to	One Berth in Cabins of 1 or 2 Berths, General Transatlantic Co.		One Berth in Cabins of 3 or more, General Transatlantic Co.	
	One Berth (Saloon), Pacific Co.		One Berth (Saloon), Pacific Co.	
	£ s. d.	francs. cent.	£ s. d.	francs. cent.
Payta	65 11 3	1665 45	60 1 3	1516 55
San José	} 69 6 3	1750 15	63 16 3	1611 25
Pimentel				
Callao	74	1868 50	68 10	1722 60
Tambo Mora	} 76 16 3	1939 50	71 6 3	1810 65
Pisco				
Chinchas				
Chala	82 8 9	2081 55	76 18 9	1942 65
Islay	85 5	2152 55	79 15	2013 70
Ilo	} 87 2 6	2199 90	81 12	2061
Arica				
Pisagua	} 89 18 9	2270 90	84 8 9	2132 05
Mejillones				
Iquique				
Tocopilla	} 91 16 3	2118 25	86 6 3	2179 40
Cobija				
Chanaral	} 93 13 9	2365 60	88 3 9	2226 70
Caldera				
Huasco	} 94 12	2289 25	89 2 6	2250 40
Corrizal Bajo				
Coquimbo	95 11 3	2412 95	90 1 3	2274 05
Valparaiso	98 7 6	2483 95	92 17 6	2345 10

Tickets are also delivered for Buenaventura, Guayaquil, Lambayeque, Huanchaco, Casma, and Huacho, that are served by intermediate steamers, at the rate of

	francs. c.	francs. c.		francs. c.	francs. c.
For Buenaventura	1347 70	1208 85	For Huanchaco	1730 15	1611 25
" Guayaquil	1608 10	1469 20	" Casma......	1773 80	1634 95
" Lambayeque.	1730 15	1611 25	" Huacho.....	1797 45	1653 60

For returning, see the Hand-book of the Company.

2d. Connection with the Steamers of the Pacific Mail Steam-ship Company, Northern Coast of the Pacific.

	One Berth in Cabins with 2 or 3 Berths, Transatlantic Co. 1st Cabins, P. M. S. S. Co.		One Berth in Cabins with 3 or more Berths, Transatlantic Co. 1st Cabins, P. M. S. S. Co.		Steerage.	
	£ s.	francs. c.	£ s.	francs. c.	£ s. d.	francs. c.
From St. Nazaire to San Francisco, and vice versâ............	69 10	1754 85	56 15	1432 95	34 17 6	880 60
From St. Nazaire to Acapulco, Manzanilla, and vice versâ...................	59	1489 75	49 10	1249 85	31 10	795 35

3d. Connection with the Central American Steamers.

	One Berth in Cabins of 1 or 2 Berths.	One Berth in Cabins of 3 or more Berths.
	francs. cent.	francs. cent.
From St. Nazaire to Punta Arena, and vice versâ	1310	1175
" " Realejo (Corinto) "	1441	1306 25
" " La Union "	1467 50	1332 50
" " La Libertad "	1493 75	1358 75
" " Acajutla "	1520	1385
" " San José "	1546 25	1411 25

Prices indicated in the three tables above do not include the fare of the railroad from Aspinwall to Panama either for travelers or baggage.

They are thus: $25 00 for adults;
$12 50 for a child twelve years old;
$ 6 25 for a child six years old.

Fifty pounds of baggage are allowed to every traveler going by the aforesaid railway; above this weight, 5 cents per pound (25 centim.) will be charged.

Travelers on the Pacific, holders of through tickets for ports to which steamships of the associated companies run, are subjected, while on board of the steamers of the Transatlantic Company, to the general rules of the Company. While on board of the other steamers, they must comply with the regulations established thereon.

On board of steamers of South Pacific, children are admitted under the same conditions as on the steamers of the General Transatlantic Company.

Male servants will pay half the rate of a cabin passage on board of the South Pacific; the same for the steerage passengers. Female servants will pay two thirds of the price.

The discount of 25 per cent. for return tickets from the southern ports of the Pacific will be allowed, and these tickets will be good for 12 months.

GENERAL TRANSATLANTIC COMPANY.

RATE OF PRICES FOR FREIGHT OF VALUABLES AND MERCHANDISE (WEST INDIAN SEA AND GULF OF MEXICO).

§ I. GOING OUTWARD (DEPARTURE FROM ST. NAZAIRE).

1st. *Tariff of Coins and Valuables.*

From St. Nazaire to all ports called at by the steamers of the Company in the West Indian Sea and Gulf of Mexico.................... 1 per cent. ad valorem.

Silver plate, Silver, and Quicksilver......... 2 per cent. ad valorem.

2d. *Tariff of Merchandise.*

From St. Nazaire to St. Thomas, Porto Rico, Hayti, Guadaloupe, Martinique, St. Lucie, St. Vincent, Granada, and Trinidad....... 100 francs a cubic metre, or 1000 kilog., at the Company's will.

From St. Nazaire to Havana, Santiago de Cuba, Jamaica, Demerara, Surinam, Cayenne, and Santa Martha................................ 125 francs a cubic metre, or 1000 kilog., at the Company's will.

From St. Nazaire to Colon (Aspinwall), Vera Cruz, Tampico, and Matamoras.......... 150 francs a cubic metre, or 1000 kilog., at the Company's will.

Merchandise will always be taxed by weight or bulk, at the will of the Company.

The Company receives at the above rates only packages weighing 350 kilogrammes, or a maximum of one cubic metre at the most.

Packages of a larger size or weight must be charged at special prices, or refused if their size or weight is such as to prevent a speedy shipment or landing.

Merchandise should be sent to St. Nazaire two days before departure, and be accompanied by the necessary documents (consular invoices, custom-house declarations, etc.) for their regular shipment and immediate landing at their destination.

In no case will a bill of lading be delivered for freight less than 25 francs.

3d. *Tariff of Parcels, Samples, etc.*

The Company receives and taxes as parcels separate packages without value whose size does not exceed 100 cubic decim. or weight of 50 kilog.

These small parcels will be received for all ports to which the steamers of the Company run.

The freight of these packages must always be paid in advance, and is fixed as follows:

By Size.

    25 cubic decimetres and below, 10 francs per parcel;
  from 25   "   to 50, 15 "   "
    " 50   "   to 75, 20 "   "
    " 75   "   to 100, 25 "   "

By Weight.

  Below 20 kilogrammes,   10 francs per parcel;
  from 20   "   to 30, 15 "   "
    " 30   "   to 40, 20 "   "
    " 40   "   to 50, 25 "   "

Parcels are taxed by size or weight, at the Company's will.

No bill of lading, but a single receipt, will be given for parcels.

In case a parcel shall be lost, the Company will not hold itself responsible to pay a sum of more than one hundred francs.

§ II. RETURNING TO FRANCE.

1st. *Tariff for Coins, Valuables, Jewels, etc.*

From the several ports called at in the West Indian Sea and the Gulf of Mexico to St. Nazaire:

Coins, precious metals, jewelry, diamonds (delivered either at the office of the Company, or at the Bank of France; or in London, at the Bank of England)	1¼ per cent. of the value.
Silver and silver plate	2 per cent. of the value.
Copper coins	175 francs per 1000 kilog.

2d. *Tariff of Merchandise.*

The rate of freight for goods to St. Nazaire will be fixed by private agreement, at the shipping ports, with the agents of the Company. These agents are also authorized to deliver, at prices fixed by the Company, direct bills of lading for Bordeaux, Paris, Havre, Antwerp, Rotterdam, Bremen, Hamburg, etc.

A primage of 5 per cent. will always be collected in addition to the rate of freight.

3d. *Tariff of Parcels and Samples.*

As to the freight of parcels and samples coming to France, the same tariff will be applied as that for goods and other objects of the same class leaving France.

CONNECTIONS AT THE ISTHMUS OF PANAMA.

By agreement with the Panama Railroad Company and the Steam-ship Companies running by the western coasts of America, in correspondence with the service from St. Nazaire to Colon, receipts and direct bills of lading from St. Nazaire to Panama, or to any of the ports designated hereafter, and vice versâ, will be delivered at the following rates:

1st. *From St. Nazaire to Panama.*

Merchandise, 227 fcs. 25 c. (£9) a ton of 40 cubic feet (1130 cubic decim.). No bill of lading delivered for less than 40 francs.

Gold, jewels, etc.	1¼ per cent. ad valorem.
Silver	1⅜ " "

No bill of lading delivered for less than 31 francs 25 cent.

PARCELS.

From 1 cubic foot and below (28 cubic decim.) 15 francs 15 c. (£0 12s.).
1 cub. ft. to 2 cub. feet (56 ") 22 francs 75 c. (£0 18s.).
2 cub. ft. to 3 " (84 ") 30 francs 30 c. (£1 4s.).

2d. *From Panama to St. Nazaire.*

Gold, jewels, etc.	1¼ per cent. ad valorem.
Silver	1⅜ " "

delivered in Paris at the office of the Company, or at the Bank of France; in London, at the Bank of England.

Pearls, emeralds, or other precious stones... 1¼ per cent. ad valorem, delivered as above.

No bill of lading given for freight less than 35 francs.

The price of freight for merchandise from Panama to St. Nazaire will be fixed by private agreement with the agents of the Transatlantic Company in Colon or Panama. These agents are also authorized to deliver, at the rates established by the Company, direct bills of lading for Bordeaux, Havre, Paris, Antwerp, Rotterdam, Hamburg, etc.

3d. *Ports of Southern Pacific Ocean to which the Steamers of the Pacific Steam Navigation Company run.*

OUTWARD.

Merchandise (a ton of 40 cubic feet, or 1^m· 130 cubic decim.).	£ s.	francs. c.
From St. Nazaire to all ports south of Callao (Valparaiso included)	15 5	385 05
From St. Nazaire to all ports south of Payta (Callao included)	14 5	359 80
From St. Nazaire to all ports south of Guayaquil (Payta included)	13 15	347 20
From St. Nazaire to Guayaquil	13 5	335 55
" " to Buenaventura	12 15	321 95
PARCELS AND SAMPLES.		
From St. Nazaire to all ports called at by the aforesaid steamers:		
1 cubic foot and below (28 cubic decim.)	1	25 25
From 1 to 2 cubic feet (56 ")	1 10	37 85
" 2 to 3 " (84 ")	1 19	49 25
COINS AND JEWELS.		
From St. Nazaire to all ports called at	2¼ per cent. ad valor.	

RETURNING.

Rates of Freight for Merchandise, Coins, and Samples shipped in the Southern Ports of the Pacific to St. Nazaire.

	Shipped in		
	Callao, Payta, and Guayaquil.	Any other Ports.	
	£ s. d.	£ s. d.	
Copper and Pewter in ingots	6 13 6	6 13 6	⎫
Copper and pewter ore in bags	8 2 8	8 19 4	⎪
Silver ore	8 16	8 16	⎪
Coffee and cocoa	9 14	10 2	⎬ 1 ton weight.
Archil	9	9 16	⎪
Peruvian bark	13 10	13 15	⎪
Cochineal and indigo	17 10	17 15	⎪
Leaf tobacco	14 6	14 18	⎭
Cotton	6 5	6 7 6	⎫
Whalebone	11 2 8	13 13 4	⎪
Panama hats	18 9 4	21 2 8	⎬ 1 cubic ton measurement.
Sarsaparilla	11 5	12 5	⎪
India-rubber	9 16	10 16	⎪
Merchandise not denominated	12 8	12 18	⎭

The price for parcels returning is the same as for those going out.

Freight for coins, precious metals, diamonds, etc., from all southern ports of the Pacific to St. Nazaire (delivered in Paris at the office of the Company, or at the Bank of France, or in London at the Bank of England) is 2¼ per cent. ad valorem.

No bill of lading given for freight less than 52 francs 50 cent. (£2 2s.).

Direct bills of lading will be delivered for Bordeaux, Havre, Paris, Antwerp, Rotterdam, Bremen, and Hamburg by the agents of the Transatlantic Company and Pacific Steam Navigation Company.

A primage of 5 per cent. will be collected in addition to the above-mentioned rates.

4th. *Ports of Central America at which the Steamers of the Panama Railroad Company call.*

Miscellaneous Merchandise.

From St. Nazaire to the ports of Central America at which the above steamers stop [Punta Arenas, Realejo (Corinto), La Union, La Libertad, Acajutla, San José de Guatemala], 290 francs 35 c. (£11 10s.) per ton of 1000 kilog., or 40 cubic feet.

Coins and Jewelry.

From St. Nazaire to all ports above-mentioned.......$2\frac{1}{4}$ per cent. ad valorem.
No bill of lading delivered for freight less than 52 francs 50 c.

Parcels going out.

1 cubic foot and below (28 cubic decim.)......20 francs 20 c. (£0 16s.)
From 1 cub. ft. to 2 cub. ft. (56 ")......30 francs 30 c. (£1 4s.)
" 2 " to 3 " (84 ")......40 francs 40 c. (£1 12s.)

Coins, Diamonds, Precious Metals.

From St. Nazaire to the aforesaid ports......$2\frac{1}{4}$ per cent. ad valorem.
No bill of lading given for freight less than 55 francs.

Merchandise returning from the Ports of Central America.

Vanilla............................$2\frac{1}{4}$ per cent. ad valorem.

Rates for merchandise not denominated will be established by private agreement with the agents of the Central American Line, or with those of the Transatlantic Company. Direct bills of lading can be delivered from the Central American ports to Bordeaux, Havre, Paris, Antwerp, Rotterdam, Bremen, and Hamburg, at the rates and conditions determined by the aforesaid agents.

Coins, Diamonds, Precious Metals.

From all the above ports to St. Nazaire......$2\frac{1}{4}$ per cent. ad valorem.

Parcels.

Same prices as above for going out.

5th. *Ports of the North Pacific at which the Steamers of the Pacific Mail Steam-ship Company call.*

From St. Nazaire to San Francisco, Acapulco, or Manzanillo.

Goods to San Francisco, 429 francs 25 cent. (£17) per ton of 1000 kilogrammes or 40 cubic feet.

Goods to Acapulco and Manzanillo, 404 francs (£16) per ton of 1000 kilogrammes or 40 cubic feet.

Jewelry and diamonds......$2\frac{1}{4}$ per cent. ad valorem,⎱ primage 5 per cent.
Silver.........................3 " " ⎰ more.

Parcels of three cubic feet and below, 52 francs 50 c. (£2 2s.).

From San Francisco, Acapulco, and Manzanillo to St. Nazaire.

Coins, gold, silver, etc., at the rates fixed by the agents of the Company, or those of the Pacific Mail Steam-ship Company.

Direct bills of lading are also delivered by the agents in San Francisco, Acapulco, and Manzanillo for St. Nazaire, Paris, Havre, Bordeaux, London, Antwerp, Hamburg, etc. (See the special Hand-book for the rates for returning.)

No bill of lading delivered for less than 55 francs.

Merchandise forwarded each way on board of the steamers of the Company according to the conditions in the manuals and bills of lading agreed upon by the Company.

MAIL LINE FROM HAVRE TO NEW YORK, CALLING AT BREST, LEAVING HAVRE, BREST, AND NEW YORK EVERY 14 DAYS.

Rates of Passage.

	1st Class. francs.	2d Class. francs.	3d Class. francs.
From Havre or Brest to New York	700	400	300
From Paris to New York (railway included)	725	415	310

Children from 2 to 10 years old pay half fare.
Servants accompanying passengers of 1st class pay the fare of 2d class.
Rates of passage include attendance, living, and table wine.
Superior wines and liquors may be procured on board at moderate prices.
Whole passage must be paid for in advance. Passengers not present at the departure lose half of the passage-money.
560 cubic decim. (20 cubic feet) are allowed to passengers of 1st class.
280 cubic decim. (10 cubic feet) are allowed to passengers of 2d class and children.
Passengers should have their names and destinations distinctly written on their baggage, and should be careful to have it on board the day before departure.
No package of any kind will be allowed in the saloons. The Company is not responsible for damages, loss, or detention of baggage. Merchandise in no case will be considered as baggage.
A passage is considered as engaged only after the payment of half of the passage-money.

List of Vessels of the Company.

Napoleon III.,	paddle-wheel,	1200	horse-power.
Washington,	"	900	"
Lafayette,	"	900	"
Europe,	"	900	"
Impératrice Eugénie,	"	900	"
France,	"	900	"
Nouveau Monde,	"	900	"
Panama,	"	900	"
Saint Laurent,	screw,	1000	"
Pereire,	"	1000	"
Ville de Paris,	"	1000	"
Louisiana,	"	600	"
Florida,	"	600	"
Tampico,	"	300	"
Vera Cruz,	"	300	"

H 2

Guyane,	paddle-wheel,	250 horse-power.
Sonora,	"	180 "
Caraïbe,	screw,	150 "
Cacique,	"	150 "
Caravelle,	"	150 "

Tugs.

At Saint Nazaire,	Belle-Isle,	100 "
" Brest,	Satellite,	80 "

Addresses.

Offices.—In Paris: 8 Place Vendôme.
" 12 Boulevard des Capucines, Grand Hôtel.
" 108 Rue du Faubourg Saint Denis.
In Saint Nazaire: Quai de la Marine.
" " M. Bourbeau, Principal Agent.

Agents and Correspondents in Europe.

Havre...............Messrs. W. Iselin & Co., Agents of the N. Y. Line.
Havre.........................Auguste Pierre.
Brest.........................Kerjégu and Villeferon.
Nantes........................Haentjens Brothers.
Bordeaux......................F. Alexandre, Agent.
Bayonne.......................J. M. Goyetche.
Marseilles....................N. Paquet & Co.
Lyon..........................Causse.
Geneva and Lausanne..........Gétaz.
Basel and Zurich............Dansaz and Minct.
Florence and Naples.......Padovani.
Rome.........................L. Fabri.
Genoa........................Vanetti.
Antwerp......................L. Hauterman & Co.
Rotterdam....................Ruys and Kellar.
Vienna .... { Austrian Co. I. R. P. of the railroads of the Empire.
Trieste......................G. and P. Ravasini.
Hamburg......................J. H. Dirks.
Bremen.......................H. G. Fisser.
London ....Pothonier & Co.
Madrid .... { Gen. Co. of the Spanish Personal Property's Bank.
Cadiz........................A. L. Sicre.
Barcelona....................Comas Salitre.
Santander....................Ruben Moïse & Co.
Bilbao.......................R. de Gaminde.

Agents and Correspondents of the Aspinwall, Guaymas, and Pacific Line.

Fort de France, Martinique......Messrs. E. Dupré, Agent.
St. Pierre, " ...... N. Montès.
Pointe-à-Pitre, Guadaloupe ...}
Basse-terre, " ...} Chabron, Laballe & Co.
Santa Martha...................... Vengoechea, Lafaurie & Co.
Colon (Aspinwall).................. Arrivet, Agent.
Panama .... Hourquet, Poylo & Co.
Guayaquil .... Poudavigne.

Jacna	Messrs. Prudhomme Brothers.
Lima	Thomas Lachambre & Co.
Valparaiso	Lequellec and Bordes.
La Union	Courtade Frères.
San José de Guatemala	Xavier du Theil.
Manzanilla	Oetling & Co.
San Francisco	Abel Guy.
St. Lucie	Belmar, Dubouloy & Co.
St. Vincent	Hugues & Co.
La Granada	L. Dill & Co.
Port of Spain (Trinidad)	O'Connor Brothers.
Demerara (English Guiana)	G. Little & Co.,
Surinam (Dutch Guiana)	Van'Praag Brother.
Cayenne (French Guiana)	G. Emler.

In the southern ports of the Pacific, apply also to the agents of the Pacific Steam Navigation Company.

In the ports of Central America, to the agents of the Central American Line Company.

In the northern ports of the Pacific, apply also to the agents of the Pacific Mail Steam-ship Company.

Agents and Correspondents of the Mexican, West Indian, and New York Lines.

Saint Thomas	Messrs. Nunes & Co.
Havana	Caro Brothers and Watson.
Vera Cruz	Lelong & Co.
Tampico	Dionisio Gamacho.
Matamoros	Droege, Oetling & Co.
Mexico	Deschamps & Co.
San Juan (Porto Rico)	Latimer & Co.
Cape Haytien	L. Vincent.
Santiago de Cuba	Ducourau & Co.
Kingston, Jamaica	W. Malabre & Co.
New Orleans	Victor Perilliat.
New York	G. Mackenzie, 58 Broadway, Agent.

N.B.—Rates given in francs ought to be divided by 4.94 in order to have dollars. The prices are always specified in gold.

1000 kilogrammes are equal to 2200 pounds avoirdupois.

THE WEST INDIA AND PACIFIC STEAM-SHIP COMPANY,

Sailing twice a month from LIVERPOOL to ASPINWALL, and three times a month from ASPINWALL to LIVERPOOL.

Head Office, the Temple, Dale Street, Liverpool; ARTHUR B. FORWARD, Managing Director.

London Offices, 117 and 118 Leadenhall Street, London.

The following steam vessels comprise the fleet:

Australian........	2400 tons.	Cuban..........	1334 tons.
Colombian.......	2250 "	Mexican..........	1279 "
Caribbean........	1852 "	Saint Thomas...	1245 "
American........	1831 "	Bolivar..........	1179 "
Californian......	1831 "	Darien..........	1171 "
West Indian.....	1804 "	Crusader.........	901 "
Venezuelan......	1682 "	Talisman.........	738 "
Chilian...........	1340 "	Plantagenet.....	694 "

The vessels call at St. Thomas and Santa Martha on their voyage from Liverpool, and at Kingston and Port-au-Prince on their return, leaving Liverpool on the 10th and 25th, and Aspinwall on the 7th, 15th, and 30th of each month. The passage occupies 27 days.

This line was established principally for the conveyance of cargo, but the steamers have accommodations for about 40 first-class passengers.

General Information.

This Company have organized a most complete system of through traffic arrangements between Europe and ports in the West Indies, Spanish Main, Gulf of Mexico, Central America, and the North and South Pacific Oceans, for the conveyance of goods, passengers, and specie.

These arrangements are in connection with the Panama Railroad Company, the Pacific Steam Navigation Company, and the Pacific Mail Steamship Company.

Steamers also leave Panama for New Zealand and Australia. Passengers are booked through at through rates.

Through bills of lading for produce and specie, shipped at the different ports on the Pacific to Europe, will be signed by the respective agents of the Companies above referred to. Shippers can also forward their merchandise by sailing vessels to Panama, consigned to the agent of the Company at Panama, who will undertake to forward it from thence, through to Europe, free of commission, charging only the expense incurred and the freight stipulated in this tariff from Panama. (Page 226.) When merchants adopt this course, they must address the agent at Panama, with full instructions as to consignees, disposition of bills of lading, etc. The agent of the Company will also effect insurance, if desired.

The agent at Colon will attend to all inquiries relating to the transmission of goods by this Company's steamers, and will furnish bills of lading and all particulars required. Bills of lading can also be obtained at the various ports on the Pacific from the agents of this and the other Steam-ship Companies trading on the Pacific Coast of America.

Produce will be received at Port-au-Prince for shipment by the steamers on board the Company's receiving-hulk at that port, free of storage, but at shipper's risk.

Shippers or consignees can arrange to have the option of forwarding their goods, on arrival in Liverpool, to any port in England or the Continent named in the freight-tables of this tariff. They will thus have the advantage of several markets.

The agents of the Company in London and on the Continent sign through bills of lading at through rates of freight.

No bills of lading will be signed except such as are made out on the Company's forms.

No rough goods, machinery, or weight will be received except by special agreement.

Silk goods, specie, jewelry, plate, watches, or any valuable or hazardous articles, can be taken only by special agreement previously made.

All goods, when sent down for shipment, must be accompanied by a shipping note on the Company's form, specifying the marks and numbers, and port the goods are for. All packages must be strongly packed, distinctly marked and numbered, and the port of destination must be painted thereon in letters of not less than two inches in size. Glass, liquids, and goods of a similar description, or of a damaging or dangerous nature, must have their contents plainly marked on the packages. The Company will not be responsible for accident or loss arising from the neglect of these precautions.

Goods of a dangerous or damaging nature to ship or cargo can only be taken under a special written agreement, and parties shipping any such goods without such arrangement will be held liable for all the consequences arising therefrom. The attention of shippers is particularly directed to the clauses of the act of Parliament in relation to this subject.

Any goods wrongly described in the bill of lading will be charged £10 per ton extra, and the goods will not be delivered until such extra freight is paid.

Goods for Maracaibo are taken on a through bill of lading, and forwarded from Curaçoa by sailing vessel, at ship's expense, but shipper's risk.

All freights outward are payable on delivery of the bills of lading.

All freights homeward are payable on the gross weights or measurements taken in Liverpool, and a deposit of the estimated amount of freight must be made before delivery.

Consular invoices for the following ports—La Guayra, Puerto Cabello, and Maracaibo, in Venezuela; Santa Martha, Carthagena, and Buenaventura, in the United States of Colombia; Vera Cruz and Tampico, in Mexico—must be presented at the respective consulates before 1 P.M. on the day previous to the advertised dates of the steamer's sailing, or an addition of 10 per cent. will be added to the freight. In the event of the necessary documents not being deposited within the time specified, the steamer is authorized to clear without them, and to land the goods at any other port, or carry them to their destination; all fines, expenses, or losses of any nature caused by their absence, to be paid by the shippers of the goods. No bills of lading for the ports above named will be signed without production of the consul's receipt for delivery of the invoices.

All letters and newspapers for conveyance by these steamers must pass through the post-office.

WEST INDIES, SPANISH MAIN, AND MEXICO.
List of Routes.

OUTWARD.		HOMEWARD.	
Leave Liverpool	10th	Leave Colon	15th
At St. Thomas	27th	At Santa Martha	17th
Leave "	29th	Leave "	19th
At San Martha	2d	At Liverpool	10th
Leave "	4th		
At Colon	6th		

OUTWARD.		C	HOMEWARD.	
Leave Liverpool	15th		Leave Vera Cruz	21st
At Port-au-Prince	5th		At Colon	29th
Leave "	7th		Leave "	7th
At Kingston	9th		At Kingston	12th
Leave "	11th		Leave "	14th
At Vera Cruz	16th		At Liverpool	5th

		D		
Leave Liverpool	25th		Leave Colon	30th
At St. Thomas	12th		At Carthagena	2d
Leave "	14th		Leave "	3d
At Santa Martha	17th		At Port-au-Prince	6th
Leave "	19th		Leave "	7th
At Colon	21st		At Liverpool	26th

Steamers will be regularly dispatched from Liverpool with goods for the undermentioned ports. For dates of sailing, etc., see the Company's advertisements.

    Barbadoes.   La Guayra.   Puerto Cabello.   Curaçoa.

The D steamer takes goods for Carthagena every alternate month.

The Company reserve to themselves the right to deviate from the above routes at any time, and do not hold themselves responsible for arriving and departing at the dates given, which are approximate.

The following are the tariffs of freight:

Outward Rates of Freight from Liverpool to Central American Ports—Panama, Punta Arenas, Realejo, La Union, La Libertad, Acajutla, and San José de Guatemala. To be paid on delivery of Bills of Lading. All free of Primage.

MEASUREMENT. Per ton of 40 cubic feet.	Panama.	All other Central American Ports.
	£ s. d.	£ s. d.
General merchandise, hardware, and all goods not specially enumerated	6 5 0	8 15 0
Wines or spirits, in bulk	6 0 0	8 0 0
" " in bottle	5 5 0	7 5 0
Common glass-ware	5 10 0	7 10 0
Beer, in bulk or bottle, and common earthen-ware	4 10 0	6 0 0
Cotton and sugar bagging	5 10 0	7 0 0
Jewelry and plate	$1\frac{1}{4}$ per cent.	$2\frac{1}{4}$ per cent.
Gold coin or bullion	$\frac{4}{8}$ "	$1\frac{4}{8}$ "
Silver " "	$1\frac{4}{8}$ "	$2\frac{4}{8}$ "
WEIGHT. Per ton of 20 cwt. gross weight.		
Iron bars, plate, rods, etc.	5 0 0	6 10 0
Bent iron, nails, zinc, steel, lead, etc.	6 0 0	7 5 0
Copper and brass, of all kinds	6 10 0	8 0 0
Common soap	5 5 0	7 5 0

THE WEST INDIA AND PACIFIC STEAM-SHIP CO. 183

SOUTH PACIFIC PORTS.

Outward Rates of Freight from Liverpool, to be paid on delivery of Bills of Lading.

PORTS.	General Merchandise.	Wines, Spirits, and Beer in bottles, Glass-ware, Earthen-ware, etc.
	£ s. d.	£ s. d.
Buenaventura...............................	10 0 0	9 10 0
Tumaco, Esmeralda, Manta, and Guayaquil...	10 10 0	10 0 0
Payta..	11 0 0	10 10 0
Lambayeque, Pacasmayo, Huanchaco, Santa, Casma, Supè, Huacho, and Callao...	11 10 0	11 0 0
Cerro Azul, Pisco, Chala, Islay, Arica, Pisagua, Mexillones, Iquique, Tocapillo, Cobija, Caldera, Carrizal-bajo, Huasco, Coquimbo, Tongoy, and Valparaiso....................................	12 10 0	12 0 0

Per ton of 40 cubic feet, or 20 cwt. gross, at ship's option.

NORTH PACIFIC PORTS.

Outward Rates of Freight from Liverpool, to be paid on delivery of Bills of Lading. All free of Primage.

Per ton of 40 cubic feet, or 20 cwt. gross, at ship's option.	San Francisco.	Manzanillo and Acapulco.
	£ s. d.	£ s. d.
General merchandise.......................	14 5 0	13 5 0
Hardware......................................	14 5 0	12 5 0
Groceries, wines, liquors, crockery, and common glass-ware........................	13 0 0	10 10 0
No bills of lading signed for less than.	1 11 6	1 11 6

CENTRAL AMERICAN PORTS.

Homeward Rates of Freight to Liverpool. All free of Primage.

ARTICLES.	At per Ton.	TO LIVERPOOL FROM	
		Panama.	Central American Ports.
		£ s. d.	£ s. d.
Balsam	Weight.	16 10 0	22 0 0
Bark...	"	8 5 0	11 0 0
Cochineal	"	12 0 0	17 7 6
Cotton	Measurement.	3 12 6	4 15 0
Coffee, in bags	Weight.	5 10 0	8 10 0
" " from Punta Arenas............	"	....	8 0 0
Cocoa...	"	5 15 0	8 15 0
Copper ore, in bags	"	8 15 0	6 0 0
Dyewoods.....................................	"	4 0 0	5 15 0
Deer and goat skins........................	Measurement.	6 5 0	10 0 0
Indigo	Weight.	12 0 0	17 7 6
India-rubber, in bags or loose	"	7 10 0	11 10 0
" in cases or casks..............	Measurement.	3 10 0	4 10 0
Hides, dried	Weight.	10 10 0	10 5 0

Homeward Rates of Freight to Liverpool—continued.

ARTICLES.	At per Ton.	TO LIVERPOOL FROM Panama.	TO LIVERPOOL FROM Central American Ports.
		£ s. d.	£ s. d.
Merchandise, not enumerated	Weight or Meas't.	10 10 0	15 5 0
Mother-of-pearl shells	Weight.	4 0 0	....
Sarsaparilla	Measurement.	3 5 0	5 5 0
Silver ore	Weight.	4 5 0	6 0 0
Sugar	"	4 0 0	6 0 0
Specie—gold	Per cent.	0 15 0	1 15 0
" silver	"	1 0 0	2 0 0
" jewelry and plate	"	1 5 0	2 5 0
Tobacco, in hide serons	Weight.	7 10 0	11 0 0
" in bales	Measurement.	8 15 0	4 15 0
No bills of lading will be signed for less than.	....	1 1 0	1 1 0

SOUTH PACIFIC PORTS.

Homeward Rates of Freight to Liverpool. All free of Primage.

ARTICLES.	At per Ton.	TO LIVERPOOL FROM Callao, Payta, and Guayaquil.	TO LIVERPOOL FROM All other Ports.
		£ s. d.	£ s. d.
Barilla, in bags	Weight.	4 10 0	4 10 0
Bark, in hide serons	"	12 5 0	12 10 0
Copper and tin, in bars or ingots	"	4 10 0	4 10 0
Coffee, in bags	"	8 0 0	8 5 0
Cocoa "	"	8 5 0	8 10 0
Cochineal	"	15 15 0	16 0 0
Cotton	Measurement.	4 10 0	4 12 6
Hides, dried	Each.	0 3 1½	0 3 4½
Indigo	Weight.	15 15 0	16 0 0
India-rubber, in cases or casks	Measurement.	4 10 0	4 15 0
" loose or in bags	Weight.	10 5 0	10 15 0
Ivory nuts	"	6 10 0	6 15 0
Merchandise, not enumerated	Weight or Meas't.	10 10 0	10 15 0
Orchilla weed, press-packed	Weight.	7 15 0	8 10 0
Panama hats	Measurement.	18 0 0	15 0 0
Rhatania root	Weight.	11 0 0	11 10 0
Silver ores, in bags	"	7 10 0	7 10 0
Sarsaparilla	Measurement.	4 10 0	4 10 0
Skins, deer and goat	"	7 10 0	7 10 0
Specie (gold)	Per cent.	1 12 6	1 12 6
Silver and valuables	"	1 17 6	1 17 6
Tobacco, in hide serons	Weight.	10 15 0	11 7 6
" in bales	Measurement.	5 10 0	5 15 0
Wool, alpaca	Weight.	18 10 0	19 5 0
" sheep's, washed	"	15 5 0	16 0 0
" " unwashed	"	13 0 0	13 15 0
" all descriptions	Measurement.	4 0 0	4 0 0
No bills of lading signed for less than	....	1 10 0	1 10 0

NORTH PACIFIC PORTS.

Homeward Rates of Freight to Liverpool. All free of Primage.

ARTICLES.	At per Ton.	TO LIVERPOOL FROM Acapulco and Manzanillo.	TO LIVERPOOL FROM San Francisco.
		£ s. d.	£ s. d.
All merchandise, not enumerated	Weight or Meas't.	12 0 0	12 0 0
Bark	Weight.	13 10 0	14 10 0
Cochineal	"	17 15 0	18 10 0
Cotton	Measurement.	6 2 6	6 2 6
Copper ore, in sacks	Weight.	6 15 0	7 0 0

Homeward Rates of Freight to Liverpool—continued.

ARTICLES.	At per Ton.	TO LIVERPOOL FROM Acapulco and Manzanillo.	TO LIVERPOOL FROM San Francisco.
		£ s. d.	£ s. d.
Dyewoods	Weight.	6 15 0	7 10 0
Hides, dried	Each.	0 2 9	0 3 0
India-rubber, loose or in bags	Weight.	12 8 0	12 8 0
" in cases or casks	Measurement.	6 5 0	6 5 0
Indigo	Weight.	17 15 0	18 10 0
Lead ore, in sacks	"	7 0 0	7 0 0
Parcels	Each.	1 10 0	1 10 0
Quicksilver [Per flask of not	exceeding 90 lbs.	0 11 0	0 12 0
Sarsaparilla	Measurement.	5 10 0	5 10 0
Silver ore, in sacks	Weight.	7 0 0	8 0 0
Skins, deer and goat, press-packed	Measurement.	5 15 0	6 0 0
Tobacco, in hide serons	Weight.	12 10 0	12 10 0
" in bales	Measurement.	6 0 0	6 0 0
Wool	"	5 15 0	5 15 0
Whalebone	"	10 0 0	10 10 0
Whale oil	Per 252 gallons.	11 0 0	12 0 0
No bills of lading will be signed for less than	....	1 10 0	1 10 0

Passenger Fares, etc., including the use of Bedding and Linen, Steward's Fees, and all other Charges, except for Wines, Spirits, Malt Liquors, etc., which will be supplied on Board at moderate Prices.

FROM LIVERPOOL.	Third Class.	Second Class.	First Class.
	£ s. d.	£ s. d.	£ s. d.
To St. Thomas	......	......	25 0 0
" Barbadoes	......	......	28 0 0
" Port-au-Prince, Kingston, La Guayra, Puerto Cabello, Curaçoa, Santa Martha, Carthagena, and Colon	......	......	30 0 0
" Vera Cruz, Tampico, and Belize	......	......	36 0 0
" Guayaquil, exclusive of railway fare*	......	48 15 0	49 18 9
" Callao, do	......	58 2 6	60 0 0
" Valparaiso, do	......	80 12 6	84 7 6
" Acapulco and Manzanillo, do.	37 10 0	40 0 0	45 0 0
" San Francisco, do	40 17 6	48 5 0	55 10 0
" Vancouver's Island, do	46 2 6	53 10 0	64 19 0

* The railway fare across the Isthmus is five guineas.

Passengers can be booked through to other ports in the South Pacific and Central America: the particulars of fares, etc., can be obtained at the Company's offices.

A deposit of £5 is required to secure a berth; the balance to be paid before embarkation.

Steamers leave Panama for New Zealand and Australia on the 24th of every month, arriving at Wellington on the 21st and Sydney on the 29th of the succeeding month. Passengers to Colon by the West India and Pacific Steam-ship Company's steamers can book forward on the Isthmus.

The second and third class accommodation shown in the above table refers to the Pacific portion of the voyage, first-class passengers only being carried between Liverpool and Colon.

186 THE WEST INDIA AND PACIFIC STEAM-SHIP CO.

Foreign Currency to be received by the pursers on board the steamers at the following rates of exchange:

Spanish dollar ....at 4s. 2d. sterl.	Mexican dollar ....at 4s. 0d. sterl.	
" doubloon...... 64 0	Bolivian " 3 1	
American eagle 41 0	French silver 5fr. piece 4 0	
" half eagle .. 20 6	French gold, at the rate	
" quar. eagle. 10 3	per 5fr. piece of...... 4 0	
" gold dollar. 4 1	Chilian condor 37 0	
" silver " 4 0	New Granadian do..... 39 0	

Rates for Intercolonial-Cabin Passengers, to be paid, before embarking, in Silver Dollars or their equivalent.

FROM	Barbadoes	St. Thomas	La Guayra	Puerto Cabello	Curaçoa	Santa Martha	Carthagena	Colon	Kingston	Port-au-Prince	Vera Cruz	Tampico
St. Thomas	25	...	30	40	50	40	50	50	30	30	...	...
La Guayra.....	...	40	...	15	20	...	...	...	...	...	...	...
Puerto Cabello	...	40	15	...	15	...	...	...	...	...	...	...
Curaçoa........	...	40	20	15	...	...	...	...	...	...	...	...
Santa Martha.	...	...	...	...	...	...	10	25	50	60	...	...
Carthagena....	...	...	...	...	...	10	...	15	50	60	...	...
Colon	...	...	...	...	...	25	15	...	25	40	...	...
Kingston.......	...	...	...	...	...	45	40	25	...	25	90	90
Port-au-Prince	...	...	...	...	...	45	50	50	25	...	100	100
Vera Cruz.....	...	...	...	...	...	...	...	100	90	100	...	...
Tampico	...	...	...	...	...	...	...	100	90	100	...	...
Barbadoes......	...	25	25	30	40	...	...	...	75	60	...	...

Male deck passengers to pay one third cabin fare, females one half, and to be messed on the same scale as the crew, but to find their own bedding, etc., and utensils. Children over three and under twelve years old to pay one half fare. Dogs to pay one eighth of the fare paid by their owners.

Return Tickets issued to adult cabin passengers, with an abatement of 25 per cent. off the passage-money, to be available for six months for West Indian ports, and twelve months for South Pacific ports. For male servants, half full cabin fare each way, and for female servants, two thirds full cabin fare out, and half full cabin fare home. Application to be made to the agent before embarking for permission to do so, and if the ship be full, the holder to have a passage by the first subsequent opportunity. None granted for intercolonial voyages.

Notice.—The Company will not be responsible for the maintenance of passengers, nor for the loss of time during any detention consequent upon the occurrence of any cause to prevent their branch steamers from meeting at the appointed places; nor for any delay arising out of accidents; nor for any loss or damage arising from perils of the sea, or accidents from machinery, boilers, or steam; from any act, neglect, or default whatsoever of the pilot, master, or mariners; nor for any consequences arising from the sanitary regulations or precautions which the Company's officers or local government authorities may deem necessary. Should such sanitary regulations or precautions prevent embarkation or disembarkation; or if, in consequence of such sanitary regulations or precautions, passengers should have to be conveyed to their destination by a circuitous route, or to remain (with the consent of the Company's officers) on board the Company's vessels, beyond the time at which, under ordinary circumstances, they would disembark, the Company will, in lieu of additional passage-money, etc., charge only at the rate of 5s. per diem for victualing during the extra time each adult cabin passenger may have been on board, and in proportion for other classes of passengers.

Should the Company's vessels be detained, from any cause whatever, more than 48 hours at any port of call, the cabin passengers to pay 5s. per diem, in addition to the passage-money, for each day the vessel is so detained.

Agencies and Correspondents.

Colon and Panama.....P. M. LEAY, Esq., Colon.
Paris ....J. M. CURRIE, Esq., Place de la Bourse, 12.
Havre.................J. M. CURRIE, Esq., Quai d'Orleans, 21.
Bordeaux............Messrs. LAFITTE & VANDERCRUYCE.
Queenstown ....Messrs. N. & J. CUMMINS & BROTHERS.

Arica......................................G. H. Nugent.
Barbadoes................................Dummett & Co.
Belize.....................................Antonio Mathé.
Bermuda..................................Musson & Co.
Cape Hayti...............................Case, Rowe, & Co.
Carthagena...............................Macia & Son.
Colon and Panama......................P. M. Leay, Colon.
Curaçoa...................................J. & H. Jones.
Demerara.................................S. Barber & Co.
Guayaquil................................Millan, Ballen, & Co.
Guatemala, for San José de Guatemala........Hockmeyer & Rittscher.
Havana....................................M. A. Herrera & Co.
Islay.......................................Gibson & Lewis.
Kinstgon..................................M'Dowell & Barclay.
La Guayra................................Rüete, Röhl, & Co.
Lima.......................................Graham, Rowe, & Co.
New Orleans..............................O. B. Graham & Co.
Nassau, N. P.............................Sawyer & Menendez.
New York.................................Ribon & Muñoz.
Port-au-Prince...........................Rowe, Brown, & Co.
Puerto Cabello...........................Rüete, Röbl, & Co.
Realejo....................................P. Eisenstuck & Co.
Sonsonaté, for Acajutla.................José, Kerferd, & Co.
San Miguel, for La Union................Kerferd, Nephew, & Co.
San Salvador, for La Libertad..........   "   "
San José de Costa Rica, for Punta Arenas....Allan, Wallis, & Co.
San Francisco............................Rodgers, Meyer, & Co.
Santa Martha.............................Manuel J. de Mier.
St. Thomas...............................Schön, Willink, & Co.
Tampico...................................Dionisio Camacho.
Trinidad...................................Hume, Bernard, & Co.
Turk's Island..............................C. R. Hinson.
Valparaiso.................................Graham, Rowe, & Co.
Vera Cruz.................................Büsing, Mertens, & Co.
Also the Agents of the....................Pacific Steam Navigation Co.
   "   "   ....Pacific Mail Steam-ship Co.
   "   "   ....Panama Railroad Co.

ROYAL MAIL STEAM PACKET COMPANY,

Under contract with Her Majesty's Government for the conveyance of the mails for the WEST INDIES, MEXICO, NEW ZEALAND, AUSTRALIA, CENTRAL AMERICA, PANAMA, and the PACIFIC.

Offices:

55 Moorgate Street, London. J. M. LLOYD, Secretary.
Canute Road, Southampton. Capt. W. VINCENT, Superintendent.

The following are some of the Agencies:

Liverpool	C. E. HAMILTON, Esq., the Temple, Dale Street.
Manchester	HUGH FLEMING, Esq., 4 York Chambers.
Paris	Messrs. PRITCHARD & MONNERON, 4 Rue Rossini. Sub-Agency, 10 Rue Castiglione.
Havre	Messrs. MARCEL & Co. (late DAVIDSON & Co.)
Hamburg	Messrs. HUNDEIKER & ABEGG.
Antwerp	W. KENNEDY, Esq.
Rotterdam	Messrs. HUDIG & BLOKHUYZEN.
Copenhagen	Messrs. F. and E. GOTSCHALK.
St. Thomas	J. B. CAMERON, Esq., Superintendent.
Colon (Aspinwall)	D. R. MARTIN, Esq., Traffic Manager.
Panama	C. A. HENDERSON, Esq., H.B.M. Consul.
Havana	J. V. CRAWFORD, Esq., H.B.M. Vice-Consul.
Vera Cruz	C. MARKOE, Esq.
Tampico	Messrs. JOLLY & Co.
Jamaica	Capt. COOPER, R.N., Superintendent.
Trinidad	FRED. J. SCOTT, Esq.
Barbadoes	Messrs. M. CAVAN & Co.
Demerara	Messrs. ROSE, DUFF, & Co.
San Francisco (California)	W. LANE BOOKER, Esq., H.B.M. Consul.
Victoria (Vancouver's Isl.)	
San José de Guatemala	WM. EVERALL, Esq., H.B.M. Vice-Consul.
La Union (San Salvador)	Messrs. MORRIS & Co.

Passengers, specie, and parcels are booked at the Company's Office, 55 Moorgate Street, London. At Southampton, passengers, specie, goods, etc., are booked by Mr. J. K. LINSTEAD, the Company's Cargo Superintendent.

The Company's steam-ships are appointed by Her Majesty's Government to leave Southampton at 2 o'clock P.M. on the 2d and 17th of each month (unless these dates should fall on a Sunday, and then on the following day), proceeding direct to St. Thomas, where mails, passengers, etc., are transferred, and conveyed thence to the places on the branch routes by the Company's Intercolonial steamers, and between Panama, New Zealand, and Australia by the steamers of the Panama, New Zealand, and Australian Royal Mail Company (limited).

ROYAL MAIL STEAM PACKET COMPANY. 189

The following are the estimated Dates of Arrival of the Outward Mails, etc., at, and of the Departure of the Homeward Mails, etc., from, the Principal Stations:

From Southampton:
2d and 17th of each month, arriving at St. Thomas .... 17th and 2d.
"   "   "   Aspinwall (Isthmus of
                                     Panama) .... 22d and 7th.
"   "   "   Jamaica .... 21st and 6th.
"   "   "   Barbadoes .... 20th and 5th.
"   "   "   Trinidad .... 22d and 7th.
"   "   "   Demerara .... 22d and 7th.
2d of each month, arriving at Havana (one mail each month) 22d idem.
"   "   "   Vera Cruz   "   26th "
"   "   "   Tampico   "   28th "
"   "   "   Carthagena   "   24th "
"   "   "   Santa Martha   "   26th "
17th   "   "   Belize   "   10th following m'th.
"   "   "   Greytown   "   10th "

The following are the estimated Dates of Departure of the homeward Mails from the principal Stations, commencing with the Mails in reply to those from Southampton March 2d.

(The mails are conveyed to St. Thomas by the Company's intercolonial ships.)

From:
Tampico (one mail each month) 29th, reaching Southampton 29th following m'th.
Santa Martha   "   27th,   "   "   29th   "
Vera Cruz   "   2d,*   "   "   29th idem.
Havana   "   8th,*   "   "   29th   "
Carthagena   "   5th,*   "   "   29th   "
Belize   "   17th,*   "   "   14th following m'th.
Greytown   "   19th,   "   "   14th   "
Demerara .... 9th* and 24th of each month. ⎫
Trinidad .... 9th* and 24th   "   "   ⎪ Reaching
Barbadoes .... 11th* and 26th   "   "   ⎬ Southampton
Jamaica .... 10th* and 25th   "   "   ⎪ 29th and 14th
Aspinwall (Isthmus of Panama).. 9th* and 24th   "   "   ⎪ respectively.
St. Thomas .... 15th* and 30th   "   "   ⎭

N.B.—The estimated dates of departure which are marked thus * above will be a day earlier when the preceding month comprised 31 days.

Notice.—The Company will not be responsible for the maintenance of passengers, or for their loss of time during any detention consequent upon the occurrence of any cause to prevent the vessels from meeting at the appointed places; nor for any delay arising out of accidents; nor for any loss or damage arising from perils of the seas, or from machinery, boilers, or steam, or from any act, neglect, or default whatsoever of the pilot, master, or mariners; nor from any consequences arising from sanitary regulations or precautions which the Company's officers or local government authorities may deem necessary, or should such sanitary regulations or precautions prevent embarkation or disembarkation; and if, in consequence of such sanitary regulations or precautions, passengers should have to be conveyed to their destination by a circuitous route, or to remain (with the consent of the Company's officers) on board the Company's vessels beyond the time at which, under ordinary circumstances, they would disembark, the Company will, in lieu of additional passage-money, etc., charge only at the rate of 10s. per diem for victualing during the extra time each adult cabin passenger may have been on board, and in proportion for other classes of passengers.

PASSENGER FARES, WHICH INCLUDE THE USE OF BEDDING AND LINEN, STEWARD'S FEES, AND ALL OTHER CHARGES EXCEPT FOR WINES, SPIRITS, MALT LIQUORS, AND MINERAL WATERS.

Atlantic Voyages (see *Regulations*, pages 193 and 194).

OUTWARD.		FARES OUT OR HOME.		HOMEWARD.	
Leaves Southampton each Month.	Destination.	Berths* in after Cabins (except outside Cabins on the main Deck) and in main Deck forward Cabins. Each Berth.†	Berths in lower Deck forward Cabins. Each Berth.	From what Places.	Due at Southampton each Month.
		£ s.	£ s.		
2d and 17th	Antigua......	38 10	33 0	Antigua......	14th and 29th
2d and 17th	Barbadoes...	38 10	33 0	Barbadoes...	14th and 29th
17th	Blewfields ...	44 0	38 10	Blewfields ...	14th
2d and 17th	Carriacou....	38 10	33 0	Carriacou....	14th and 29th
2d	Carthagena..	44 0	38 10	Carthagena..	29th
2d and 17th	Aspinwall ...	44 0	38 10	Aspinwall....	14th and 29th
2d and 17th	Demerara ...	38 10	33 0	Demerara....	14th and 29th
2d and 17th	Dominica....	38 10	33 0	Dominica....	14th and 29th
		18 14	18 14	Fayal (if touched at)	
2d and 17th	Granada	38 10	33 0	Granada......	14th and 29th
17th	Greytown....	44 0	38 10	Greytown....	14th
2d and 17th	Guadalonpe.	38 10	33 0	Guadaloupe.	14th and 29th
2d	Havana	44 0	38 10	Havana	29th
17th	Honduras....	44 0	38 10	Honduras....	14th
2d and 17th	Jacmel	38 10	33 0	Jacmel	14th and 29th
2d and 17th	Jamaica......	38 10	33 0	Jamaica......	14th and 29th
2d and 17th	Martinique..	38 10	33 0	Martinique..	14th and 29th
2d and 17th	Porto Rico ..	38 10	33 0	Porto Rico ..	14th and 29th
2d and 17th	St. Kitts......	38 10	33 0	St. Kitts......	14th and 29th
2d and 17th	St. Lucia.....	38 10	33 0	St. Lucia.....	14th and 29th
2d and 17th	St. Thomas..	38 10	33 0	St. Thomas..	14th and 29th
2d and 17th	St. Vincent..	38 10	33 0	St. Vincent..	14th and 29th
2d	Sta. Martha.	44 0	38 10	Sta. Martha.	29th
2d	Tampico.....	49 10	44 0	Tampico.....	29th
2d and 17th	Tobago.......	38 10	33 0	Tobago.......	14th and 29th
2d and 17th	Trinidad	38 10	33 0	Trinidad	14th and 29th
2d	Vera Cruz...	49 10	44 0	Vera Cruz...	29th

* A whole after cabin secured for the exclusive use of one passenger (not being an outside cabin on the main deck) is to be charged as a berth and a half, calculated at the rate shown in the column marked † above.

† For an outside cabin, or for a berth therein on the main deck aft, an additional charge of £5 is to be made to each passenger beyond the fares indicated respectively in the preceding clause and in the column marked † above.

In future, no whole cabins on the main deck forward, or on the lower deck forward, of any of the Company's ships, are to be let as single cabins.

The above distinctions in accommodation apply more particularly to the Atlantic voyages between Southampton and St. Thomas, and *vice versa*, but they will also be adhered to as far as practicable on board the intercolonial vessels.

The difference in the rates of passage-money shown above refers merely to the sleeping-cabins; in all other respects the passengers will be precisely on the same footing.

Return Tickets.—Return tickets issued to cabin passengers for Atlantic voyages with an abatement of 25 per cent. on the passage-money. Such tickets to be paid for when issued, and not to be transferable. To be available if the parties holding the same embark on the return voyage within six calendar months (but in the case of Colon [Aspinwall] within twelve calendar months) from the date of their first embarkation; and no allowance will be made to such parties if they do not make the return voyage by the Company's vessels. Should there be no available accommodation in the ship by which the holder wishes to embark on the return voyage, he will be entitled to a passage by the first subsequent opportunity. In all such cases certificates must be obtained from the Company's agents or captains, specifying the dates of application, and that no accommodation could then be afforded.

Children.—Of the children of cabin passengers under three years of age, one to be carried free of charge; any other under that age to be charged as three years and under eight; those three years and under eight years, to pay one fourth the cabin-passage rate paid by their parents, and four such children to be entitled to one berth.

Passengers on Warrant-officers' Scale.—A limited number of artisans, emigrants, etc., to be victualed on the same footing as the ship's warrant-officers, and supplied with bunks and bedding, will be conveyed, when there is room for them, from Southampton to the West Indies, Colon (Aspinwall), or Mexico for £25 each.

Return tickets are not to be issued to passengers of this class.

Servants.—Passengers' servants can not be booked as deck passengers.

Passengers' male servants to pay one half, and female two thirds of the lowest rates established for adult saloon passengers, and no abatement to be made on account of age. Men servants will be berthed in the fore part of the ship; women servants will have beds made up in the ladies' saloon.

Deck Passengers can only be conveyed intercolonially.—Only troops, common sailors, or laborers to be conveyed as deck passengers; to find their own provisions and bedding, and not admitted abaft the chimney, and to pay one fourth the cabin fare. Children of deck passengers to pay half the deck fare, when three years or above, and not exceeding twelve years of age, and when under three years to be taken free. N.B.—No deck passenger is to be booked for St. Thomas.

Dogs, Carriages, Horses, Cattle, etc.—Dogs to be charged at one eighth the fare paid by their owners.

Carriages, horses, live-stock, etc. (for the shipment of which special permission must be obtained from Captain W. Vincent, the Company's superintendent at Southampton), will be conveyed only under special form of ticket, which provides for the owner's undertaking all risk of conveyance whatsoever, as the Company will not be responsible for any injury or damage (however caused) occurring while on board the Company's ships, or in embarkation, transfer, or disembarkation; and the shippers must in all cases provide food, boxes, pens, or coops.

Carriages measuring 3 tons or under, £12 each.

Carriages measuring above 3 tons, at the rate of £4 per ton measurement.

Horses, colts, and heifers, to St. Thomas, £20 each; to other West Indian ports, £25 each. Rams, sheep, and pigs, £5 each; poultry, 15s. each.

☞ In all cases where passengers are subject in the ordinary course of the mail service, as per tables, to a detention of more than four days, that is, while waiting the arrival of the vessel by which they are to prosecute their voyage, they will have to defray the expenses of their victualing during such period of detention.

192   ROYAL MAIL STEAM PACKET COMPANY.

Intercolonial Voyages.—Fares in Silver Dollars for Cabin Passengers. (Return Tickets are not granted to Intercolonial Passengers.)

Places.	Antigua	Barbadoes	Blewfields	Carriacou	Carthagena	Aspinwall	Demerara	Dominica	Grenada	Guadaloupe	Greytown	Havana	Honduras	Jacmel	Jamaica	Martinique	St. Juan's	St. Kitts	St. Lucia	Sta. Martha	St. Thomas	St. Vincent	Tampico	Tobago	Trinidad	Vera Cruz
Antigua........	...	25	85	25	65	65	40	12	25	8	75	65	80	40	50	15	25	10	15	65	15	25	115	35	30	110
Barbadoes.....	20	...	100	15	80	80	20	15	15	20	90	80	95	55	65	15	40	25	10	80	30	12	130	25	20	125
Blewfields.....	110	120	...	120	50	80	135	115	120	110	10	135	150	110	120	115	95	105	115	60	85	120	185	130	130	180
Carriacou......	25	20	100	...	80	20	35	20	5	20	90	80	95	55	65	20	40	25	20	80	30	5	130	25	12	125
Carthagena....	85	95	40	95	...	15	110	90	95	85	30	110	125	85	95	90	70	80	90	10	60	95	160	105	105	155
Colon (Aspinwall)...	85	95	25	95	15	...	110	90	95	85	15	110	125	85	95	90	70	80	90	35	60	95	160	105	105	155
Demerara......	40	20	120	30	100	100	...	35	30	40	110	100	115	75	85	35	60	45	30	100	50	30	150	35	30	145
Dominica......	12	25	85	25	75	75	40	...	25	8	85	75	90	50	60	20	35	15	8	75	20	25	125	35	10	120
Granada.......	25	20	95	5	75	75	35	25	...	20	85	75	90	50	60	8	40	25	20	75	30	10	130	20	30	125
Guadaloupe....	8	25	80	25	70	70	40	8	20	...	80	70	85	45	55	8	30	12	12	70	20	25	120	35	10	115
Greytown.....	100	110	10	110	40	15	125	105	110	100	...	125	140	100	110	105	85	95	105	50	75	110	175	120	120	170
Havana........	85	95	130	95	110	110	110	90	95	85	120	...	95	85	95	90	70	80	90	110	60	95	45	105	105	40
Honduras......	110	120	155	120	135	135	135	115	120	110	145	95	...	60	40	115	80	105	115	135	85	120	180	130	130	175
Jacmel.........	55	65	100	65	80	80	95	75	80	70	105	60	50	...	20	75	40	65	75	80	45	80	125	75	75	120
Jamaica........	70	80	115	80	95	95	95	75	85	75	85	20	30	20	...	75	30	40	60	95	25	80	140	90	90	135
Martinique....	12	25	95	25	75	75	40	8	25	8	70	60	90	50	60	...	35	15	8	75	25	25	125	35	25	120
St. Juan's, Pto. Rico.	85	50	95	50	60	60	60	40	50	30	85	30	60	25	30	40	...	20	40	60	12	50	105	60	55	100
St. Kitts......	12	30	80	30	60	60	50	20	30	15	70	50	75	35	50	20	20	...	20	60	12	30	115	40	35	110
St. Lucia.....	15	10	80	20	60	60	30	10	15	12	70	60	90	55	65	8	40	20	...	60	12	20	115	30	35	110
Santa Martha.	85	95	120	95	8	25	110	90	95	85	90	110	125	85	95	90	70	80	90	...	60	95	160	105	105	155
St. Thomas...	25	35	95	35	50	50	50	30	35	20	60	50	65	25	35	30	10	20	30	50	...	35	95	45	45	90
St. Vincent...	20	15	105	5	85	85	30	15	10	25	95	85	100	60	70	15	45	25	15	85	35	...	135	25	15	130
Tampico......	145	155	190	155	170	170	170	150	155	145	180	65	185	145	155	150	115	140	150	170	120	155	...	165	165	12
Tobago........	30	25	110	25	90	90	35	25	15	30	100	90	105	65	75	25	50	35	25	90	40	25	140	...	10	135
Trinidad......	30	25	110	12	90	90	30	30	15	10	105	90	105	65	75	25	50	35	25	90	40	15	140	15	...	135
Vera Cruz.....	140	150	185	150	165	165	165	145	150	140	175	60	180	140	150	145	110	135	145	165	115	150	12	160	160	...

Dogs, when conveyed intercolonially, to be charged one eighth of the fare paid by their owners.

Horses, colts, and heifers, when conveyed intercolonially, to be charged five sixths of the saloon passenger rate.

Carriages, ditto, measuring three tons or under, £9 each. Ditto, ditto, above three tons, at the rate of £3 per ton measurement.

Rams, sheep, and pigs, £3 each. Poultry, 10s. each.

For Conditions of Conveyance, see pages 189, 190.

PASSENGER REGULATIONS, ETC.

Each ship carries an experienced surgeon.

No berth is considered engaged until the whole fare is paid.

Passengers not proceeding after taking their passage, to forfeit half the passage-money.

Passengers are earnestly recommended to conform to established regulations as respects passports, etc.

Passengers are not allowed to take on board wines, spirits, or other liquors for use during the voyage, an ample stock thereof being provided on board at moderate prices.

There are French and English cooks on board.

No person can be received on board the Company's ships when suffering from any infectious disorder; and if, in the course of the voyage, any passenger should be found to be suffering from a disorder of that character, he will be required, at his own expense, to find accommodation at any port in which the vessel may happen to be at the time of, or at the first port she may reach after discovery of the existence of the disorder, it being understood that, when sufficiently recovered, such passenger will be conveyed to his destination in one of the Company's vessels.

The captains will be most careful to avoid all personal preference or partiality in allotting accommodation on board the Company's ships. Within the prescribed limits, priority is always to be given according to the dates on which passengers were originally booked and the passage-money paid. If paid through the Company's agent, he will be careful, when he hands the money to the captain, to furnish also the date when it is paid for notation on the passage ticket.

The respective classes of cabin accommodation in the homeward steamer from St. Thomas will be apportioned as follows, viz.: the passengers from routes Nos. 2 and 4, and those booked at St. Thomas, are to be allowed priority of berths on the starboard side, according to the date of their tickets, that is to say, the oldest date from No. 2 route to have the first allotment, the oldest date from No. 4 route the second, and the oldest date from St. Thomas the third; this plan to be repeated until the whole of the cabin accommodation on that side has been disposed of. The passengers from all other sources are to be allowed berths on the port side in the same manner. Should there be an excessive demand on the one side and a deficiency on the other, the available berths are to be allotted to passengers from each route alternately according to priority in date of tickets.

No passenger booking for a berth in a cabin is to be accommodated in a cabin by himself, so long as he can be placed in a cabin of the same class or price with another passenger not booked for a whole cabin.

Transatlantic passengers are always to have priority of cabins over intercolonial passengers, whether previously booked or not. This is not, however, to extend to the displacing of any intercolonial passenger while any other cabin berth of similar description is vacant.

Transatlantic passengers desiring it may, on taking their tickets, secure to themselves the privilege of remaining at an intermediate port from the time of arrival at such port till the next steamer of the Company calls there, viz., for a fortnight or a month, as the case may be, but in such cases the place must be specified, and a corresponding notation made on the ticket, upon the understanding, moreover, that on re-embarking the passenger must be content with inferior accommodation if there should be none vacant similar to that originally engaged. In the event of there being no room on board the vessel by which the passenger may be entitled to proceed, they will be allowed accommodation by the first subsequent vessel able to afford it.

Homeward passengers taking a whole or single after cabin are not to have another passenger intruded upon them, unless the number of passengers should accumulate by successive transhipments so as to render it unavoidable to occupy the remaining berth or berths in the cabin, in which case the charge will be only as for one berth in a cabin throughout. Passengers, however, may secure to themselves the exclusive right to a whole cabin by the payment of £10 extra at or prior to their first embarking.

Should any homeward-bound passenger, upon subsequent transhipment, fail to obtain accommodation similar to that for which he originally paid, he is to be charged the inferior fare throughout.

Whenever there may be more passengers than can be accommodated with cabin berths, and who may, in consequence, be obliged to sleep in cots, or otherwise not in any cabin, an abatement of £5 from the lowest cabin rate will be made upon such occasions, but no passenger will be allowed this abatement so long as there is a cabin bed berth unoccupied.

When passengers fail to obtain on board the ship conveying them to England the same sort of accommodation as that for which they originally paid, the captains will furnish to each of such persons a certificate specifying the description of berth paid for and the accommodation subsequently afforded on the voyage to Southampton, which document will entitle the respective parties, on its production at the Company's office in London, to payment of the abatements. Certificates are likewise to be granted to contract passengers when *compelled* to share *fore* cabin accommodation with others.

Should any outward-bound passenger upon subsequent transhipment fail to obtain accommodation similar to that for which he originally paid (as this can only occur when the voyage is nearly finished), he is to be allowed a deduction of five shillings per day for every day he is compelled to occupy such inferior accommodation.

Should any outward or homeward bound passenger shift from the accommodation for which he was originally booked to a berth for which a higher charge is established, or from a berth in a cabin to a whole cabin, he is to be charged the superior fare throughout.

There is to be no difference in the fares between the fore, after, and main deck cabins, nor between a whole cabin and a berth in a cabin, so far as mere intercolonial passages are concerned; the difference of fares being only intended to apply to transatlantic passages out and home.

Although ladies may have sleeping berths allotted to them in the ladies' saloon, yet it is to be open for the use of all the ladies on board between 9 A.M. and 9 P.M. every day.

Intercolonial passengers must not be booked farther than they can be conveyed by the vessel in which they embark, or by other vessels, expected to be met with, to which they can be directly transferred.

Passengers intending to embark abroad will apply to the agents, but the passage-money is to be paid on board, either by the agents (if they have received it) or by the passengers themselves.

Embarkation at Southampton.—The Company's steam tender will convey passengers on board free of charge at Southampton, leaving the docks for that purpose not later than 30 minutes after 11 A.M. on the day of sailing.

Baggage, except carpet-bags and hat-boxes, must be shipped the previous day. No heavy baggage will be received on board on the day of sailing.

Baggage.—Any passenger is liable to a penalty of £100 who carries gunpowder or other goods of a dangerous nature (stat. 17 and 18 Vic., c. 104); for example, lucifer matches, chemicals, or any articles of an inflammable or damaging nature.

Baggage for shipment at Southampton must be addressed to the care of shipping agents there, and, as before stated, must be shipped the day previous to the ship's departure.

Arrangements have been made by which passengers can effect insurance on their baggage at the Company's office in London.

Each adult saloon passenger allowed to carry luggage free of charge to the extent of 20 cubic feet measurement, children and servants in proportion; and each adult passenger on the warrant-officers' or artisans' scale, 10 cubic feet. With a view to prevent mistakes on landing or transhipment, passengers are strongly recommended to label each parcel of their luggage with their name and destination.

Each deck passenger is allowed 56 lbs. of baggage.

All luggage will have to pass through the Custom-house at the port of destination.

All extra luggage to be charged as for measurement goods, but without primage.

Merchandise can not be carried under the name of luggage, but must be shipped according to the Company's regulations for cargo, etc. Whenever an attempt may be discovered to carry merchandise as luggage, freight will be charged at the rate of 4s. per cubic foot. All specie, bullion, or other treasure carried by passengers, above the value of £150, to be shipped as treasure, and charged for at the established rates of freight.

The Company will not be responsible for any loss, damage, or detention of luggage under any circumstances; nor for specie, bullion, jewelry, or other treasure belonging to passengers, unless the same be shipped as such at the established rates of freight.

Foreign Currency.—The Spanish dollar is to be taken every where at the rate of 4s. 2d. sterling; the doubloon at 64s.; the American eagle and its fractional parts at the rate established by H. M. proclamation, dated 19th of August, 1853, viz.: the eagle at 41s. sterling; the half eagle at 20s. 6d., the quarter eagle at 10s. 3d.; and the gold dollar at 4s. 1d.

In foreign ports the fares specified in the intercolonial table are to be paid in silver dollars, or their equivalent in other current coin; this rule applies also to the British colonies, except that notes of the West India Colonial Bank are to be taken as equivalent. Gold or silver five-franc pieces are to be received at the rate of four shillings each when tendered in payment of passage-money, but only by persons embarking at or for Martinique or Guadaloupe.

SPECIE, TREASURE, CARGO, AND PARCELS.

Outward.

For through rates to ports in the Pacific, see pages 200, 201.

Specie and treasure may be forwarded by the packets from Southampton to any port at which they touch at the following rates, viz.:

Quicksilver .... 2 per cent. on value from Southampton.
Plate.. 2   "   "   "   "
Specie, Jewelry, and Precious } 1   "   from Southampton, or 1½ when
  Stones........................... }   received by the Company in London.
Copper Coin .... £7 per ton from Southampton.

For particulars, apply at 55 Moorgate Street, or to Mr. W. Ritchie, the Company's Cargo Superintendent, Southampton.

When packages of specie or treasure are sent to Southampton, they must be forwarded to the care of shipping agents there.

No bills of lading will be given for less freight than £1 1s.

Packages for Aspinwall will not be received when consigned "to order," but a consignee must be named.

Outward Cargo.

A limited quantity of goods can be forwarded by the packets of the 2d and 17th of each month from Southampton to Barbadoes, Granada, Jamaica, Demerara, Trinidad, St. Thomas, Aspinwall; by the packet of the 2d of each month to Carthagena and Santa Martha; and by that of the 17th to Honduras and Greytown.

For through rates to ports in the Pacific, see pages 200, 201.

No package above five hundred weight to be received, and none to exceed a cube of 27 feet, nor in length 4 feet 4 inches.

Packages cubing more than 4 feet can not be taken to Greytown.

No bills of lading will be given for less freight than £1 1s.

Packages for Aspinwall will not be received when consigned "to order," but a consignee must be named.

Wine and beer can be shipped at Southampton only by special permission from Captain Vincent, the Company's superintendent there.

The following are the *Rates of Freight*, which must be prepaid: By measurement, £6 per ton, or 3s. per cubic foot, with 5 per cent. primage; by weight, £5 per ton and 5 per cent. primage—the Company reserving the right to charge by measurement or by weight. Cinnamon, 1d. per pound.

Goods for shipment must be addressed to the care of agents at Southampton, and must be there, at latest, at noon on the last day of each month if for shipment by the steamer of the 2d, and at noon on the 15th if for shipment by the steamer of the 17th of the month; but when the day of departure falls on a Monday, the latest period will be one day previous to the above dates.

For particulars, apply to Mr. W. Ritchie, the Company's Cargo Superintendent, Southampton.

Outward Parcels and Periodicals are received at the Company's offices in London and Southampton for transmission by the steamers of the 2d and 17th of each month, to St. Kitts, Antigua, Guadaloupe, Dominique, Martinique, St. Lucia, Tobago, St. Vincent, Barbadoes, Demerara, Granada, Trinidad, Jacmel, Jamaica, St. Thomas, and Aspinwall; by the steamer of the 17th for Honduras and Greytown; and by the steamer of the 2d for Havana, Vera Cruz, Tampico, Santa Martha, and Carthagena. The weight of a package or parcel for St. Kitts, Antigua, Guadaloupe, Dominique, Martinique, St. Lucia, Tobago, and St. Vincent, must not exceed half a hundred weight. The cube of a package or parcel for Greytown must not exceed 4 feet.

To Havana, Vera Cruz, and Tampico, parcels containing only samples and periodicals can be conveyed.

Packages and parcels (not exceeding 5 cubic feet) must be delivered at the London office before noon upon the 14th if intended for transmission by the steamer leaving Southampton upon the 17th of the month, and before noon upon the 28th if intended for shipment by the vessel leaving upon the 2d of the following month.

Periodical publications, with the covers open at both ends, can be booked at the London office until 2 o'clock on the day previous to the sailing of the packet, excepting when the day of sailing falls on Monday, in which case not later than 2 o'clock on the previous Saturday.

Parcels and periodicals, if sent to the care of an agent at Southampton, can be received at the Company's cargo office at that place until 10 A.M. on the day of the departure of the steamers for the West Indies.

Rates (which must be prepaid).

For through rates to Panama and ports in the South Pacific, see pages 202, 203.

The following rates include all charges except insurance (which, however, can be effected at the Company's office in London), whether the packages are received at London or Southampton: By measurement, 1 cubic foot and under, 7s. 6d. per package; above 1 foot and not exceeding 2, 11s. 6d.; above 2 feet and not exceeding 3, 15s.; above 3 feet, 5s. per foot, up to 14 feet, beyond which measurement no packages can be received at the parcel rate.

Packages can not be received at the London office if they exceed 5 cubic feet, but in that case they must be sent to Southampton.

By weight, at the rate of 10s. per cwt.

No package weighing more than 5 cwt. can be received at the parcel rate.

The Company reserves to itself the right to charge by measurement or by weight.

Quarterly publications and pamphlets, 2s. each; monthly publications, 1s. each.

Each package must be fully and distinctly addressed, and contents and value declared.

No parcels are to contain letters or bills.

The Company will not be responsible for the act of God, the queen's enemies, fire on shore or afloat, or any other dangers and accidents of the seas, rivers, and steam navigation. All parcels must be applied for to the agents of the Company at the port of delivery, except those for St. Thomas and Carthagena, which must be taken from alongside at consignee's risk and expense. At Martinique, the landing charges are to be paid by the consignee, and at Greytown the packages will be landed by the Company, but at the consignee's risk. All parcels subject to duty must be cleared from the Custom-house in the usual manner by the parties to whom they are addressed, they paying all duties and other expenses attendant upon the same. The Company will not be answerable for any package, in case of loss, damage, or detention, beyond the value of £5, unless by special agreement.

REGULATIONS IN REGARD TO CARGO AND PARCELS.

Packages, of whatever description, sent to Southampton, must be forwarded to the care of shipping agents there for delivery by them to the Company.

Shippers are earnestly recommended to have their goods packed securely in tin or wooden cases, to prevent the possibility of damage in shipment, transfer, or disembarkation.

Brown paper parcels will not be received, and the use of canvas wrappers is strongly recommended to shippers as a means of security.

All deeds must be packed in tin cases.

The Company decline to take on board their vessels medicinal fluids, oil, balsam, sugar, molasses, cotton, spirits, gunpowder, vitriol, tar, pitch, turpentine, acids, ether, chloroform, Lucifer matches, percussion caps, or any other articles of a dangerous, damaging, or inflammable nature. Any person or persons forwarding such commodities for shipment, without giving notice to the Company, will be liable, by the Merchant Shipping Act of 1854, to a penalty of £100.

Wine and beer can not be shipped at Southampton except by special permission of the Company's superintendent there.

Packages containing plants can not be shipped, unless by special agreement exempting the Company from all liability in the event of damage.

Double freight will be imposed in all cases of detection, where attempts may be made, by smuggling specie, etc., to evade the Company's established charges.

No article of any kind to be received on board without going through the established Customs' regulations and formalities.

Packages on arrival at destination will be lodged in the Custom-house, whence they will have to be retired by the consignees, or by agents commissioned by them to do so, at their expense.

All packages must have the port of destination distinctly marked thereon, or they can not be received for shipment.

No package above five hundred weight to be received, and none to exceed a cube of 27 feet, nor in length 4 feet 4 inches.

Homeward and Intercolonial Freight.

☞ It is to be understood that all regulations or notices relating to outward traffic will hold good, where applicable, to homeward and intercolonial traffic, although they may not be repeated under the latter heads.

Homeward Specie and Treasure can be shipped at any of the ports touched at by the Company's steamers at the following rates, viz.:

Specie, bullion, platina, diamonds, pearls, emeralds, and all other precious stones, unset, being exempt from duty, deliverable at the Bank of England or Southampton, and jewelry subject to duty deliverable at Southampton only.....on value $1\frac{1}{8}$ per cent.
Ditto ditto, deliverable at the Branch Bank of France, Havre.. $1\frac{5}{16}$ "
Specie or bullion, from Martinique or Guadaloupe, deliverable ditto..on value
    Consignments under £50 in value........................... £1 1s.
    " " £100 " .... £1 10s.
    " " £150 " .... £2 2s.
    " of and above £150 in value................. $1\frac{5}{16}$ per cent.
Plate, subject to duty, deliverable at Southampton.....on value 2 "
Ditto, deliverable at the Branch Bank of France, Havre......... $2\frac{3}{16}$ "
Copper coin, deliverable at Southampton......................£7 per ton weight.
Copper ore, mineral sand, etc.............................see Homeward Cargo.

No primage is charged on the foregoing.

For rates on treasure from the Pacific, see pages 172–174.

No package of specie, jewelry, etc., to be conveyed, and no bills of lading to be granted, for less freight than £1 1s., or five silver dollars.

Homeward Cargo can be shipped for Southampton at the following ports, viz.: Barbadoes, Jamaica, St. Thomas, Porto Rico, Tampico, Vera Cruz, Havana, Honduras, Trinidad, Carthagena, Santa Martha, Aspinwall, Greytown, Demerara, Granada.

No bills of lading granted for less freight than £1 1s.

The following are the rates payable on delivery of the goods at Southampton, viz.:

Copper ore, copper and silver alloy, cupel stuff, and mineral sand .... £5 per ton weight.
Alpaca wool .... { $1\frac{1}{2}d.$ per lb. or 1s. 9d. per foot measurement.
Ginger .... £7 per ton weight.
Coffee, cocoa, and arrow-root........................ £5 " "

India-rubber in solid pieces	£5 per ton weight.	
Sarsaparilla, jalap, and other dry drugs	1½d. per lb.	
Divi divi	1d.	"
Peruvian bark	1d.	"
Pimento, cochineal, indigo, gums, and beeswax	1d.	"
Plantain fibre	1½d.	"
Pines, oranges, or other green fruits or plants, packed in hampers, barrels, or boxes	£5 per ton measurement of 40 cubic feet.	
Cigars and leaf tobacco	£5 per ditto ditto.	
Measurement goods	3s. 6d. per cubic foot.	
Cases containing preserved turtle	2s. 6d. " "	
Turtle, on the quantity landed alive at Southampton; but the Company not liable for losses by death or disaster	£1 5s. per cwt.	
Vanilla	on value 1½ per cent.	
" deliverable at Havre	" 1 4/16 "	
Cochineal, "	1¼d. per lb.	

Five per cent. primage is charged on all homeward freight except vanilla. Balsam will not be received on board the Company's steamers.

Homeward Parcels and Periodicals, including small parcels of succades, arrow-root, etc., will be charged at the same rates as outward parcels, but deliverable at Southampton.

Freight must be prepaid. For rates, etc., see pages 197.

Intercolonial Specie, Cargo, and Parcels.

Specie can be shipped for any port touched at by the packets.

No package of specie is to be conveyed, and no bills of lading are to be granted, for less freight than five silver dollars.

Freight on specie, jewelry, pearls, diamonds, and other precious stones, to be prepaid at the port of shipment: Exceeding 2500 miles, 1 per cent.; exceeding 1000 miles, and not above 2500 miles, ¾ per cent.; not exceeding 1000 miles, ½ per cent.

The distance between St. Thomas or intermediate places and Demerara is to be considered as not exceeding 1000 miles.

No sums under 5000 dollars are to be conveyed, however short the distance, at a lower rate than ½ per cent.; but when larger amounts are to be remitted from one British colony to another, or between any places visited by the Company's vessels eastward of Jamaica, provided, in either case, the distance is within 800 miles, the rate will be ¼ per cent. The tables of routes to determine the distances.

Copper coin, £7 per ton weight.

Intercolonial Rates on Goods to be prepaid at Port of Shipment.

Goods can be forwarded between Barbadoes, St. Thomas, Aspinwall, Demerara, Jamaica, Greytown, Trinidad, Granada, Carthagena, Honduras, Santa Martha, and to these places from Havana and other foreign ports; but cargo can not be carried to foreign ports, with the before-mentioned exceptions, except by special permission.

£3 10s. per ton measurement of 40 cubic feet.

Cocoa and coffee, £3 10s. per ton, on the gross weight.

Indigo and other dry drugs, cochineal, 1d. per lb.

Divi divi, ½d. per lb.

Beeswax, ¾d. per lb.

Dry and wet provisions,	From St. Thomas to Barbadoes, Trinidad, Demerara, or Jamaica	1 silver dollar per barrel.
	From St. Thomas to Greytown	1½ do. do.

No primage is charged.

No bills of lading for merchandise will be granted for less freight than 2½ silver dollars.

Balsam will not be received on board the Company's steamers.

Intercolonial Parcels carried to all the places named under the head of "Outward Parcels," to be prepaid at the port of shipment, to be charged one fifth less than the transatlantic scale, and to be restricted in size and weight, as indicated under that head for different ports. See p. 195.

Preference is always to be given to transatlantic over intercolonial cargo.

ISTHMUS OF PANAMA AND THE PACIFIC.

Trains now run daily across the Isthmus of Panama, thus affording an easy means of transit for passengers, specie, goods, etc.

Under arrangement with the Pacific Steam Navigation Company, whose vessels run from Panama southward, through tickets (comprising the privilege of stopping at an intermediate port, as stated in "General Passenger Regulations," page 165) can be obtained to or from Southampton and ports on the west coast of South America, but not including the providing or expense of the transit of passengers or their luggage across the Isthmus of Panama. Also, return tickets to or from those ports (including Panama), with an abatement of 25 per cent. on the Royal Mail Steam Packet Company's proportion of passage-money, available for twelve months, under the conditions mentioned in page 191.

Goods, etc., for San Francisco and Victoria (British Columbia).

The Royal Mail Steam Packet Company have completed arrangements for granting *through bills of lading* for measurement goods, jewelry, and plate, shipped by their steamers leaving Southampton on the 2d and 17th of each month, to be delivered at San Francisco and Victoria (British Columbia) at the following rates of freight:

To be paid on shipment of goods, etc.:

Goods: From Southampton to Aspinwall, £6 per ton measurement, with 5 per cent. primage.

Jewelry, on value: From London to Aspinwall, 1¼ per cent.; from Southampton to Aspinwall, 1 per cent.

Plate, on value: From Southampton to Aspinwall, 2 per cent.

And in addition,

To be paid on delivery of goods, etc., at destination.

Goods: From Aspinwall to San Francisco, $80 per ton measurement, with 5 per cent. primage; from Aspinwall to Victoria, $100 per ton measurement, with 5 per cent. primage.

Jewelry, on value: From Aspinwall to San Francisco, 2 per cent.; from Aspinwall to Victoria, 2¼ do.

Plate, on value: From Aspinwall to San Francisco, 4 per cent.; from Aspinwall to Victoria, 5 per cent.

No bill of lading will be issued for less freight than one guinea to Aspinwall.

Specie, Goods, etc., from England or the West Indies, for Ports in the Pacific south of Panama, viz., Buenaventura, Tumaco, Guayaquil, Payta, Lambayeque, Huanchaco, Callao, Islay, Arica, Iquique, Cobija, Caldera, Coquimbo, Valparaiso.

Cargo for Lambayeque and Huanchaco is carried on to Callao, where it is transhipped to the steamer proceeding northward.

The Royal Mail Steam Packet Company have effected an arrangement with the Panama Railroad Company and the Pacific Steam Navigation

Company for the delivery of treasure, measurement goods, and quicksilver, from Southampton and the West Indian ports hereafter specified,* under *through bills of lading*, at ports in the South Pacific, and at the respective rates of freight under-mentioned, which must be paid on shipment of the goods, whether at Southampton or in the West Indies.

Measurement Goods from Southampton, shipped by Steamer of 2d and 17th of each Month.

Per ton measurement (with 5 per cent. primage):
To Buenaventura..£12 15s.
To ports south of Buenaventura, including Guayaquil..... 13 5
To Payta 13 15
To ports south of Payta, including Callao..................... 14 5
To ports south of Callao, including Valparaiso.............. 15 5

No bill of lading for goods to any of the above ports will be granted for less freight than £2 2s.

From the West Indies, viz., *St. Thomas, Havana, Jamaica, Barbadoes, Trinidad, Demerara, Greytown, Carthagena, and Santa Martha.*

To any of the above-mentioned Pacific ports south of Panama, the rate of freight for measurement goods will be £2 10s. per ton less than from Southampton to those places, and no primage will be charged.

No bill of lading for goods from the West Indies to any of the above ports will be granted for less freight than £1 11s. 6d.

Treasure from England, or the before-mentioned West Indian ports, at a uniform rate, viz.: For specie (gold) and jewelry, when received in London, 2¾ per cent. on value.

No bill of lading for gold or jewelry will be granted in London for less freight than £2 7s. 6d.

Of jewelry only small packages will be received in London.

For specie (gold) and jewelry, when received in Southampton or the West Indies, 2¼ per cent. on value.

No bill of lading for gold or jewelry will be granted in Southampton or the West Indies for less freight than £2 5s.

For specie (silver), one eighth per cent. is to be added to the above respective rates for gold.

Quicksilver, which must be delivered to the Company at Southampton for shipment: To ports as far as Callao inclusive, 5¼ per cent. on value; to ports beyond Callao, 5¾ per cent. on value.

No bill of lading for quicksilver will be granted in Southampton for less freight than £5 5s. in the one case, and £5 15s. in the other.

Parcels not exceeding three cubic feet in measurement will be received at the Company's offices in London and Southampton for the ports above-mentioned at the under-mentioned rates, which must be paid on shipment, and which include all charges except insurance (which, however, can be effected at the Company's office in London), whether the packages are received at London or Southampton: One cubic foot and under, £1; above 1 cubic foot and not exceeding 2, £1 10s.; above 2 feet and not exceeding 3, £2.

Under arrangement between the Royal Mail Steam Packet Company and the Panama Railroad Company, *through bills of lading* are granted at Southampton as follows: To Central American (Pacific) ports, touched at by the steamers of the Panama Railroad Company, viz., Punta Arenas, Realejo, La Union, La Libertad, Acajulta, San José de Guatemala.

For goods, at £13 per ton measurement (with 5 per cent. primage), which must be paid on shipment.

No bill of lading will be granted for less freight than £2 2s.
There is no through parcel or specie rate to these ports.

Through bills of lading are also granted at Southampton, and in the West Indies at St. Thomas, Havana, Jamaica, Barbadoes, Trinidad, Demerara, Greytown, Carthagena, and Santa Martha, as far as Panama, for specie, jewelry, measurement goods, and quicksilver, destined for Panama and the North Pacific, at the following rates of freight, which must be paid on shipment:

For goods, etc., from Southampton, £10 per ton measurement (with 5 per cent. primage).

No bill of lading will be granted for less freight than £1 11s. 6d.

For goods, etc., from the above West Indian ports, £7 10s. per ton measurement (without primage).

No bill of lading will be granted for less freight than £1 1s.

For specie (gold) and jewelry, when received in London, 1⅜ per cent.

No bill of lading will be granted for less freight than £1 7s. 6d.

For specie (gold) and jewelry, when received in Southampton or at the above West Indian ports, 1¼ per cent.

No bill of lading will be granted for less freight than £1 5s.

For specie (silver), one eighth per cent. is to be added to the above respective rates for gold.

For quicksilver, which must be delivered to the Company at Southampton for shipment, 3¼ per cent. on value.

No bill of lading will be granted for less freight than £3 5s.

Parcels for Panama not exceeding 3 cubic feet in measurement will be received at the Company's offices in London and Southampton at the following rates, which must be paid on shipment, and which include all charges except insurance (which, however, can be effected at the Company's office in London), whether the packages are received at London or Southampton: One cubic foot and under, 12s.; above 1 foot and not exceeding 2, 18s.; above 2 feet and not exceeding 3, £1 4s.

NOTE.—For farther information as to when goods, etc., must be ready for shipment, and general regulations in regard to cargo and parcels, etc., see pages 166, 167, and 168, or apply to 55 Moorgate Street, or to Mr. J. K. Linstead, the Company's Cargo Superintendent, Southampton.

No package above 5 cwt. to be received, and none to exceed a cube of 27 feet, nor in length 4 feet 4 inches.

Specie, etc., from Panama and the South Pacific.

The following rates have been established by the Royal Mail Steam Packet Company, in addition to the freight charged by the Pacific Steam Navigation Company, or other parties delivering treasure to the agent of the Royal Mail Steam Packet Company at Panama, for conveyance to the under-mentioned places, such charges to include transport across the Isthmus, and all other expenses thence to the place of destination:

		To Branch Bank of France, Havre.
Specie and bullion from Panama to Southampton or Bank of England..................	1¾ per cent.	1⁷⁄₈ per cent.
Pearls, emeralds, and all other precious stones, unset being exempt from duty, from Panama to Southampton or the Bank of England, on value..................	1⅞ "	2¹⁄₁₆ "
Jewelry, subject to duty, from Panama to Southampton, on value..................	1⅞ "	1⁹⁄₁₆ "

ROYAL MAIL STEAM PACKET COMPANY.

Specie, bullion, precious stones, etc., from Panama to British
Guiana, Vera Cruz, and Tampico.................................... 1¼ per cent
Dito ditto to St. Domingo, Porto Rico, St. Thomas, Windward Islands, Havana, Honduras, and Jamaica................. 1⅛ "
Ditto ditto to Carthagena and Greytown........................ ⅞ "

N.B.—The Pacific Steam Navigation Company's charge on specie, etc., from any port in Chili or Peru, etc., to Panama, for transfer to the Royal Mail Steam Packets, is ⅞ per cent., which, being added to the rates from Panama above stated, will make the charges by *through bill of lading*,

To Southampton or the Bank of England.......... 2¼ per cent.
To the Branch Bank of France, Havre.............. 2 7/16 "

The through charge on jewelry, pearls, and all other precious stones from the South Pacific ports is the same as that on specie and bullion.

Double freight will be imposed in all cases of detection where attempts may be made, by smuggling, etc., to evade the Company's established charges.

Gold, etc., from San Francisco (California).

Gold, etc., can be shipped at San Francisco, under the *through bills of lading* of the United States Pacific Mail Steam-ship Company and the Royal Mail Steam Packet Company, for conveyance to England, Havre, or the West Indies.

For particulars as to through rates of freight, etc., apply in San Francisco to W. L. Booker, Esq., H.B.M. Consul, or at the office of the Pacific Mail Steam-ship Company.

Goods from South Pacific Ports to Southampton.

Through bills of lading are granted at South Pacific ports by the Pacific Steam Navigation Company, in conjunction with the Panama Railroad Company and the Royal Mail Steam Packet Company, at the following through rates of freight, payable on delivery of the goods at Southampton:

Description of goods, etc.	Shipped at ports between Payta and Panama, including Payta.	Shipped at ports between Callao and Payta, including Callao.	Shipped at ports between Valparaiso and Callao, incl. Valparaiso.
	Per ton weight. £ s. d.	Per ton weight. £ s. d.	Per ton weight. £ s. d.
Copper and tin, bars...............	7 2 8	7 9 4	7 19 4
Copper and tin ore, in bags.....	8 2 8	8 9 4	8 19 4
Silver ore.............................	8 16 0	9 4 0	9 16 0
Coffee, cocoa, and India-rubber	9 16 0	10 4 0	10 16 0
Orchilla...............................	9 0 0	9 6 5	9 16 0
Bark*.................................	15 8 8	15 18 8	16 8 8
Tobacco in leaf....................	15 16 0	16 8 0	17 6 0
	Per ton measurement.	Per ton measurement.	Per ton measurement.
Whalebone.........................	11 2 8	11 13 4	12 9 4
Panama hats.......................	18 9 4	19 10 8	21 2 8
Sarsaparilla........................	11 16 0	12 8 0	13 6 0
General merchandise............	13 8 0	14 0 0	15 0 0

Primage at the rate of 5 per cent. will be charged in addition to the above rates of freight.

* Bills of lading will be granted for bark to Havre at an advance of a farthing per lb. on the above rates.

Parcels from South Pacific ports to Southampton at the same rates as "Outward Parcels" to those places (see pages 201, 202).

From Central American (Pacific) Ports to Southampton.

Through bills of lading are granted by the Panama Railroad Company, in conjunction with the Royal Mail Steam Packet Company, at the following ports, touched at by the Panama Railroad Company's steamers, namely, Punta Arenas, Realejo, La Union, La Libertad, Acajutla, San José de Guatemala.

The through rates of freight from the above places to Southampton are as under-mentioned, and the freight is payable on delivery of the goods at that port:

On silver ore, £9 per ton weight, with 5 per cent. primage.
On coffee, £10 per ton weight, with 5 per cent. primage.
On cochineal and indigo, $2\tfrac{8}{16}d.$ per lb., with 5 per cent. primage.
Measurement goods, 7s. 6d. per foot, with 5 per cent. primage.

Also on treasure (gold and silver) from the above places to Southampton or the Bank of England, London, $2\tfrac{1}{4}$ per cent. on value, payable on delivery of the treasure.

Cochineal and indigo, deliverable at Havre, $2\tfrac{7}{16}d.$ per lb., with 5 per cent. primage.

Balsam will not be received on board the Company's steamers.

ISTHMUS OF PANAMA AND THE PACIFIC, INCLUDING NEW ZEALAND AND AUSTRALIA.

Colon (Aspinwall) is the port of disembarkation for passengers proceeding to Panama and ports on the West Coast of South America, San Francisco, British Columbia, Central American (Pacific) Ports, New Zealand, and Australia.

Trains now run daily across the Isthmus of Panama, thus affording an easy means of transit for passengers.

SOUTH AMERICA (WEST COAST).

Under arrangement with the Pacific Steam Navigation Company, whose vessels run from Panama southward, through tickets (comprising the privilege of stopping at an intermediate port, as stated in "Passenger Regulations," p. 193) can be obtained to or from Southampton and ports on the West Coast of South America, but not including the providing or expense of the transit of passengers or their luggage across the Isthmus of Panama; also, return tickets to or from these ports, with an abatement of 25 per cent. on the Royal Mail Steam Packet Company's proportion of passage-money, available for twelve months, under the conditions mentioned on page 191.

The table of through rates of fare can be obtained on application.

Passengers for Panama and the South Pacific can obtain Panama Railroad Company's transit tickets at the Royal Mail Steam Packet Company's offices in London and Southampton.

NEW ZEALAND AND AUSTRALIA.

Under an agreement with the Panama, New Zealand, and Australian Royal Mail Company (limited), through tickets (including the Panama Railroad fare) are issued for passages from Southampton to the following ports of New Zealand and Australia, viz.: Wellington, Auckland, Taranaki, Napier, Nelson, Picton, Canterbury, Otago, the Bluff, Sydney, and Melbourne, and *vice versâ*.

Return tickets are also issued at an abatement of 25 per cent., available for twelve months.

For farther information as to fares, baggage, etc., see separate Hand-book.

For through passages from Southampton to San Francisco, Victoria (Vancouver's Island), and British Columbia, application should be made to Messrs. H. Starr & Co., 145 Cheapside, London.

PANAMA, NEW ZEALAND, AND AUSTRALIAN ROYAL MAIL COMPANY (Limited).

NEW ZEALAND AND AUSTRALIAN MAIL SERVICE viâ PANAMA.

Offices.

Chief Office, 41 Moorgate Street, London, E.C. JAMES WORLEY, Secretary.
Head Colonial Office, Wellington, New Zealand. Capt. JOHN VINE HALL, General Manager; HENRY LAWSON, sub-Manager.

Agencies.

Liverpool.............. C. E. HAMILTON, the Temple, Dale Street.
Manchester .... HUGH FLEMING, 4 York Chambers.
Glasgow ....
Paris ....
Havre ....
Panama................ W. G. SEALY.
Colon (Aspinwall)...
New York............. E. E. MORGAN & SON.
San Francisco ....
New Zealand—
   Auckland.......... H. M. JERVIS, Queen Street.
   Napier .... ROUTLEDGE & Co.
   Taranaki .... CHARLES BROWN, Beach.
   Nelson .... THOMAS CAWTHRON, Wharf.
   Picton.............. A. BEAUCHAMP, Wharf.
   Canterbury........ MILES & Co., Lyttelton.
   Otago .... G. S. BRODRICK, Dunedin.
   Bluff................. T. G. TANTON, Wharf.
Australia—
   Sydney .... Grafton Wharf.
   Melbourne .... C. J. LEWIS & Co., Elizabeth Street, South.

Screw Steamers employed on the Main Line.

No.	Names.	Tonnage Register.	Horse Power, Nominal.	Names of Commanders.
1	Mataura.......	1767	400	G. E. Bird.
2	Kaikoura......	1501	400	Edward Wheeler.
3	Ruahine.......	1503	350	T. S. Beal.
4	Rakaia.........	1450	350	S. H. Wright.

Screw Steamers employed in the Performance of the Mail Services between Australia and New Zealand, and between the Provinces of the latter Colony.

No.	Names.	Tonnage, B. M.	Horse Power.
5	Prince Alfred	900	180
6	Tararua	850	160
7	Auckland	850	150
8	Otago	800	150
9	Claud Hamilton	800	120
10	Rangitoto	650	140
11	Phœbe	650	120
12	Lord Ashley	500	90
13	Egmont	500	90
14	Airedale	400	80

NEW ZEALAND AND AUSTRALIA *viâ* PANAMA.

The Company's steamers carrying Her Majesty's mails are appointed to run between Panama, Wellington (New Zealand), and Sydney, commencing in June, 1866, in continuation of the present line of steamers of the Royal Mail Steam Packet Company between Southampton and Colon (Aspinwall). The latter vessels run *twice* a month; but the New Zealand and Australian steamers will run only *once* a month, connecting with the mail packets leaving Southampton *for* Colon on the 2d, and sailing *from* Colon on the 7th.

The main-line steamers of the Panama, New Zealand, and Australian Royal Mail Company will leave Wellington on or about the 8th, on the arrival of the branch steamer from Sydney, sailing from that place on the 31st or 1st of the month, and will arrive at Panama on or about the 5th. The departures from the Isthmus will be on or about the 24th of the month, the vessels will be due on the 21st at Wellington, and the branch steamer will arrive at Sydney about the 29th.

The through service between Southampton and New Zealand and Sydney will be performed thus:

Outward.

Leave Southampton on or about the 2d of the month.
Arrive at St. Thomas " 17th "
Leave " " 18th "
Arrive at Colon " 22d "

} Royal Mail Steam Packet Co.

Leave Panama " 24th "
Arrive at Wellington " 21st "
Leave " " 22d "
Arrive at Sydney " 29th "

} Panama, New Zealand, and Australian Royal Mail Co.

Time to Wellington, 49 days.
Time to Sydney, 57 "

Homeward.

Leave Sydney on or about the 31st or 1st of the month.
Arrive at Wellington the 7th "
Leave " " 8th "
Arrive at Panama " 5th* "

} Panama, New Zealand, and Australian Royal Mail Co.

Leave Colon, *viâ* Jamaica
 and Hayti, on or about } the 7th* of the month.
Arrive at St. Thomas " 13th*   "
Leave   "   " 15th*   "
Arrive at Southampton " 29th*   "
} Royal Mail Steam Packet Co.

Time from Wellington, 51 days.
Time from Sydney, 59 "

N.B.—The dates of arrival and departure marked thus * will be one day earlier when the preceding month comprises thirty-one days.

Passengers for Auckland, Tasmania, Napier, Nelson, Picton, Canterbury, Otago, and the Bluff, and for Sydney and Melbourne, will be conveyed per the Company's steamers appointed to sail north and south, and direct to Sydney, immediately on the arrival of the main-line packets at Wellington; and the local steamers will leave the above places in time to tranship mails, passengers, and cargo into the homeward Panama vessel.

For farther information concerning intercolonial and interprovincial services, see local time-tables and advertisements in the Sydney and New Zealand newspapers.

Through Passages.

Under an agreement with the Royal Mail Steam Packet Company, tickets will be issued for through passages from Southampton and any of the ports visited by the steamers of that Company, to all parts of New Zealand and Australia, and *vice versâ*.

Notice.

The respective Companies will not be responsible for any detention consequent upon any occurrence of whatever kind which may prevent the vessels meeting at the appointed places, nor for postal changes, nor for any delay arising out of accidents, nor for any loss or damage arising from perils of the seas, or from machinery, boilers, or steam, or from any act, neglect, or default whatsoever of the pilot, master, or mariners, nor for any consequences arising from sanitary regulations or precautions which either or both of the respective Companies or local government authorities may deem necessary, or in the event of such sanitary regulations or precautions preventing embarkation or disembarkation. If, in consequence thereof, passengers should have to be conveyed to their destination by a circuitous route, or to remain (with the consent of the commander) on board the vessels of the Royal Mail Steam Packet Company beyond the time at which, under ordinary circumstances, they would disembark, the last-named Company will, in lieu of additional passage-money, etc., charge only at the rate of 10*s*. per diem for victualing during the extra time each adult cabin passenger may have been on board, and in proportion for second-cabin passengers.

PASSENGER FARES

Between Southampton and the Principal Ports in New Zealand and Australia, and between Panama and New Zealand and Australia.

The rates for *chief* cabin include the use of bedding and linen, stewards' fees, etc., etc., but are exclusive of wines, spirits, malt liquors, and mineral waters.

Second-class passengers are supplied with berths and bedding, and other ordinary requisites.

The *through* fares of both classes *include* the railway transit across the Isthmus of Panama. Outward passengers will be provided with the requisite passes before leaving England; but homeward passengers will not receive their tickets until their arrival at Panama, when they will be handed to them by the Company's agent at that place.

The rates mentioned in column A are for a berth in any of the after cabins of the Panama, New Zealand, and Australian Royal Mail Company's ships, and for a berth in the after cabins on the main or lower deck of the Royal Mail Steam Packet Company's ships (excepting only the outside cabins on the *main* deck), or in the main-deck *forward* cabins.

Passengers occupying a berth in one of the *outside* cabins on the main deck aft of the Royal Mail Steam Packet Company's ships have to pay an additional charge of £5 each, which should be paid to the purser on board the Southampton steamer.

The rates stated in column B are for a berth in one of the forward cabins of the Panama, New Zealand, and Australian Royal Mail Company's vessels, and for a berth in the *lower* deck forward of the Royal Mail Steam Packet Company's ships.

The rates mentioned in column C are for a chief-cabin berth in any of the after cabins, and those stated in column D for a berth in any of the forward cabins of the Panama, New Zealand, and Australian Royal Mail Company's ships.

The difference in the rates for a chief-cabin passage to any particular place refers merely to the sleeping-cabins; in all other respects the passengers will be on precisely the same footing.

	From Southampton to the following places, or *vice versâ*. Inclusive of Railway Transit across the Isthmus of Panama.			From Panama to the following places, or *vice versâ*.		
	Chief Cabin.		2d Cabin.	Chief Cabin.		2d Cabin.
	A. Each Berth.	B. Each Berth.	Each Berth.	C. Each Berth.	D. Each Berth.	Each Berth.
	£	£	£	£	£	£
Wellington.......	100	90	60	55	50	30
Auckland.........	104	94	64	59	54	34
Taranaki	103	93	63	58	53	33
Napier	102	92	62	57	52	32
Nelson	102	92	62	57	52	32
Picton.............	102	92	62	57	52	32
Canterbury.......	102	92	62	57	52	32
Otago	104	94	64	59	54	34
Bluff	104	94	64	59	54	34
Sydney	105	95	65	60	55	35
Melbourne	105	95	65	60	55	35

A *whole after cabin*, ordinarily used for two persons, in the Panama, New Zealand, and Australian Royal Mail Company's ships, and a whole after cabin in the Royal Mail Steam Packet Company's ships (not being an outside cabin on the main deck), for the exclusive use of *one* passenger, will be charged as a berth and a half, calculated at the rate shown in column A above. The sum of £5 extra is payable to the Royal Mail Company for an outside cabin on the main deck.

Any person desiring to occupy, exclusively, a cabin in the Panama, New Zealand, and Australian Royal Mail Company's ships, fitted up for three or four passengers instead of two, and a whole after cabin in the Royal Mail

Steam Packet Company's ships, as above, must pay double the rate mentioned in the foregoing table.

No *whole cabins* on the *main* or *lower deck forward* of any of the Royal Mail Company's ships are let as *single cabins*.

The Royal Mail Steam Packet Company have undertaken to reserve accommodation in the vessels performing the Atlantic portion of the service for a given number of passengers from the Australasian colonies, so that parties taking through tickets in Sydney, Melbourne, or Wellington can make sure of obtaining comfortable berths for the entire voyage.

Return Tickets.

Return tickets between Sydney, Melbourne, the various ports in New Zealand, and Panama and Southampton, are issued to chief-cabin passengers, and to their servants accompanying them both ways, at an abatement of 25 per cent. on the total passage-money. Such tickets are to be paid for at the time of being issued, and *not* to be transferable. To be available if the parties holding the same embark on the return voyage within twelve calendar months from the date of the commencement of their first voyage. No allowance will be made if such parties do not make the return passage by the vessels of the respective Companies. Should there be no available accommodation in the ships of either Company by which the holder wishes to embark in the return trip, he will be entitled to a passage by the first subsequent opportunity. In all such cases a certificate must be obtained from the agents or captains of either of the Companies, specifying the date of application, and that no accommodation could then be afforded. Return tickets are not issued to second-class passengers.

Children.

Of the children of cabin passengers under three years of age, one is to be carried free of charge; any other under that age to be charged as three years and under eight; those three years and under eight years to pay one fourth the cabin-passage rate paid by their parents, and four such children are to be entitled to one berth; eight years and under twelve years to pay one half ditto, and two such children are entitled to one berth; but when their parents have paid the £5 extra for a berth in an aft outside cabin, and a similar additional berth is not assigned to the children also, the latter are only to be charged at the proportion of the inner aft rate.

Of the children of second-class passengers under three years of age, one is to be carried free of charge; any other under that age to be charged as three years and under eight; those three years and under eight years to pay one fourth the rate paid by their parents; eight years and under twelve years to pay one half ditto.

Servants.

Passengers' servants can not be booked as "servants" unless they accompany their employers.

Passengers' male servants to pay *one half*, and female *two thirds* of the lowest rate established for adult saloon passengers, and no abatement to be made on account of age. Men-servants will be berthed in the fore part of the ship; women-servants will have beds made up in the ladies' saloon.

PASSENGER REGULATIONS, ETC.

Transatlantic and Transpacific Services.

Each ship carries a surgeon.

No berth is considered engaged until the whole fare is paid.

Passengers not proceeding after taking their passage, to forfeit half the passage-money.

Passengers are not allowed to take on board wines, spirits, or other liquors for use during the voyage, an ample stock thereof being provided on board at moderate prices.

The attention of passengers is directed to the "notice" on page 207.

No person can be received on board a vessel when suffering from any infectious disorder. If, in the course of the voyage, any passenger should be found to be suffering from a disorder of that character, he will be required, at his own expense, to find accommodation at any port in which the vessel may happen to be at the time of, or at the first port she may reach after discovery of the existence of the disorder, it being understood that, when sufficiently recovered, such passenger will be conveyed to his destination in the Companies' vessels.

The captains will be most careful to avoid all personal preference or partiality in allotting accommodation on board of the Companies' ships. Within the prescribed limits, priority is always to be given according to the dates on which passengers were originally booked and the passage-money paid. If paid through an agent of either Company, he will be careful, when he hands the money to the captain, to furnish also the date when it is paid for notation on the passage ticket.

No passenger booking for a berth in a cabin is to be accommodated in a cabin by himself so long as he can be placed in a cabin of the same class or price with another passenger or not booked for a whole cabin.

Passengers desiring it may, on taking their tickets, secure to themselves the privilege of remaining at an intermediate port, between Southampton and Wellington, from the time of arrival at such port till the next steamer of the Royal Mail Company calls there, viz., for a fortnight or a month, as the case may be; but in such cases the place must be specified, and a corresponding notation made on the ticket; upon the understanding, moreover, that on re-embarking, the passengers must be content with inferior accommodation if there should be none vacant similar to that originally engaged. In the event of there being no room on board the vessel by which the passengers may be entitled to proceed, they will be allowed accommodation by the first subsequent vessel able to afford it.

Should any homeward-bound passenger, upon subsequent transhipment, fail to obtain accommodation similar to that for which he originally paid, he is to be charged the inferior rate throughout.

Whenever there may be more passengers than can be accommodated with cabin berths, and who may, in consequence, be obliged to sleep in cots, or otherwise not in any cabin, an abatement of £5 from the lowest cabin rate will be made upon such occasions; but no passengers will be allowed this abatement so long as there is a cabin bed-berth unoccupied.

When passengers fail to obtain on board the ship conveying them to England from Panama the same sort of accommodation as that for which they originally paid, the captain will furnish to each of such persons a certificate specifying the description of berth paid for, and the accommodation subsequently afforded on the voyage to Southampton, which document will entitle the respective parties, on its production at the office of the Royal Mail Company in London, to payment of the abatement.

Should any outward-bound passenger upon subsequent transhipment fail to obtain accommodation similar to that for which he originally paid (as this can only occur when the voyage is nearly finished), he is to be allowed a deduction of 5s. per day for every day he is compelled to occupy such inferior accommodation.

Should any outward or homeward bound passenger shift from the accommodation for which he was originally booked to a berth for which a higher charge is established, or from a berth in a cabin to a whole cabin, he is to be charged the superior fare throughout.

Although ladies may have sleeping-berths allotted to them in the ladies' saloon, yet it is to be open for the use of all the ladies on board between 9 A.M. and 9 P.M. every day.

Passengers intending to embark abroad will apply to the agents, but the passage-money is to be paid on board, either by the agents (if they have received it) or by the passengers themselves. Second-class passengers are not to frequent the saloon or to go on the quarter-deck.

Embarkation at Southampton.

The Royal Mail Company's steam tender will convey passengers on board free of charge at Southampton, leaving the docks for that purpose not later than 30 minutes after 11 A.M. on the day of sailing. Baggage, except carpet-bags and hat-boxes, must be shipped the previous day. No heavy baggage will be received on board on the day of sailing.

ISTHMUS OF PANAMA.

Trains now run frequently every day across the Isthmus, between Colon (Aspinwall) on the east side, and Panama City on the west side, and the transit occupies only four hours; the railway stations at both places are close to the landing-piers, and the arrangements made by the Panama Railroad Company are most complete in every respect.

As the Company's vessels will be compelled to lie off about four or five miles from the shore at Panama, a steam tender, comfortably fitted up and of good capacity, has been specially provided for the conveyance of passengers and goods, etc., to and from the steamers.

On the other side of the Isthmus, Colon (Aspinwall), the vessels lie alongside the pier.

Baggage.—Any passenger who carries gunpowder or other goods of a dangerous nature, for example, lucifer matches, chemicals, or any articles of an inflammable or damaging nature, is liable not only to a penalty of £100 (stat. 17 and 18 Vic., c. 104), but also for all damages resulting from carrying such articles.

Baggage for shipment at Southampton must be addressed to the care of shipping agents there, and, as before stated, must be shipped the day previous to the ship's departure.

Arrangements have been made by which passengers can effect insurance on their baggage at the office of the Royal Mail Steam Packet Company in London.

Each adult saloon passenger is allowed to carry luggage, free of charge, to the extent of 20 cubic feet measurement, children and servants in proportion; and each adult second-class passenger 15 cubic feet. With a view to prevent mistakes on landing or transhipment, passengers are strongly recommended to label each parcel of their luggage with their name and destination.

All extra luggage to be charged as for measurement goods, but without primage.

Merchandise can not be carried under the name of luggage, but must be shipped according to the Companies' regulations for cargo, etc. Whenever an attempt may be discovered to carry merchandise as luggage, freight will be charged at the rate of 12s. 6d. per cubic foot. All specie, bullion, jewelry, or other treasure carried by passengers must be shipped as treasure, and paid for at the established rates of freight.

The respective Companies will not be responsible for any damage to, loss, or detention of luggage, under any circumstances; nor will they be responsible for specie, bullion, jewelry, or other treasure belonging to passengers, unless the same be shipped as such at the established rates of freight.

All luggage will have to pass through the Custom-house at the port of destination.

Regulations.—Cargo, Specie, and Parcels.

In virtue of an arrangement with the Royal Mail Steam Packet Company and the Panama Railroad Company, through bills of lading and through receipts for parcels are issued in England, and at certain ports in the West Indies, Wellington, and the other ports in New Zealand, and for Sydney and Melbourne.

Packages, of whatever description, sent to Southampton, must be forwarded to the care of shipping agents there, for delivery by them to the Royal Mail Company.

Shippers are earnestly recommended to have their goods packed securely in tin or wooden cases, to prevent the possibility of damage in shipment, transfer, or disembarkation.

Brown paper parcels will not be received. The use of canvas wrappers is strongly recommended to shippers as a means of security.

All deeds must be packed in tin cases.

The respective Companies decline to take on board their vessels medicinal fluids, oil, balsam, molasses, spirits, gunpowder, vitriol, tar, pitch, turpentine, acids, ether, chloroform, lucifer matches, percussion caps, or any other articles of a dangerous, damaging, or inflammable nature. Any person or persons forwarding such commodities for shipment, without giving notice to the Companies, will be liable, by the Merchant Shipping Act of 1854, not only to a penalty of £100, but also for all damage resulting from such shipments.

The respective Companies will not be responsible for the act of God, the queen's enemies, fire on shore or afloat, or any other dangers and accidents of the seas, rivers, and steam navigation; nor will either Company be answerable for any parcel or package, in case of loss, damage, or detention, beyond the value of £5, unless by special agreement.

All goods and parcels must be applied for to the agents of the respective Companies at the port of delivery, except those for St. Thomas, Havana, Carthagena, Greytown, and Santa Martha, which must be taken from alongside by the consignees at their risk and expense. All goods and parcels subject to duty must be cleared from the Custom-house in the usual manner by the consignees or parties to whom they are addressed, they paying all duties, and other expenses attendant upon the same.

Wine and beer can be shipped at Southampton only by special permission of the superintendent of the Royal Mail Company at that place.

Packages containing plants can not be shipped unless by special agreement, exempting the Companies' from all liability in the event of damage.

Double freight will be imposed in all cases of detection where attempts may be made, to smuggling specie, etc., to evade the established charges.

No article of any kind to be received on board without going through the established Custom's regulations and formalities.

Packages on arrival at destination will be lodged in the Custom-house, whence they will have to be retired by the consignees, or by agents commissioned by them to do so, at their expense.

PANAMA, NEW ZEALAND, AND AUSTRALIAN MAIL CO. 213

All packages must have the port of destination distinctly marked thereon, or they can not be received for shipment.

Primage at the rate of £5 per cent. is charged on cargo and quicksilver.

No bills of lading will be given for a less freight than £2 2s.

The Companies reserve the right to charge for cargo and parcels by measurement or by weight, entirely at their option.

Of jewelry only small packages are received in London.

Packages of treasure, cargo, or parcels, etc., forwarded to Southampton for shipment, must be sent to the care of the shipping agents there, to be delivered by them to the Royal Mail Steam Packet Company.

Each package must be fully and distinctly addressed, and contents and value declared. Parcels must not contain letters or bills. Packages for Colon (Aspinwall) will not be received when consigned to order, but a consignee must be named.

No package above five hundred weight to be received, and none to exceed a cube of 27 feet, nor in length 4 feet 4 inches.

For farther particulars respecting the shipment of treasure, cargo, etc., from England, apply at 55 Moorgate Street, or to Mr. J. K. Linstead, the cargo superintendent of the Royal Mail Company at Southampton.

The foregoing regulations are to hold good, where applicable, to homeward and colonial traffic equally with outward traffic.

TIME FOR DELIVERY OF GOODS, ETC., TO THE ROYAL MAIL STEAM PACKET COMPANY.

Cargo must be sent to Southampton (to the care of a shipping agent), and must be there at latest at noon on the last day of each month, if for shipment by the steamer of the 2d; but when the day of departure falls on a Monday, the latest period will be one day previous to the above dates.

Parcels and periodicals, if sent to the care of an agent at Southampton, can be received at the Company's office there until 10 A.M. on the day of sailing.

Packages and parcels (not exceeding 5 cubic feet) must be delivered at the London office before NOON upon the 28th if for the vessel of the 2d of the following month.

Periodical publications, with the covers *open at both ends*, can be booked in the London office until noon on the day previous to the sailing of the packet, *excepting when the day of sailing falls on Monday, in which case not later than noon on the previous Saturday.*

Table of Rates for Bills of Lading and Parcel Receipts between Panama and New Zealand and Australia, and for Through Bills of Lading and Parcel Receipts between England, the West Indies, and New Zealand and Australia.

TREASURE.

From the ports named below to any of the places mentioned in the following column, or *vice versâ*.	Specie, Jewelry, and Precious Stones.	Plate.	Quicksilver.	Copper Coin
	On value.	On value.	Per ton weight. £	Per ton weight. £
From Panama......	1 per cent.	2 per cent.	10	12
" London........	1¼ "	—	—	—
" Southampton.	1¼ "	3½ per cent.	16	18
" West Indian Ports...............	1¼ "	3 "	16	18

214 PANAMA, NEW ZEALAND, AND AUSTRALIAN MAIL CO.

GENERAL MERCHANDISE.

To or from	From or to Panama.		From or to Southampton.		From or to West Indian Ports.*		
	Light Goods, per ton measurem't.	Heavy Goods, per ton weight.	Light Goods, per ton measurem't.	Heavy Goods, per ton weight.	Goods, per ton measurem't.	Coffee, per ton weight.	Cochineal and Indigo, per ton weight.
	£	£	£	£	£	£	£
Wellington...	12	10	20	16	18	16	30
Auckland....							
Taranaki.....							
Napier........							
Nelson........	13	11	21	17	19	17	31
Picton........							
Canterbury..							
Otago.........							
Bluff..........							
Sydney.......	14	12	22	18	20	18	32
Melbourne...	14	12	22	18	20	18	32

* St. Thomas, Havana, Jamaica, Barbadoes, Trinidad, Demerara, Greytown, Carthagona, and Santa Martha.

PARCELS.

	From London or Southampton to Ports in New Zealand and Australia, or *vice versâ*.	From Panama to Ports in New Zealand and Australia, or *vice versâ*.
	Per package.	Per package.
1 cubic foot and under....................	20s.	10s.
Above 1 cubic foot, and not exceeding 2 feet	30s.	15s.
Above 2 cubic feet, and not exceeding 3 feet...	40s.	20s.
Above 3 cubic feet, up to 14 feet, beyond which measurement no package can be received as a parcel......	12s. 6d. per foot.	7s. per foot.
By weight, up to 5 cwt.	22s. 6d. per cwt.	12s. per cwt.

NEW YORK, CANADA, BRITISH COLUMBIA, SAN FRANCISCO, CALLAO, VALPARAISO, ETC., ETC.

Arrangements for through traffic to the above places are being made with the Panama Railroad Company, the Pacific Steam Navigation Company, and the United States Pacific Mail Steam-ship Company, and the rates will be announced in due course.

The steamers of the Pacific Steam Navigation Company leave Panama for the West Coast of South America on the 2d, 9th or 10th, and 25th of the month, and arrive *at* Panama on the 4th or 5th, 20th, and 28th.

The vessels of the Pacific Mail Steam-ship Company on the *Pacific* route leave Panama for San Francisco on the 9th, 19th, and 29th, and arrive *at* Panama on the 1st, 12th or 13th, and 22d or 23d of the month. On the *Atlantic* route, the steamers leave Colon (Aspinwall) on the 1st, 12th or 13th, and 23d for New York, and leave the latter place on the 1st, 11th, and 21st, or on previous Saturday when these days fall on Sunday, arriving at Colon on the 9th, 19th, and 29th.

THE PACIFIC STEAM NAVIGATION COMPANY. 215

Although eight days are allowed for the passage between New York and Aspinwall, the run is frequently performed in six days.

The passenger fares between New York and Aspinwall are as follows: Chief cabin, £16; second cabin, £10.

For the information of passengers coming to England *viâ* New York, it may be mentioned that the steamers of the Cunard (British Mail) Line leave, every Wednesday, New York and Boston alternately for Liverpool, and those of the Inman Line sail from New York every Wednesday and Saturday.

The chief cabin fares per the former are from £22 to £26; ditto per the latter, £15 15s.

The Cunard vessels perform the voyage to Liverpool ordinarily in 10 days, and the Inman vessels in 12 days.

THE PACIFIC STEAM NAVIGATION COMPANY,

Plying between PANAMA, CALLAO, VALPARAISO, and the INTERMEDIATE PORTS.

The steam-ships destined for the service are the following: Bogotá, 1600 tons; Lima, 1600 tons; Callao, 1200 tons; Valparaiso, 1200 tons; Guayaquil, 1000 tons; San Carlos, 1000 tons; Bolivia, 800 tons; Anne, 500 tons; Cloda, 900 tons; New Granada, 750 tons; Inca, 300 tons; Morro, 150 tons.

Voyage to the South.

		Days of each Month.
Departure from	Panama	9th and 24th.
Arrival at	Guayaquil	13th and 28th.
Departure from	Guayaquil	14th, 29th, and 2d.
Arrival at	Payta	15th, 30th, and 3d.
"	Lambayeque	17th and 4th.
Departure from	Lambayeque	18th and 5th.
Arrival at	Pacasmayo	18th and 5th.
"	Huanchaco	19th and 6th.
"	Santa	20th.
"	Samanco	7th.
"	Casma	20th and 7th.
"	Supe	21st and 8th.
"	Huacho	21st and 8th.
"	Callao	18th, 22d, 2d or 3d, and 9th.
Departure from	Callao	20th, 26th, 5th, and 11th.
Arrival at	Cerro Azul	27th and 12th.
"	Islas de Chincha	21st, 27th, 6th, and 12th.
"	Pisco	21st, 27th, 6th, and 12th.
"	Chala	29th and 14th.
"	Islay	23d, 30th, 8th, and 15th.
"	Arica	24th, 31st or 1st, 9th, and 16th.
"	Pisagua	1st or 2d, and 17th.
"	Mejillones	1st or 2d, and 17th.
"	Iquique	1st or 2d, and 17th.
"	Tocopillo	2d or 3d, and 18th.
"	Cobija	25th, 2d or 3d, 10th and 18th.
"	Caldera	27th, 4th or 5th, 12th, and 20th.
Departure from	Caldera	27th, 4th or 5th, 12th, and 20th.
Arrival at	Carrizal bajo	5th or 6th, and 21st.

		Days of each Month.
Arrival at	Huasco	5th or 6th, and 21st.
"	Coquimbo	28th, 6th or 7th, 13th, and 22d.
"	Tongoy	6th or 7th, and 22d.
"	Valparaiso	29th, 7th or 8th, 14th, and 23d.

Voyage to the North.

		Days of each Month.
Departure from Valparaiso		3d, 11th, 18th, and 27th.
Arrival at	Tongoy	12th and 28th.
"	Coquimbo	4th, 12th, 19th, and 28th.
"	Huasco	13th and 29th.
"	Carrizal bajo	13th and 29th.
"	Caldera	5th, 14th, 20th, and 30th.
"	Cobija	7th, 16th, 22d, 1st or 2d.
"	Tocopillo	16th, and 1st or 2d.
"	Iquique	17th, and 2d or 3d.
"	Mejillones	17th, and 2d or 3d.
"	Pisagua	17th, and 2d or 3d.
"	Arica	8th, 18th, 23d, and 3d or 4th.
"	Islay	9th, 19th, 24th, and 4th or 5th.
"	Chala	20th, and 5th or 6th.
"	Pisco	11th, 21st, 26th, and 6th or 7th.
"	Islas de Chincha	11th, 21st, 26th, and 6th or 7th.
"	Cerro Azul	21st, and 6th or 7th.
"	Callao	12th, 22d, 27th, and 7th or 8th.
Departure from Callao		14th, 24th, 29th, and 13th.
Arrival at	Huacho	25th and 14th.
"	Supe	25th and 14th.
"	Casma	26th and 15th.
"	Samanco	26th.
"	Santa	15th.
"	Huanchaco	27th and 16th.
"	Pacasmayo	27th and 16th.
"	Lambayeque	28th and 17th.
"	Payta	17th, 19th, and 1st or 2d.
"	Guayaquil	30th.
"	Panama	22d, and 6th or 7th.

Rates of Passage.

		First Saloon.	Second Saloon.			First Saloon.	Second Saloon.
Panama to	Guayaquil	$105	$100	Panama to	Islay	$220	$210
"	Payta	115	110	"	Arica	230	220
"	Lambayeque	135	130	"	Iquique	245	230
"	Huanchaco	135	130	"	Cobija	255	240
"	Casma	140	135	"	Caldera	265	250
"	Huacho	145	140	"	Huasco	270	255
"	Callao	160	150	"	Coquimbo	275	260
"	Pisco	175	165	"	Valparaiso	290	270

Passage for any of the above ports can be secured at the office of the Panama Railroad Company, 88 Wall Street, New York.

The Pacific Steam Navigation Company will issue *through bills of lading* for produce from the above-mentioned ports—To New York, to be conveyed from Aspinwall by sailing vessels of the Panama Railroad Company; to Liverpool, to be conveyed from Aspinwall by the vessels of the West India and

Pacific Steam-ship Company; to Southampton, to be conveyed from Aspinwall by steamers of the Royal Mail Steam Packet Company.

An arrangement has also been made by which produce can be shipped under *through bills of lading* from ports in Central America touched at by steamers Guatemala and Columbus to the above ports on the west coast.

Rates of Freight in Dollars from Panama to Valparaiso and intermediate Ports.

	Buenaventura.	Guayaquil.	Payta.	Lambayeque.	Huanchaco.	Casma.	Huacho.	Callao.	Pisco.	Islay.	Arica.	Iquique.	Cobija.	Caldera.	Huasco.	Coquimbo.	Valparaiso.
Panama........per ton.	20	25	25	25	25	30	30	30	30	35	35	40	40	40	45	45	45
Buenaventura.... "	...	20	20	25	25	25	25	25	30	30	35	35	35	40	40	40	40
Guayaquil........ "	...	...	12	15	15	15	15	15	20	20	20	25	25	25	25	25	25
Payta............ "	...	...	...	15	15	15	15	15	20	20	20	25	25	25	25	25	25
Lambayeque..... "	...	...	...	...	15	15	15	15	20	20	20	20	20	20	20	20	20
Huanchaco....... "	...	...	...	...	...	15	15	15	20	20	20	20	20	20	20	20	20
Casma........... "	...	...	...	...	...	...	15	15	20	20	20	20	20	20	20	20	20
Huacho.......... "	...	...	...	...	...	...	...	12	15	20	20	20	20	20	20	20	20
Callao........... "	...	...	...	...	...	...	...	...	15	20	20	20	20	20	20	20	20
Pisco............. "	...	...	...	...	...	...	...	...	...	20	20	20	20	20	20	20	20
Islay............. "	...	...	...	...	...	...	...	...	...	...	15	20	20	20	20	20	20
Arica............ "	...	...	...	...	...	...	...	...	...	...	...	15	15	20	20	20	20
Iquique.......... "	...	...	...	...	...	...	...	...	...	...	...	...	20	20	20	20	20
Cobija........... "	...	...	...	...	...	...	...	...	...	...	...	...	...	20	20	20	20
Caldera.......... "	...	...	...	...	...	...	...	...	...	...	...	...	...	...	12	12	12
Huasco.......... "	...	...	...	...	...	...	...	...	...	...	...	...	...	...	...	12	12
Coquimbo........ "	...	...	...	...	...	...	...	...	...	...	...	...	...	...	...	...	12

Rates of Freight in Dollars from Valparaiso to Panama and intermediate Ports.

	Coquimbo.	Huasco.	Caldera.	Cobija.	Iquique.	Arica.	Islay.	Pisco.	Callao.	Huacho.	Casma.	Huanchaco.	Lambayeque.	Payta.	Guayaquil.	Buenaventura.	Panama.
Valparaiso.......per ton.	12	12	12	20	20	20	20	20	20	25	25	25	25	25	25	30	30
Coquimbo........ "	...	12	12	15	15	15	15	15	15	18	18	18	18	18	18	25	25
Huasco.......... "	...	...	12	15	15	15	15	15	15	18	18	18	18	18	18	25	25
Caldera.......... "	...	...	...	15	15	15	15	15	15	18	18	18	18	18	18	25	25
Cobija........... "	...	...	...	...	15	15	15	15	15	18	18	18	18	18	18	25	25
Iquique.......... "	...	...	...	...	...	15	15	15	15	15	18	18	18	18	18	25	25
Arica............ "	...	...	...	...	...	...	15	15	15	15	15	15	15	15	18	25	25
Islay............. "	...	...	...	...	...	...	...	15	15	15	15	15	15	15	18	25	25
Pisco............ "	...	...	...	...	...	...	...	...	12	15	15	15	15	15	18	25	25
Callao........... "	...	...	...	...	...	...	...	...	...	12	12	12	12	12	15	20	20
Huacho.......... "	...	...	...	...	...	...	...	...	...	...	12	12	12	12	12	18	18
Casma........... "	...	...	...	...	...	...	...	...	...	...	...	12	12	12	12	18	18
Huanchaco....... "	...	...	...	...	...	...	...	...	...	...	...	...	12	12	12	18	18
Lambayeque..... "	...	...	...	...	...	...	...	...	...	...	...	...	...	12	12	18	18
Payta............ "	...	...	...	...	...	...	...	...	...	...	...	...	...	...	12	15	18
Guayaquil........ "	...	...	...	...	...	...	...	...	...	...	...	...	...	...	...	15	15
Buenaventura.... "	...	...	...	...	...	...	...	...	...	...	...	...	...	...	...	...	15

K

Through Rates of Freight from New York to Valparaiso and intermediate Ports.

The Panama Railroad Company are now prepared to issue *through bills of lading* to all the ports touched at by the steamers of the Pacific Steam Navigation Company, at the following rates:

	To Buenaventura, Guayaquil, Payta, and intermediates.	To Callao, Valparaiso, and intermediates, south of Payta.
General merchandise, and all goods embraced in first class of Panama Railroad tariff, per ton of 40 cubic feet, or 2240 lbs. gross weight, at the option of the Company	$40 00	$50 00
Beef and pork, per barrel	5 00	7 00
" " per half barrel	2 75	3 75
Flour, per barrel	4 00	5 00
" per half barrel	2 25	2 75
Biscuit, per 100 lbs.	2 50	3 50
Butter, lard, hams, bacon, cheese, salt fish, tallow, and rice, per ton of 2000 lbs.	30 00	40 00
Refined sugar, per ton of 2000 lbs.	40 00	45 00
Wines and other liquors, in boxes and barrels, per ton of 40 cubic feet	30 00	40 00
Manufactured tobacco, per ton of 40 cubic feet	30 00	40 00
Cigars, per ton of 40 cubic feet	35 00	45 00
Unbleached domestics, per ton of 40 cubic feet	25 00	32 00
Soap, per ton of 2000 lbs.	30 00	40 00
Candles, per ton of 40 cubic feet	30 00	40 00
Carriages and furniture, per ton of 40 cubic feet	30 00	40 00
Agricultural implements, per ton of 40 cubic feet	25 00	35 00
Pitch, tar, and rosin, per barrel	3 00	4 00
Earthen-ware and glass-ware (coarse), in crates and boxes, per ton of 40 cubic feet	25 00	35 00
Turpentine and oil in cases, per ton of 40 cubic feet	30 00	40 00
Turpentine and oil in tins only, per ton of 40 cubic feet	35 00	45 00

All weights to be the gross weight.

Articles not enumerated to be charged at rates assimilating to the above.

From New York to Aspinwall shipments are made by the sailing vessels of the Panama Railroad Company, leaving at intervals of from eight to ten days.

All freight to be prepaid.

No bill of lading signed for less than five dollars.

Farther particulars may be learned on application to the secretary at the office of the Panama Railroad Company, No. 88 Wall Street, New York.

Weekly Line between Callao, Lambayeque, and Guayaquil.

Departure from Callao	6th, 13th, 19th, and 24th	of each month.	
Arrival at Huacho	7th, 14th, 20th, and 25th	" "	
" Supe	7th, 14th, 20th, and 25th	" "	
" Casma	8th, 15th, 21st, and 26th	" "	
" Samanco	.... 26th	" "	
" Santa	...... 15th	" "	

Arrival at Huanchaco...... 9th, 16th, 22d, and 27th   of each month.
"   Malabrigo....... 9th and 22d   ......   "   "
"   Pacasmayo...... ...... 16th, ... and 27th   "   "
"   Lambayeque.... 10th, 17th, 23d, and 28th   "   "
"   Payta.............. .... 29th   "   "
"   Guayaquil........ .... 30th   "   "
Departure from Guayaquil .... 2d or 3d   "   "
Arrival at Payta............. .... 3d or 4th   "   "
"   Lambayeque.... .... 4th or 5th   "   "
Departure fr. Lambayeque 10th, 17th, 23d, and 4th or 5th   "   "
Arrival at Pacasmayo...... ...... 18th ...... and 5th or 6th   "   "
"   Malabrigo....... ...... 18th ...... and 5th or 6th   "   "
"   Huanchaco...... 11th, 19th, 24th, and 6th or 7th   "   "
"   Santa.............. ...... 20th ....   "   "
"   Samanco........ .... 7th or 8th   "   "
"   Casma........... 12th, 20th, 25th, and 7th or 8th   "   "
Departure from Casma.... 12th, 20th, 25th, and 7th or 8th   "   "
Arrival at Supe............ 13th, 21st, 26th, and 8th or 9th   "   "
"   Huacho........ 13th, 21st, 26th, and 8th or 9th   "   "
"   Callao............ 14th, 22d, 27th, and 9th or 10th   "   "

Rates of freight: From Callao to Guayaquil and the intermediate ports, $8 per ton; from Guayaquil to Callao and the intermediate ports, $10 per ton; from Guayaquil, and the intermediate ports as far south as Callao, to Valparaiso, $15 per ton.

Semi-monthly Line between Valparaiso, Talcahuano, and Puerto Montt.

Departure from Valparaiso.. 10th and 30th   of each month.
Arrival at Constitucion....... 11th   ......   "   "
"   Tomé.............. 12th and 31st or 1st   "   "
"   Talcahuano........ 12th and 31st or 1st   "   "
"   Coronel............ ...... 1st or 2d   "   "
"   Lota................ 13th   ......   "   "
"   Valdivia............ 14th   ......   "   "
"   Ancud.............. 15th   ......   "   "
"   Calbuco............ 16th   ......   "   "
"   Puerto Montt..... 16th   ......   "   "
Departure from Puerto Montt 18th   ......   "   "
Arrival at Calbuco............ 18th   ......   "   "
"   Ancud.............. 18th   ......   "   "
"   Valdivia............ 20th   ...... ,   "   "
"   Lota................ 21st   ......   "   "
"   Coronel............ ...... 1st or 2d   "   "
"   Talcahuano........ 22d and 2d or 3d   "   "
Departure from Talcahuano. 22d and 3d or 4th   "   "
Arrival at Tomé............. 22d and 3d or 4th   "   "
"   Constitucion....... 23d   ......   "   "
"   Valparaiso......... 24th and 4th or 5th   "   "

Monthly Line between Panama and Guayaquil—Steam-ship Anne.

Departure from Panama...................... 12th of each month.
Arrival at Buenaventura...................... 14th   "   "
Departure from Buenaventura.............. 15th   "   "
Arrival at Tumaco.......................... 16th   "   "
"   Esmeraldas........................ 17th   "   "
"   Manta.............................. 18th   "   "
"   Guayaquil.......................... 20th   "   "

PACIFIC STEAM NAVIGATION COMPANY.

Departure from Guayaquil................... 24th of each month.
Arrival at Manta............................... 26th " "
" Esmeraldas......................... 28th " "
" Tumaco.............................. 29th " "
" Buenaventura...................... 30th " "
Departure from Buenaventura.............. 31st " "
Arrival at Panama............................. 2d or 3d "

Prices of Passage by the Anne.

	Buenaventura.	Tumaco.	Esmeraldas.	Manta.	Guayaquil.
From Panama to............	$50 00	$60 00	$70 00	$80 00	$85 00
" Buenaventura to.....		30 00	40 00	50 00	60 00
" Tumaco to................			20 00	30 00	40 00
" Esmeraldas to.........				20 00	30 00
" Manta to..................					25 00

	Manta.	Esmeraldas.	Tumaco.	Buenaventura.	Panama.
From Guayaquil to.........	$25 00	$30 00	$40 00	$50 00	$85 00
" Manta to...................		20 00	30 00	45 00	80 00
" Esmeraldas to.........			20 00	35 00	70 00
" Tumaco to................				30 00	60 00
" Buenaventura to.....					50 00

Rates of Freight.

From Guayaquil and intermediate ports to Panama......$10 00 per ton.
" Panama " " Guayaquil.. 12 00 "

The Pacific Steam Navigation Company was organized in April, 1839, but the charter of incorporation was not obtained until February, 1840. In November, 1839, the directors, under assurance that the charter would be granted, contracted for two steam vessels, which were completed and dispatched from England for service on the Pacific in July, 1840, and commenced their voyages on the coasts of the Pacific in November of the same year, since which time the line has been in regular and successful operation. Its business has increased to such an extent that a fleet of eleven large steam-ships, with a semi-monthly service, are now employed on the through route between Panama and Valparaiso, besides a monthly steam-ship (the Anne) plying between Panama and Guayaquil, a weekly line of four steamships plying between Callao and Guayaquil, and a semi-monthly line between Valparaiso and Puerto Montt, touching at the intermediate ports for the collection of freight, which, from the increase of the through business, caused too much delay for the ships of the through line.

The machine and repair shops, and other facilities for keeping the vessels of the Company in order, are very extensive and well appointed. They are situated on the island of Toboga, in the Bay of Panama.

The head-quarters of the Company are at
Liverpool.............. WILLIAM JUST, *General Manager.*
Callao.................. GEORGE PETRIE, *Resident Manager on the Pacific.*
Panama .... *Agent.*

CALLAO DOCK COMPANY.

DIRECTORS:

In England.	At Callao.
S. R. GRAVES, Esq., M. P. for Liverpool.	General MEDINA, Lima, Chief of the Staff of the Army of Peru.
CHARLES ROWE, Esq. (Messrs. Graham, Rowe, & Co., Liverpool.	FRANCIS BRYCE, Esq., Callao.
	HENRY HIGGINSON, Esq., Callao.
WILLIAM JUST, Esq., Managing Director of the Pacific Steam Navigation Company, Liverpool.	S. D. GREGORIO HURTADO, Callao.
	GEORGE PETRIE, Esq., General Manager of the Pacific Steam Navigation Company, Callao.

Principal Dimensions of the Iron Floating Dock.

Length .... 300 feet.
Extreme breadth .... 100 "
Inside .... 76 "
Height .... 38 " 3 inches.
Can be sunk to a depth of .... 33 "
And take in a ship drawing .... 21 "
 Or weighing up to 6000 tons.

RATES FOR THE USE OF DOCK.

Steamers and Ships of War.

First day .... 1 sol per ton.
Four following days .... 75 centimes per ton.
All subsequent days .... 50 " "

Sailing Vessels.

First day .... 50 centimes of a sol per ton.
All subsequent days ... 25 " " "

The tonnage of a vessel will be reckoned according to the following rule:

Double-decked Vessels.

Take the length of every vessel, if double-decked, from the fore part of the main stem to the after side of the stern-post above the upper deck, the breadth at the broadest part above the main wales; and half such breadth shall be accounted the depth of every double-decked vessel. Then deduct from the length three fifths of the breadth; multiply the remainder by the breadth, and the product by the depth; divide the last product by 95, and the quotient is the true tonnage of such vessel.

Single-decked Vessels.

Take the length from the fore part of the main stem to the after side of the stern-post above the upper deck, and the breadth at the broadest part above the main wales, and deduct from the length three fifths of the breadth; take the depth from the under side of the deck-plank to the ceiling of the hold; multiply the remainder by the breadth, and the product by the depth; divide this last product by 95, and the quotient is the tonnage of such single-decked vessel.

[Ten tons of ballast, cargo, and (in the case of men-of-war) of guns and ammunition, will be allowed for every 100 tons of the above measurements; any excess being charged at the rate as tons' measurement.]

In docking and undocking, all vessels must conform strictly to the orders of the dock-master.   JAMES B. AIKEN, Secretary.

JAMES ANDERSON, Dock-master.

THE PANAMA RAILROAD COMPANY'S CENTRAL AMERICAN LINE OF STEAM-SHIPS,

Running semi-monthly between the PORTS OF GUATEMALA, SAN SALVADOR, COSTA RICA, NICARAGUA, and PANAMA.

The steam propellers Guatemala, 1021 tons, J. M. Dow, commander, and Salvador, 1200 tons, J. W. Rathbun, commander, arrive at and depart from Central American ports on or about the following days of each month, forming a semi-monthly line:

Departure.			Arrival.		
From	Salvador.	Guatemala	At	Salvador.	Guatemala
Panama............	15th	30th	Punta Arenas....	17th	2d
Punta Arenas....	18th	3d	Realejo............	19th	4th
Realejo............	20th	5th	La Union.........	20th	5th
La Union.........	21st	6th	La Libertad......	22d	7th
La Libertad......	22d	7th	Acajutla...........	22d	7th
Acajutla...........	22d	7th	San José.........	23d	8th
San José	25th	10th	Acajutla...........	25th	10th
Acajutla...........	26th	11th	La Libertad......	27th	11th
La Libertad......	27th	12th	La Union.........	28th	13th
La Union.........	30th	15th	Realejo............	30th	15th
Realejo............	1st	16th	Punta Arenas....	2d	17th
Punta Arenas....	3d	18th	Panama............	5th	20th

Prices of Passage.

From Panama to Punta Arenas........................... $40 00
"   "   Realejo 65 00
"   "   La Union................................. 70 00
"   "   La Libertad............................. 75 00
"   "   Acajutla................................... 80 00
"   "   San José de Guatemala............... 85 00

Payable in American gold.

The Company has recently added to its service the steamer Parkersburgh, 700 tons, to run during portions of the year when freights are abundant.

PANAMA RAILROAD CO.'S CENTRAL AMERICAN LINE.

Prices of Freight (including Lighterage in Panama).

From Panama to	Punta Arenas,	per ton measurement			$14 00
" "	Realejo,	"	"		16 00
" "	La Union,	"	"		16 00
" "	La Libertad,	"	"		18 00
" "	Acajutla,	"	"		18 00
" "	San José,	"	"		18 00

And five per cent. primage.

Prices of Return Freight (including Lighterage at Panama).

From San José, Acajutla, and La Libertad, to Panama: For cochineal and indigo, 1¼ cents per lb. on the net weight; hides, 32 cents each; other merchandise in cases, bales, etc., 45 cents per cubic foot; and 5 per cent. primage.

From La Union and Realejo to Panama: Cochineal and indigo, 1¼ cents per lb. net weight; hides, 30 cents each; merchandise in cases, bales, etc., 40 cents per cubic foot; and 5 per cent. primage.

From Punta Arenas to Panama: Coffee, ⅜ cent, gross weight; hides, 24 cents each; merchandise in cases, bales, etc., 35 cents per cubic foot.

Produce and other merchandise for Panama will be landed at the railroad wharf, where it must be received by the consignees immediately; in default of which, it will be taken to the depôt at the expense and risk of the owner.

All freight and passage payable in American gold or its equivalent.

Prices of Freight from the Ports of Central America to Aspinwall (Colon), including the Expense of Landing and Transportation by the Railroad.

From San José, Acajutla, and La Libertad: Indigo and cochineal, 2¾ cents per lb. net weight; hides, 47 cents each; merchandise in cases, etc., 45 cents per cubic foot, and the regular transportation charges established by the tariff of the railroad.

From La Union and Realejo: Indigo and cochineal, 2¾ cents per lb. net weight; hides, 45 cents each; merchandise in cases, etc., 40 cents per cubic foot, and the transportation charges established by the tariff of the railroad.

From Punta Arenas: Coffee, 1⅛ cents per lb. gross weight; hides, 39 cents each; merchandise in cases, etc., 35 cents per cubic foot, and the transportation charges established by the tariff of the railroad.

Through Rates of Freight from Central America to the South American Ports.

To Guayaquil,	cochineal,	per ceroon		$3 75
" Callao,	"	"		4 75
" Valparaiso,	"	"		5 75
To Guayaquil,	coffee,	per pound		1½ cts.
" Callao,	"	"		1¾ "
" Valparaiso,	"	"		2¼ "
To Guayaquil,	crude sugar			1½ cts.
" Callao	"			1¾ "
" Valparaiso,	"			2¼ "

Rates of Through Freight from New York, by the Company's sailing Vessels to Aspinwall, including Lighterage in Panama.

	To Punta Arenas.	Realejo, La Union.	La Libertad, Acajutla, San José (Guatemala).
Dry-goods, hats, boots, shoes, drugs, and other goods, included in railroad tariff as first class, per ton of 40 feet	$40 00	$42 00	$44 00
Unbleached domestics, per ton of 40 feet	32 00	34 00	36 00
Furniture, carriages, agricultural implements, wooden-ware, clocks, etc., per ton of 40 feet	30 00	32 00	34 00
Iron in bars, sheets, and bundles, iron castings, nails, spikes, copper, zinc, and lead, per ton of 2000 lbs.	30 00	32 00	34 00
Steel in bars and bundles, coarse machinery, common hardware, earthen-ware, sugar-mills, -moulds, and -pans, shot, etc., per ton of 2000 lbs	34 00	36 00	38 00
Butter, cheese, lard, fish, ham, soap, and candles, per ton of 2000 lbs.	35 00	37 00	39 00
Refined sugar, per ton of 40 feet	30 00	32 00	34 00
Flour and rice, per barrel	4 20	4 50	4 80
" " per half barrel	2 20	2 35	2 50
Wine in boxes and baskets, per ton of 40 feet	32 00	34 00	36 00
" in casks, and other liquors, per ton of 40 feet	35 00	37 00	39 00
Tobacco, manufactured, per ton of 40 feet	40 00	42 00	44.00
" unmanufactured, per ton of 40 feet	32 00	34 00	36 00
Ship-bread, crackers, etc., per ton of 40 feet	28 00	30 00	32 00

Rates of Return Freights, by the Company's sailing Vessels from Aspinwall to New York, including Lighterage in Panama.

	To Panama.	Aspinwall.	New York.
Lumber, from La Union, per M.	$20 00		
" " Punta Arenas, per M.	18 00		
Cochineal and indigo, from either port, per lb net.	1⅛	$0 02¾	$0 03½
Hides, from San José, Acajutla, and La Libertad, each	32	47	62
Hides, from La Union and Realejo, each	30	45	60
" " Punta Arenas	24	39	54
Coffee, from Punta Arenas, per lb. gross	⅝	1⅛	1½
Deer and goat skins, from Punta Arenas, per lb...	1	1¾	2½
" " " other ports, " ...	1½	2¼	3
Cigars, balsam, and first class goods, per railroad tariff, per foot	50	1 00	1 16
India-rubber	1	1¾	2¼
Cotton	¾	1½	2
Sugar	⅝	1⅜	1¾
Silver ore to New York, in lots of 25 tons and upward, $25; less than 25 tons, $30 per ton of 2240 lbs.			

No primage on through rates.

Through bills of lading are given from Central American ports to Liverpool (by the steamers of the West India and Pacific Steam-ship Company, limited) at 4 cents per lb. on net weight of indigo and cochineal, and 2½ cents per lb. on gross weight of coffee; and to London (by the Royal Mail Steam

CALIFORNIA, OREGON, AND MEXICO STEAM-SHIP CO. 225

Packet Company's steamers) at 2¾ pence sterling per lb. on gross weight of indigo and cochineal.

Produce and other merchandise for Panama will be landed at the railroad wharf, where it must be received by the consignees immediately; in default of which, it will be taken to the dépôt at the expense and risk of the owner.

All freight and passage payable in American gold or its equivalent.

For farther information, apply to

    Jos. F. Joy, *Secretary*, 88 Wall St., New York.
    Wm. Nelson, *Commercial Agent*, Panama.
    Crisanto Medina, Punta Arenas.
    Courtade y Clavera, La Union.
    H. J. Foote and J. Mathi, Sonsonate.
    J. Saragia, San José de Guatemala.
     Or to the commanders on board.

For a description of the countries touched at by the Central American Line, also an account of the ports, port regulations and charges, tariffs, commerce, etc., etc., see page 222, et seq.

THE CALIFORNIA, OREGON, AND MEXICO STEAM-SHIP COMPANY,

Running between San Francisco and the Ports of Oregon, Washington Territory, and Vancouver's Island, tri-monthly, with a Southern Branch, Monthly Service, between San Francisco and the Mexican Pacific Coast.

This line was established early in 1861 by Messrs. Holliday & Flint, of San Francisco, who purchased the steam-ships Panama, of 1087 tons, Cortez, 1117, Republic, 850, Columbia, 777, and Sierra Nevada, 1247 tons, from the Pacific Mail Steam-ship Company, and took charge of the San Francisco, Oregon, Washington Territory, and Vancouver Route, heretofore managed by the Pacific Mail Steam-ship Company, besides establishing a new branch of service between San Francisco and the ports of Cape St. Lucas, Guaymas, San Blas, Mazatlan, Acapulco, and other Mexican ports.

In 1866 it was formed into a joint-stock company, under the laws of New York, with the title of the "Oregon, California, and Mexico Steam-ship Company," with a capital of $2,000,000.

Officers.

    Ben. Holladay, President.
    George Dennison, Vice-President.
    John E. Russell, Secretary.

Directors.

Ben. Holladay.	W. R. Travers.
Paul S. Forbes.	George Dennison.
S. L. M. Barlow.	John E. Russell.
Wm. B. Duncan.	

This Company own the following steamers, running between San Francisco and Portland, Oregon (connecting at Portland with steamer Active from Victoria, Vancouver's Island):

Steam-ship Oriflamme,	Steam-ship Oregon,
" Sierra Nevada,	" Continental,

making three trips per month.

Also steamer John L. Stephens, making a monthly trip to Cape St. Lucas, La Paz, Mazatlan, and Guaymas, connecting at Mazatlan with steamer Panama for Acapulco.

Also the fine new steamer Del Norte (built at San Francisco), making tri-monthly trips between San Francisco and Crescent City and Humboldt Bay.

Principal office of the Company, No. 35 William St., New York.

THE PANAMA RAILROAD COMPANY'S LINE OF SAILING VESSELS BETWEEN NEW YORK AND ASPINWALL.

To accommodate shippers and facilitate trade, especially with the Pacific coast, the Panama Railroad Company have established a line of sailing vessels between New York and Aspinwall, composed of the following:

Bark Idaho	Captain Chapman	410 tons.
" Bolivia	" Whiteberry	346 "
" Xantho	" Conway	213 "
" American Eagle	" Harford	305 "
" Magdalena	" Searle	260 "
Brig Bogota	" Lindsley	243 "
" Costa Rica	" Cassidy	243 "

These vessels are all of the first class, sailing at intervals of from a week to ten days. The average passage from New York to Aspinwall is twenty days, and from Aspinwall to New York twenty-five days.

The freight from New York to Aspinwall is 15 cents per cubic foot, and 5 per cent. primage. The freight from Aspinwall to New York is from $6 to $8 per ton.

Whale-oil will be received and forwarded from Panama to New York by the road and the Company's Line of Sailing Vessels, at the rate of 7 cents per gallon, if received in the harbor alongside from ship's tackles, and at 6 cents per gallon if received at the pier, in full of all expenses, charging for the capacity of the cask, without allowing for wantage.

Whalebone will be taken from ship at Panama through to New York at 1½ cents per lb.

By these vessels the Panama Railroad Company issue *through bills of lading* to the ports of South America touched at by the steam-ships of the Pacific Steam Navigation Company, at the following rates:

	To Buenaventura, Guayaquil, Payta, and intermediates.	To Callao, Valparaiso, and intermediates, south of Payta.
General merchandise, and all goods embraced in first class of Panama Railroad tariff, per ton of 40 cubic feet, or 2240 lbs. gross weight, at the option of the Company	$40 00	$50 00
Beef and pork, per barrel	5 00	7 00
" " per half barrel	2 75	3 75
Flour, per barrel	4 00	5 00
" per half barrel	2 25	2 75
Biscuit, per 100 lbs	2 50	3 50
Butter, lard, hams, bacon, cheese, salt fish, tallow, and rice, per ton of 2000 lbs	30 00	40 00
Refined sugar, per ton of 2000 lbs	40 00	45 00
Wines and other liquors, in boxes and barrels, per ton of 40 cubic feet	30 00	40 00
Manufactured tobacco, per ton of 40 cubic feet	30 00	40 00
Cigars, per ton of 40 cubic feet	35 00	45 00
Unbleached domestics, per ton of 40 cubic feet	25 00	32 00
Soap, per ton of 2000 lbs.	30 00	40 00
Candles, per ton of 40 cubic feet	30 00	40 00
Carriages and furniture, per ton of 40 cubic feet	30 00	40 00
Agricultural implements, per ton of 40 cubic feet	25 00	35 00
Pitch, tar, and rosin, per barrel	3 00	4 00
Earthen-ware and glass-ware (coarse), in crates and boxes, per ton of 40 cubic feet	25 00	35 00
Turpentine and oil in cases, per ton of 40 cubic feet	30 00	40 00
Turpentine and oil in tins only, per ton of 40 cubic feet	35 00	45 00

All weights to be the gross weight.
Articles not enumerated to be charged at rates assimilating to the above.

The Pacific Steam Navigation Company will issue *through bills of lading* for produce *from* the above ports.

Goods arriving at Aspinwall by the Company's vessels, and consigned to parties at Panama, under *through bills of lading*, will be forwarded to them free of charges and commissions by the Company other than such as are expressed in the bills of lading.

Residents and agents at Panama can forward goods through the commercial agent of the Company at Panama to foreign ports beyond Aspinwall, on *through bills of lading*, by the Company's line of sailing vessels to New York, or by any other lines or vessels with which the Company has made the necessary arrangements.

WELLS, FARGO, & CO.'S EXPRESS.

The express system, which had long been an indispensable necessity in the Atlantic United States, became, on the discovery of gold in California, an equally valuable medium of transportation between the Atlantic and Pacific.

Prompt, reliable, and responsible, the Express Company occupies the middle ground between the shipper and the railroad and steam-ship companies.

Issuing "through receipts," and giving careful supervision to the business, it insures to its customers the most speedy delivery of their consignments, and, in case of loss or damage, prompt and liberal adjustment.

The house of Wells, Fargo, & Co. has been engaged in this business for the past fifteen years. Its first operations were limited to California; but with the extension and development of our states and territories, and the demands of commerce in the Pacific, they have been gradually and successfully extended, until they now reach all the republics, states, and territories bordering the eastern shores of that ocean, together with Japan, China, the Sandwich Islands, New Zealand, and Australia, and their connections.

Its capital, originally $300,000, has, with these requirements, been gradually increased to $10,000,000, with its Board of Direction and principal office in New York City.

The Company owns and operates, under contract with the Post-office Department of the United States, about 4000 miles of passenger and express stage-routes, extending from the Missouri River westward through Denver and Salt Lake City, to all the cities and towns of the interior territories of Colorado, Utah, Idaho, Montana, and Washington, and the states of California, Oregon, and Nevada.

Over these extensive routes passengers are carried, and an "express" organized for the transportation and delivery of treasure, packages, letters, and freight.

A prominent feature in their business is the "Collection and General Agency Department," for the collection and payment of money, attending to the execution, record, and delivery of valuable papers and documents, the purchase and sale of merchandise, receiving and transmitting property subject to charges to be paid on delivery (C.O.D.)—in fine, executing every conceivable commission.

Another prominent department is their "Banking and Exchange" (domestic and foreign). They also make TELEGRAPHIC TRANSFERS OF MONEY between San Francisco and intermediate points and New York.

This Company is also the sole freight agent of the "*Pacific Mail Steam-ship Company*," and, as such, receives and forwards by their steamers, *via* Panama, all freight destined for the ports of the Pacific reached by that line and its extended connections.

For this purpose, "through bills of lading" are issued in connection with the various steam-ship companies radiating from Panama, viz.:

The "Pacific Steam Navigation Company," touching at all the ports on the West Coast of South America.

The "Panama, New Zealand, and Australian Royal Steam-ship Company," to all ports of New Zealand and Australia.

The "Panama Railroad Company's Steamer Line," touching at all the ports of Costa Rica, Nicaragua, San Salvador, and Guatemala, and the "California, Oregon, and Mexican Steam-ship Company."

At Aspinwall connection is made with the various steam-ship lines to Liverpool and Southampton, England, and St. Nazaire, France.

Under this system, prompt and reliable shipments can be made in all directions, and, in like manner, return freights can be made by the above lines, extending from New York to Europe by the Cunard, Inman, and other steamers.

By each California steamer Wells, Fargo, & Co. dispatch a "fast package and letter express," which is made up at their principal office, No. 84 Broadway. This express extends through all the steamer connections at Panama before referred to.

Freight is received at pier 42 North River, foot of Canal Street, where the tariff of rates and all other information is furnished.

Officers of the Company.

LOUIS McLANE, President.
ASHBEL H. BARNEY, Vice-Pres.
GEORGE K. OTIS, Secretary.
CALVIN GODDARD, Treasurer.

Directors.

LOUIS McLANE,
ASHBEL H. BARNEY,
JAMES C. FARGO,
BEN. HOLLADAY,
DANFORTH N. BARNEY,
BENJAMIN P. CHENEY,
JOHNSTON LIVINGSTON,
WILLIAM H. FOGG,
EUGENE KELLY,
WILLIAM G. FARGO,
JOHN BUTTERFIELD.

The principal offices and agencies of Wells, Fargo, & Co. are

New York	84 Broadway.
Boston	39 and 40 Court Square.
San Francisco . .	Wells, Fargo, & Co., corner of Montgomery and California Streets.
London	Messrs. Erves & Macy.
Havre	Messrs. Marcel & Co.
Havana	E. Ramirez & Co.
Aspinwall . . .	S. McNider.
Panama	
Hong Kong . .	P. H. Dumaresq.

Their minor agencies are to be found in every city and town reached by their business.

The American-European Express, Forwarding, Commissioners, and Banking Agency,

For all Parts of the United States, Great Britain, Canada, California, and the Continent of Europe.

(ESTABLISHED IN 1849.)

The AMERICAN-EUROPEAN EXPRESS has special arrangements with the various lines of transatlantic steamers for the conveyance of

Parcels, Merchandise, Jewelry, Personal Effects, &c., &c.,

between Europe and America; and being the oldest of the transatlantic Expresses, and long known for the regularity and promptitude of its transactions, is now recognized as the leading and legitimate Express Conveyance between the two Continents.

Besides its own offices and branches, this Express is connected with and supported by the

"Adams," "American," "United States," and other great inland Expresses of America.

"**The London and Northwestern Railway Company,**"

"**The Continental Daily Parcels Express,**" and

"**Wheatley's Oriental & Australian Agency.**"

The A. E. EXPRESS also undertakes the collection of bills, drafts, invoices, &c., and commissions of a general nature appertaining to the Express business.

New York: AUSTIN, BALDWIN & CO., 72 Broadway.
Boston: STONE & DOWNEY (Agents), 28 State Street.
Philadelphia: H. L. LEAF (Agent), 320 Chestnut Street.
Paris: LHERBETTE, KANE & CO. (Agents), Place de la Bourse.
Havre: LHERBETTE, KANE & CO. (Agents), 21 Rue Corneille.
Liverpool: STAVELEY & STARR, 9 Chapel Street.
London: WHEATLEY, STARR & CO., 156 Cheapside (Agents Pacific Mail Steamship Co. and Panama Railroad Co.)

Great Mail Route

BETWEEN

Europe and the North Pacific,

VIA THE

Royal Mail (West India) Steam Packet Company,
Panama Railroad,

AND

Pacific United States Mail Steamship Company.

Leaving Southampton, England, on the 2d and 17th of each Month, and arriving at San Francisco in about

35 days.

For the comfort and convenience of passengers, arrangements have been made for issuing "through tickets" from England to San Francisco, including transit across the Isthmus of Panama, at

Greatly Reduced Fares.

This is now, in consequence of its being the shortest and most direct, the favorite route for travelers between the above countries; and intending passengers will please take notice that those only holding "through tickets" will have the benefit of the reduction in fares, which tickets can only be had in England of the undersigned, who are authorized by the Companies to issue them.

For rates of passage and further information, apply to

WHEATLEY, STARR & CO.,
Agents,
156 Cheapside, LONDON.

(Office of American-European Express.)

TOWER OF SAN JEROME, AT OLD PANAMA.

BRIEF ACCOUNT

OF THE

REPUBLICS OF CENTRAL AMERICA,

CONNECTED WITH THE PANAMA RAILROAD BY THE STEAMERS OF THE CENTRAL AMERICAN·LINE.

THE course of the Panama Railroad Company's Central American steamers, for their upward voyages from Panama, is due south across the Bay of Panama to Point Mala, its western boundary: from thence, following the coast-line, within distinct view of the rugged mountain range which bounds it, a northwesterly course is pursued to San José de Guatemala, the terminus of the route.

. The 1st port of entry is Punta Arenas, in the Republic of COSTA RICA, distant from Panama 450 miles.

The 2d port of entry is Realejo, in the Republic of NICARAGUA, distant from Panama 692 miles.

The 3d port of entry is La Union, in the Republic of SALVADOR, distant from Panama 762 miles.

The 4th port of entry is Libertad, in the Republic of SALVADOR, distant from Panama 862 miles.

The 5th port of entry is Acajutla, in the Republic of SALVADOR, distant from Panama 902 miles.

The 6th port of entry is San José de Guatemala, in the Republic of GUATEMALA, distant from Panama 966 miles.

COSTA RICA.

THE Republic of Costa Rica, lying between 8° 30′ and 10° 40′ N. latitude, and 82° and 85° W. longitude, has an area of about 23,000 sq. miles. Population about 150,000, composed of whites of Spanish descent, Indians, Negroes, and Mestizoes, the latter estimated at about one fifth of the whole. Costa Rica is politically divided into five departments, viz., San José, Cartago, Heredia, Alajuela, and Punta Arenas.

The prevailing religion is Roman Catholic. There are about 50 churches in the republic. Protestants are protected from molestation or annoyance on account of their religion by treaties with Great Britain and the United States. Its educational facilities consist of a University, with a government endowment of $46,310, besides one fourth of the receipts of the tobacco monopoly; there are also reported about 80 primary schools in the republic.

The city of San José, the capital of the republic, is situated in the department of the same name, about midway between the Atlantic and Pacific Oceans, on a table-land 4500 feet above their level. It is regularly laid out. The buildings are generally of one story, on account of the frequency of earthquakes. The University is located at San José; there are also a government palace, a hospital, a mint, a national bank, and several churches. The city is connected with Punta Arenas, the sea-port, by a cart-road 70 miles in length. On this road, five leagues from the capital, is the government custom-house, at a place called Garita del Rio Grande.

Punta Arenas, the only available sea-port of the Republic of Costa Rica, is situated on a small peninsula in the Gulf of Nicoya. This peninsula is a low sandy point a little more than four miles in length by from one fourth to a mile in breadth, its highest point about 16 feet above the level of the sea. Upon this the town is situated, and contains about 3000 inhabitants, one tenth of whom are Spanish, the remainder a mixed race of Spanish, Indian, and Negro.

The soil of Costa Rica is exceedingly productive. On

the "tierras calientes," or torrid lands, which run back from the Pacific up to an elevation of 3000 feet, almost all the tropical productions abound. Above these are the "tierras templadas," which are terraces making out from the main Cordilleras (following very nearly the longitudinal axis of the state in a northwest and southeast direction), and are from 3000 to 5000 feet above the level of the sea, producing sugar-cane, potatoes, corn, coffee, oranges, etc., etc., in great perfection.

Still above the tierras templadas are the tierras frias, or frigid lands, which are from 5000 to 6000 feet above the ocean level, among which several volcanoes shoot up, varying from 8000 to 11,000 feet in height. The forests, which extend over a large portion of the republic, abound in timber suitable for ship-building; also mahogany, Brazil, and various other valuable dye-woods.

The cultivated portion of Costa Rica lies principally within the valley of the Rio Grande, which flows down the western slope of the main mountain range into the Gulf of Nicoya. "Fully seven eighths of all the inhabitants are here concentrated, in a district not exceeding fifty miles in length by an average of twenty in breadth."

CLIMATE.

"The topographical features of the country indicate the variety of climate to be found in this state. In the district around the capital the thermometer generally ranges during the forenoon from 65° to 75° of Fahrenheit; from noon until 3 P.M., during the hottest season, sometimes as high as 82° Fahrenheit; during the night, at the coldest periods, never below 57°. Upon both the Atlantic and Pacific coasts the average mean temperature is, of course, much higher, but on the Pacific the thermometer seldom rises above 85° Fahrenheit. The seasons are well defined. On the Pacific the dry season lasts from November to April, and the rainy from April to November. On the Atlantic slope these periods are nearly reversed. Here, too, a much larger amount of rain falls, and the climate is hot and insalubrious."* The Pacific coast has, however, the reputation of being much more healthy, and the table-lands and upland valleys are, for a tropical country, said to be especially salubrious.

The mineral wealth of Costa Rica is almost wholly undeveloped. Mines of gold, copper, iron, lead, and coal have been discovered, but no intelligent efforts have as yet been made to ascertain their value.

The commercial products of Costa Rica are coffee, hides, dye-woods, sarsaparilla, tortoise-shell, pearl-shells, and mahogany. The principal of these, however, is coffee, which is of very fine quality, and scarcely second to the celebrated Mocha. The cultivation of this great staple was introduced in 1829. By 1845 about five millions of pounds were exported; in 1848, ten millions; and in 1850, fourteen millions. Up to the year 1856 the coffee was transported by a tedious and expensive voyage around Cape Horn to European markets. Since the establishment of the Central American Steam-ship Line, in connection with the Panama Railroad, much of the coffee-crop has been exported through this direct channel, and not a small portion has thereby found its way to the United States. Large quantities have been sent to Panama for reshipment on the Pacific mail steamers for the California market. The impetus given by greatly increased facilities and increased demands have, notwithstanding the disturbed political condition of the country, resulted in a growing increase in the number and extent of the coffee estates; and almost solely by means of its coffee trade, from one of the poorest, Costa Rica has become, relatively, one of the richest of the Central American states. The present export of coffee from Costa Rica yearly is estimated

* Squier's Central America.

at over a million of dollars, and, with all its other exports combined, about $1,350,000. Its imports, which are chiefly from Great Britain and the United States, present a total of about $1,200,000 per annum. A bank of discount, deposit, and loans on real estate was established at the capital in 1858, and its notes are the legal currency of the republic. The specie currency is mostly made up of American half eagles, British sovereigns, and French Napoleons: the two former have a fixed value of $5 25, the latter a conventional one of $4 25. The silver currency of the country is the peso = $1, the real = 12½ cents, ½ and ¼ reals.

HARBOR AND COMMERCIAL REGULATIONS.

The harbor at Punta Arenas is separated into two anchorage grounds by the point of land on which the town is located. That between the town and the main land affords accommodation only to vessels under seven feet draught. Those drawing more anchor in the outer harbor, which is protected by two small islands lying to the westward. Goods from thence are brought by lighters to the landing-place in the inner harbor, a distance of about two miles, at a cost of about $1 per ton.

Port Charges for both National and Foreign Vessels.

No anchorage or tonnage dues are imposed.
1. Quarantine fees, 75 cents for each foot of depth.
2. Clearance duty, $3.
3. Hospital dues, 50 cents per head.

No fees are exacted for the landing of passengers or their baggage, and a free permit is granted except when the latter exceeds 2 cwt., when all above that weight is subject to inspection.

All foreign merchandise in packages, when landed, is required to be deposited in the public warehouses for the purpose of registry; and, after being duly entered, may again be withdrawn, the party interested presenting the required certificates. The charge made for the above is 1 real (12½ cents) on each gross cwt.

Merchandise may be deposited on storage for any length of time on payment of ¼ real (6¼ cents) per month per cwt.; subject, however, to existing laws.

Open articles of merchandise, such as iron in bars and unpacked goods, are exempt from registry.

Light-house dues are 6¼ cents per ton.

Any vessel, whether foreign or national, may compromise the hospital and light-house dues for $25 annually, paid in advance.

Municipal and bridge tolls (intended for turnpikes), 37½ cents for each quintal (of 101 pounds).

A fine of $25 is imposed for violation of any one of the above regulations.

There is, besides, a heavy penalty for sealing in packages of powder or tobacco in quantities over 2 cwt.

CUSTOM-HOUSE REGULATIONS OF COSTA RICA (1857).

FREE LIST.

1st. All printed books for instruction or entertainment, if not in opposition to religion and morals; all periodicals and papers.

2d. Foreign music and musical instruments.

3d. Foreign seeds and plants.

4th. Gold and silver in coins and dust.

5th. All kinds of complete machines, and iron wheels with teeth.

6th. Quicksilver, stone coal, pack-thread, empty sacks or sacking materials.

7th. Instruments of art and science.

8th. All kinds of carriages, coaches, cars, etc.

PROHIBITED LIST.

Imports.

1st. Tobacco in leaf or manufactured.

2d. All spirits of molasses or rum, such as is manufactured in Costa Rica; all books and other things offending public morals; eatables of spoiled or bad quality; fire-arms and munitions of war, if not ordered by government.

By a decree bearing date September 21st, 1857, all foreign spirits are placed upon the same footing as gunpowder, rum, and tobacco, which are contraband except when imported on account of the government.

The authorities are required to prosecute and punish those who sell liquor clandestinely, and without previous permission.

The government will cause to be procured, on account of the state, all the various kinds of foreign spirits in common use, in order that the same may be expended in such public places as shall be instituted for this purpose, and the proprietors of hotels and restaurants will purchase at wholesale in those places for the supply of their establishments.

Exports.

Tobacco in leaves or stems, unless by especial permit.

Gold in coin pays at exportation 2 per cent. ad valorem; in ingots, dust, or jewelry, 4 per cent. ad valorem; silver in coin, 8 per cent. ad valorem.*

Coffee pays export duty 12½ cents on 101 pounds, duty paid in 3, 6, or 9 months, according to amount.

All vessels arriving at Punta Arenas having any prohibited articles on board are required to deposit them in a government store-house at a cost of $2 per month for each cwt. (although they may be destined for other ports), or to leave the port within twelve hours.

Coins and Weights.

Coins.—1 peso fuerto, $1; 1 real, 12½ cents.

Weights.—1 quintal = 4 arrobas = 101$\frac{44}{100}$ lbs.; 1 arroba = 25 lbs. 7 oz.; 1 libra = 1$\frac{014}{1000}$ lb.; 1 onza = 1 oz.

Measure.—1 vara, 33½ inches.

Tariff on Articles received in Costa Rica from the United States.

Denomination of Merchandise.	Number, Weight, or Measure.	Rate of Duty.
Bread, ship................................	1.014 lb.	$0 03
Brandy in bottles........................	of sugar-cane,	prohibited.
" " barrels	1.014 gall.	11
Candles, tallow	1.014 lb.	02
" stearine	"	03
Cider	in bbls. of 101 lbs.	1 00
Copper, manufactures of................	101 lbs.	(stills)10 00
Cotton goods, white....................	1.014 lb.	07
" " colored	"	08
Cheese	"	04
Cloths and cassimeres, fine............	"	25
Fish in oil..................................	101 lbs.	2 00
Flour		free.
Gold and silver coin		"
Glass, window............................	101 lbs.	1 50
Hides and skins		not defined.
Indigo	1.014 lb.	03½
Pork, salt..................................	101 lbs.	62½
Printing-presses		free.
Paper, writing............................	101 lbs.	3 00
Rice..		not defined.
Soap, common............................	1.014 lb.	02
Silk, raw....................................	"	20
Shoes, calf-skin, for men................	"	25
" patent-leather....................	"	25
Sheathing, metal	"	06
Spirits in casks	see Brandy.	
Teas	101 lbs.	2 00

* A recent act is reported abolishing the export duties upon gold and silver in coin or bullion, and jewels.

Denomination of Merchandise.	Number, Weight, or Measure.	Rate of Duty.
Tobacco, unmanufactured.......... " manufactured..............	} prohibited.	
Tin, crude.................................	101 lbs.	$2 00
Wines in casks	"	2 00
Wood, manufactured as furniture....	"	5 00

Price Current of Commodities exported to the United States.

Coffee, per cwt., $8 to $10.
Lumber, cedar and mahogany, per M. ft., $45 to $50.
Sarsaparilla, per cwt., $14.

Hides, dry, per cwt., $6 50 to $7.
Turtle-shell, per lb., $4 50
Old copper, per cwt. $15.

Freight to Atlantic States, $25 per ton; California, $20; Lumber to California, $10 to $12 per ton. Terms: Cash on delivery.

Rates of Wages.

Clerks, $500 per annum; engineers, $1000 to $1500; wheelwrights, $5 per day; carpenters, $3 50; blacksmiths, $2 to $3 per day; seamen, $25 per month.

NICARAGUA.

THE Republic of Nicaragua has the states of Honduras and Salvador on the north, and Costa Rica on the south, the Pacific Ocean on the west, and the Caribbean Sea on the east, and lies between 83° 20′ and 87° 30′ west longitude, and 9° 45′ and 15° north latitude, embracing an area of about 48,000 square miles, and is estimated to contain a population of 300,000 souls:*

Whites...	30,000
Negroes...	18,000
Civilized Indians	96,000
Mestizoes..	156,000

This republic, like Costa Rica, is divided administratively into five departments:

---

* The last census, however, taken in 1846, shows only 257,000; but it fell short of the true number, as the people feared it a preliminary step to taxation or conscription.

	Population.
The Oriental (census of 1846)	95,000
" Occidental	90,000
" Meridional	20,000
" Septentrional of Matagalpa	40,000
" " Segovia	12,000

The prevailing religion is Roman Catholic, although all other religious denominations receive the protection of the government.

The educational interests are at a very low ebb. There are reported two universities, one of which has a library of 15,000 volumes. Their course of instruction is said to be extremely defective. The expenses are paid partly by old endowments, and partly by a fee of $12 from each pupil. Besides the universities there are sixty primary schools, with a total of 2800 pupils, and five schools for females in the entire republic.

Its chief city and capital (though not invariably the seat of government) is Leon, in the Occidental department, about a day's journey from Realejo, the Pacific sea-port of the republic. It was, under the ancient Spanish rule, one of the finest cities of Central America, but has greatly declined, though many marks of its former estate remain. It is regularly laid out, the houses usually of one story. The public edifices are numerous and imposing: the great Cathedral of St. Peter covers an entire square, and is said to have cost $5,000,000; besides this there are sixteen churches, two hospitals, and a University. Population about 35,000. The capitals of the different departments are,

	Population.
Rivas, in the Meridional department (census of 1846)	20,000
Granada, in the Oriental "	10,000
Matagalpa, in the Septentrional of Matagalpa	2,000
Segovia, in the Septentrional of Segovia	8,000
Other considerable towns { Massagua	15,000
{ Managua	12,000
{ Granada	10,000
{ Chinandega	11,000
{ Realejo	1,200

Realejo, the principal sea-port town, is situated at the head of an estuary about three miles from the harbor of the same name; the low and swampy coast-lands prevented its establishment at a nearer point. It contains about 1200 inhabitants. The transportation between the harbor and the town is by bongoes and canoes.

TOPOGRAPHY, CLIMATE, AGRICULTURE, AND NATURAL PRODUCTIONS.

The northeastern portion of the republic is mountainous in its character, with a climate of the temperate zone. It abounds in mines of gold, silver, copper, iron, and lead. Precious stones, such as the opal and jasper, have been discovered; also extensive beds of anthracite coal. None of these deposits have yet been effectively worked, on account of the ignorance and indolence of the inhabitants. The great Sierra Madre range (bristling with high volcanic peaks, several of which are active) passes through the western portion of the republic; it is broken, however, by a broad valley, 300 miles in length by 150 in width, which contains the Lakes of Managua and Nicaragua, the latter well known as traversed by the old San Juan transit-route in former times. This valley is made up of fertile slopes, beautiful and productive plains, well adapted to agricultural and grazing purposes, and contains within its limits the chief cities and the greater portion of the inhabitants of the republic. It has a tropical climate. The seasons are divided into the wet and dry, the wet embracing the months from May to November, and the dry the remaining part of the year. The temperature is equable, seldom rising above 90°, or falling below 74°.

The soil is admirably adapted to the growth of all the great staples of the tropics. Indigo, sugar, cacao, tobacco, rice, coffee, cotton, etc., may all be successfully grown, but ignorance, indolence, and political disturbance have so

NATIVE BONGO, PANAMA.

dwarfed the agricultural interests of the republic that at present few articles are raised in amount beyond the immediate necessities of the people. The chief exports are indigo, sugar, cotton, hides, dye-woods, and bullion; small quantities of sarsaparilla, cacao, ginger, gum acacia, gum copal, and caoutchouc are also exported. Crude sulphur is obtained in considerable quantities from the vicinity of the volcanoes, also nitre and sulphate of iron; but the entire exports of the republic do not exceed one million of dollars annually.

The imports in manufactured goods and liquors amount to about half that sum.

From Great Britain are imported calicoes and other manufactured cottons, hardware, lead, gunpowder, etc., etc.; and from the United States, soap, candles, hardware, brandy, gunpowder, etc.

SAN SALVADOR.

THE Republic of San Salvador has Guatemala on the north and west, and Honduras on the east. It is separated from Nicaragua on the southeast by the Bay of Conchagua. It lies between 13° and 14° 10' north latitude, and 87° and 90° west longitude, embracing an area of about 9600 square miles, and is estimated to contain 294,000 inhabitants — Spanish whites, Indians, and mixed races. It is divided into eight departments:

Departments.	Capitals.	Population.
San Miguel	San Miguel	80,000
San Vicente	San Vicente	56,000
La Paz	Sacatecoluca	28,000
Chalaltenango	Chalaltenango }	75,000
Suchitoto	Suchitoto }	
San Salvador	San Salvador	80,000
Sonsonate	Sonsonate }	75,000
Santa Ana	Santa Ana }	

The capital of the republic is San Salvador, situated about twenty-two miles from the port of La Libertad, on the Pacific coast. Formerly it contained about 25,000 inhabitants, having eight or ten fine church edifices, a flourishing University, a female seminary, several hospitals, and the buildings of the general government, and was a place of considerable trade; but in 1854 it was almost totally destroyed by an earthquake, when it was deserted by many of its inhabitants, and the seat of government transferred to Cojutepeque, twelve leagues distant. San Salvador is now in process of rebuilding, its inhabitants having mostly returned, and it promises speedily to regain its former condition.

TOPOGRAPHY.

San Salvador has a coast-line on the Pacific 160 miles in length, along which, for the most part, lies a belt of low alluvial land, varying in breadth from ten to twenty miles; back of this is a broad plateau, about 2000 feet above the ocean level, and along which numerous high volcanic peaks arise. Farther beyond is a broad and beautiful valley, from twenty to thirty miles in width, and over one hundred in length, drained by the Lempa (a large river, navigable for vessels of light draught for upward of 100 miles, and emptying into the Pacific). The northern border of the state rises up into a range of mountains, which separates it from Honduras. In the eastern and western portions are also well-watered valleys of great beauty and considerable extent.

The soil of the mountain slopes, the valleys, and the coast alluvions is fertile and productive in the highest degree, and well adapted to the growth of the tropical staples. Cotton is cultivated to some extent along the coast, and with good results. The chief productions, however, are indigo, sugar, tobacco, balsam, cacao, maize, and frijoles. The usual fruits of the tropical and several of the temperate zones are abundant. Indigo is the chief article of export. Under the Spanish rule this product was exported to the amount of over $3,000,000 per annum, but since the independence of the state, owing to intestine wars and political disturbances, but little more than $1,000,000 per annum has been produced. A district along the coast, between the ports of La Libertad and Acajutla, called "Costa del Balsimo," produces an article known commercially as the "balsam of Peru." It is collected solely by the aboriginal Indians who inhabit that district. About 20,000 pounds (valued at 50 cts. per pound) are obtained for annual export.

The mineral productions of San Salvador are not extensive. It has, however, in the northeastern part of the state, valuable mines of silver and gold. Iron of a very superior quality is abundant. Vast deposits of coal are also said to exist there.

In general, the inhabitants of Salvador have more intelligence and industry than those of the previously-described states of Central America. Their government is more liberal, and the rights of person and property are more respected, and the privileges extended to foreigners are greater than those above mentioned. Under a treaty negotiated by Mr. Squier, United States minister to Salvador in 1850, all the rights, privileges, and immunities of the citizens of Salvador in commerce, navigation, mining, holding and transferring property, are extended to the citizens of the United States in that republic.

"The commerce of San Salvador is chiefly carried on through means of fairs established by the government in the districts best suited for the exhibition of the products of the state. The principal fairs are held at Chalaltenango, San Vicente, and San Miguel. The two former take place on the first of November of each year; the latter, called

'Fair of La Paz,' on the 21st of the same month. It lasts about two weeks, and is far the most important of any held iu the country. It attracts buyers and sellers not only from all parts of Central America, but from nearly every part of the Pacific coast, as well as from England, Germany, France, and the United States. England sends calicoes, shirtings, drills, linens, hosiery, cutlery, iron, and steel; France, silks, cambrics, wine, and spirits; the United States, coarse cottons, sperm-oil, and hardware; Spain, paper, wine, oil, and spirits; Germany, glass, hardware, and toys; Italy, oil, preserves, and liquors; Chili and Peru, hats, hammocks, pellons, etc. About the only product given in exchange for them is the staple of the state, indigo. A second fair, called 'Ceniza,' takes place in San Miguel about the beginning of February. To both of these fairs large numbers of cattle are brought from Honduras and Nicaragua. In 1857 the number amounted to 17,844, averaging in value from $5 to $8 each."* The amount and value of the imports and exports of the state may be estimated from the following table:

Years.	Imports.	Exports.
1854	$1,015,925	$ 786,711
1855	698,219	765,824
1856	1,046,720	1,285,485
1857	860,104	1,304,102

TARIFF REGULATIONS.

Import Duties of San Salvador on Articles received from the United States. Rate of Duty 24 per cent. ad valorem.

Denomination of Merchandise.	Number, Weight, or Measure.	Rate of Duty.
Bread, ship	101 lbs.	$3 00
Brandy in bottles	dozen,	2 50
" in barrels	gallon,	1 00
Candles, tallow		prohibited.
" stearine	1.014 lb.	30
Cider in bottles	dozen,	2 00
Copper, manufactures of	101 lbs.	25 to 37 cts.
Cotton goods, white	yard,	12
" colored	"	12

* Squier's Central America.

Denomination of Merchandise.	Number, Weight, or Measure.	Rate of Duty.
Cheese	25 lbs. 7 oz.	$4 00
Cloths and cassimeres, fine	yard,	1 00
Fish in oil	101 lbs.	4 00
Flour	barrel,	4 00
Gold and silver coin		free.
Glass, window	dozen panes,	38 cts. to $1.
Hides and skins	dozen,	$12 to $24.
Indigo		not defined.
Pork, salt	101 lbs.	5 00
Printing-presses		free.
Paper, writing	ream,	2 00
Rice	25 lbs. 7 oz.	3 00
Soap, common	101 lbs.	8 00
Silk, raw		not defined.
Shoes, calf-skin, for men	dozen,	$6 to $18.
" patent-leather	"	"

HARBORS.

San Salvador has three ports of entry:

1st. That of *La Union*, at the southeastern extremity of the state, in the Bay of Fonseca. This possesses an excellent and extensive anchorage-ground, from three to twelve fathoms deep, free from shoals, and nearly ten miles in diameter. It is surrounded on three sides by high lands, and its entrance is protected by a number of islands. It is decidedly the best harbor in Central America. Its waters abound in fine fish and excellent oysters.

2d. *La Libertad*, 100 miles from La Union, is an open roadstead. It is connected with the city of San Salvador by a cart-road 26 miles in length.

3d. *Acajutla*, 40 miles from La Libertad, is also a roadstead. It is protected from all winds except from the southwest; but there is frequently a heavy swell prevailing, which often renders the landing difficult. It is connected by a good road with Sonsonate (chief city of one of the richest districts in the state), 12 miles distant.

COMMERCIAL REGULATIONS.

All vessels of the United States, no matter whence they may have come or how laden, are to be treated in all the ports of San Salvador, as to all duties of tonnage, lighthouse, or any other charges of whatsoever denomination or character, as national vessels. From this equality the coasting-trade is excepted, which is reserved to the national flag; but should any favors of navigation be hereafter granted to any other foreign nation, it will immediately apply to the United States.

Imports into San Salvador in vessels of the United States, no matter whence imported or of what origin, to be subject to the same duties, charges, and fees of every description as similar imports in vessels of San Salvador; and if these imports consist of articles the growth, produce, or manufacture of the United States, to be subject to no higher or other duties than other similar imports the growth, produce, or manufacture of any other foreign nation.

PORT CHARGES.

All sea-going vessels, without distinction of burden or flag, pay $17, in full of tonnage and other port dues. There are no pilots.

GUATEMALA.

THE State of Guatemala, lying between latitude 14° and 18° north, and longitude 89° and 93° west, is bounded north by the Mexican provinces of Tobasco, Chiapas, and Yucatan, east by the British establishment of Honduras, south by the states of Honduras and Salvador, and west by the Pacific Ocean, and embraces an area of 43,380 square miles. It is estimated to contain about 907,500 inhabitants, made up of between 7000 and 8000 whites (principally of Spanish descent), 150,000 Ladinos, or mixed bloods, and 750,000 Indians.

The Pacific coast-line of Guatemala is about 250 miles in

length, trending northwest, and is bordered by a strip of alluvial land from twenty to thirty miles in width, broken, however, by occasional spurs from the coast-range of mountains by which it is bounded, and which, spreading out into broad table-lands, form the greater portion of the surface of the state. These great plateaux in the southern part have an elevation of from 2000 to 5000 feet, gradually attaining a still greater height toward the northeastern part, where they are more than 8000 feet above the ocean level. They are frequently separated by deeply-cut and extensive valleys of great fertility. Toward the eastern boundary they subside into the low lands bordering the coast of the Bay of Honduras. Along the Pacific several volcanic peaks arise, the highest of which is more than 14,000 feet above the level of the sea.

There are several lakes in the interior, the largest of which, that of Atitlan, in the department of Solola, is said to be thirty miles in length by ten or fifteen in breadth, and no less than 1800 feet in depth.

There are also numerous rivers in the state. These, for the most part, flow into the Bay of Honduras or the Gulf of Mexico. The rivers emptying into the Pacific are small and few. None have much importance in a commercial point of view.

CLIMATE.

The climate of Guatemala varies greatly with its varying elevations, from the tropical heat of the coast-lands and lower valleys, through the intermediate spring-like temperature of the interior plateaux and higher valleys, to the cold and sometimes almost wintry climate of the most elevated table-lands and mountains. The plateau on which the capital is situated is in the interior, about 90 miles from the Pacific coast. There the average maximum temperature throughout the year is 88.7° Fahrenheit, and the average minimum is 38.9°. The average mean is 65°. The average temperature of the coast-lands is probably between 80° and 85° Fahr., but data do not exist for exact calculation of this. On the highest table-lands and mountains in the northeastern part, ice and snow are not uncommon in certain seasons of the year. Here the productions of the temperate zones abound. Wheat of a superior quality is produced, and sheep are raised extensively. The wool-crop for 1857 was 1,500,000 pounds, but, from the lack of roads, the expense of getting these products to market bars their being raised for exportation. Cattle-raising is also carried on to a considerable extent. On the lower plateaus and valleys coffee, cochineal, tobacco, sugar-cane, and indigo are luxuriantly grown, also the vegetables and fruits of both tropical and temperate zones. On the low coast-lands cotton and rice flourish. The chief staple production of the state is the cochineal insect. The yearly produce of this is variable, on account of various contingencies to which it is subject. The crop in 1849 was 1,469,100 lbs.; in 1851, 1,231,610 lbs.; in 1852, 567,000 lbs.; in 1853, 312,700 lbs.; in 1854, 1,757,300 lbs.; in 1855, 1,204,510 lbs. It is nevertheless abundantly profitable, as its cultivators aver that if one crop is successfully gathered out of three raised, the receipts from its sale repay for the entire labor and capital expended on the whole. Cacao, silk, dye-woods, balsam, various gums, and many other minor articles, are produced to some extent.

The mineral productions of Guatemala are not extensive. Deposits of gold, silver, copper, lead, and iron exist. Some have been worked with considerable profit, but the mining interest is greatly neglected.

The seasons are divided into the wet and dry, the former commencing at about the middle of May, and continuing until the middle or end of October; the dry season then sets in, and lasts for the remainder of the year.

POLITICAL DIVISIONS.

Guatemala is divided into seven departments, those of Guatemala, Solola, and Quezaltenango extending along the Pacific coast; Sacatepequez and Totonicapam in the interior; Vera Paz, the largest of all, in the northern part; and Chiquimula in the eastern. The chief towns are:

In the Department of Guatemala—Guatemala City; Escuintla, population 6000; Amatitlan, population 15,000; and Jalpatagua.

In the Department of Solola—Solola; Atitlan; Masatenango.

In the Department of Quezaltenango—Quezaltenango, population 25,000; San Marcos; Tejutla; Tapachula.

In the Department of Sacatepequez—Old Guatemala (or Antigua), population 20,000; Chimaltenango; Patsun.

In the Department of Totonicapam—Totonicapam, population 15,000; Momostenango; Gueguetenango; Jacaltenango.

In the Department of Vera Paz—Salama; Rabinal; Copan, population 14,000; Cajabon, population 4000.

In the Department of Chiquimula—Chiquimula, population 6000; Zacapa, population 5000; Gualan, population 4000; Casaguastlan; Esquipulas, population 1800; besides many other large towns.

Guatemala City, the capital of the state, is 90 miles distant from San José, the sea-port of the Pacific coast, and 220 from Izabal, on the Atlantic, and has a population of about 40,000. It is beautifully situated on a broad tableland 4372 feet above the ocean level. The volcanoes of Agua and Fuego, 12,000 and 14,000 feet in height, tower up on the northern side 40 miles distant; the other sides present low mountains and hills in beautiful variety. The climate is one of perpetual spring, the thermometer averaging 65° Fahrenheit, and perfectly salubrious. It is regularly laid out in a quadrilateral form, with its sides facing the cardinal points; the streets are forty feet broad, crossing each other at right angles. The main plaza is 150 yards square, the east side occupied by the Cathedral, the palace of the archbishop, and other buildings of the Church authorities; on the west is the government house, offices, etc., of the government officials; on the north, the cabildo, or town-hall, prison, etc.; and on the south a range of stores of various kinds. In the middle of the square is a fountain, elaborately and artistically sculptured of gray stone, furnishing an abundant supply of water; besides this, in each of the seven or eight lesser squares are fountains well supplied with water, which is brought to the city by two aqueducts a distance of five and six miles. The dwellings are all of one story. There are twenty-six churches, some of large size, with elegantly ornamented interiors; to several are attached monasteries and convents; a University, two colleges, one public and several private elemental schools, three hospitals, one alms-house, two theatres (one of which, just finished, is a large and elaborate Corinthian building, said to have cost $200,000), and a large amphitheatre for bull-fights.

CHARACTER OF THE INHABITANTS.

The Indians are the cultivators of the lands, and are, in general, industrious and peaceable; some are owners of estates, but the landholders are principally whites. The mixed bloods are mostly mechanics and petty traders. As a people the Guatemaltecos are courteous, affable, and hospitable to strangers.

The prevailing religion is the Roman Catholic, and there are few countries in the world where the exercises and ceremonials of that Church are more universally and elaborately practiced.

THE PORTS OF GUATEMALA.

The commerce of Guatemala previous to the establishment of the Panama Railroad Company's line of steamers on the Pacific coast of Central America was almost entirely carried on through the port of Izabal, on the Atlantic. This port is inaccessible except to vessels of very light draught. It is over 200 miles from the capital (surrounding and to the westward of which the great proportion of the staples of the country are principally produced), and is reached by mule-paths, through a mountainous and uninhabited region, with great labor and expense. It is now, however, rapidly losing its importance, on account of the more accessible port of San José, on the Pacific, through which much of the commerce of the state is already carried on. San José lies in latitude 18° 56' north, and longitude 90° 42' west. It is an open roadstead. The coast is very clear, running east and west. The anchorage is about three quarters of a mile from shore, in eleven to fifteen fathoms of water. The swell breaks very heavily upon the shore, and out as far as forty or fifty fathoms, making it necessary to use a girt-line for landing and leaving. The currents are very strong, and vary with each change of the moon, the variations sometimes taking place within the short period of six hours. From November to February the landing is easy. In March the ebb and flow of the tide extends from 90 to 100 yards, and at the flood tide the surf is so heavy as to dash up the beach a distance of 100 to 120 yards; after March the sea is again calm until July, and from July to December it is again rough, and the landing difficult. An iron screw-piled pier is now, however, in process of construction at this place by the government of Guatemala (if it is not already finished), which will extend from the shore to a point beyond the breakers, thus enabling the transportation between ship and shore to be performed at every season of the year with facility and safety.

The town of San José has a population of between two and three hundred. Supplies for vessels are, however, procured with much difficulty here, unless provision be previously made to obtain them from Escuintla, a town forty miles distant, on the road to the capital. There are no means at this port for refitting or repairing vessels at present. The modes of conveyance from the port of San José to the interior are by mules and stages, and the arrangements are convenient and ample. Diligences for the transportation of passengers are in waiting on the arrival of the Panama Railroad Company's steamers for conveyance to the capital, 90 miles distant, and the intermediate points, and the roads throughout the dry season are excellent. In the wet season the journey from San José to Escuintla is performed on mules, owing to the deep mud on the low land to that place; from thence to Guatemala City the diligence is in operation throughout the year.

A small trade is carried on through the minor ports of Santa Tomas on the Atlantic and San Luis on the Pacific.

HARBOR REGULATIONS.

"Every vessel which shall anchor in the ports of this republic, no matter whence it may come, shall pay a tonnage duty of two reals (25 cents) for each ton of measurement. This measurement shall be ascertained from the register, the certificate of nationality, the patent or clearance under which it sails."

"*Shall be free of tonnage duty:* 1st. Small vessels engaged in transporting merchandise from one port to another of the republic; 2d. Vessels which shall anchor in ballast to take in water, provisions, or fruits of the country, provided they discharge no cargoes; 3d. Vessels of war, and regular mail or steam packets, provided they do not discharge merchandise over twenty tons; 4th. Merchant vessels which, exceeding 150 tons measurement, discharge not exceeding twenty tons of merchandise; 5th. Vessels which receive on board for exportation produce of the country, excepting *cochineal.*" Cochineal pays an export duty of five reals on each ceroon to the Church.

TARIFF REGULATIONS OF GUATEMALA.

PROHIBITED LIST.

Guns, muskets, and all other arms for military purposes; munitions of war, as lead, balls, gunpowder, and rifles; prints, cuts, pictures, etc., bearing against public morals and religion; books, manuscripts, etc., especially interdicted.

FREE LIST.

Anchors, cable, rigging, and all other articles belonging to ships' material not comprehended in the tariff; quicksilver, barometers, fire-engines, staves and heading of all kinds; scientific instruments and agricultural implements; books, music, maps, and geographical charts; machines and steam-engines; gold and silver coins; barrels, hogsheads, etc., etc., for exporting the products of the country.

Duties on Articles received from the United States.

Denomination of Merchandise.	Number, Weight, or Measure.	Rate of Duty.
Bread, ship	arroba of 25 lbs. 7 oz.	$0 50
Brandy in bottles	dozen,	72
" in barrels	15 to 18 gallons,	3 44
Candles, tallow	1.014 lb.	03
" stearine	"	05
Cider	dozen bottles,	05
Copper, manufactures of	1.014 lb.	12½
Cotton goods, white	yard,	02¼
" colored	"	03
Cheese	101 lbs.	2 88
Cloths, cassimeres, fine	yard,	78
Fish in oil	1.014 lb.	04½
Flour	25 lbs. 7 oz.	25
Gold and silver coin		free.
Glass, window	box of from 137 to 150 lbs.	3 60
Hides and skins	1.014 lb.	12
Indigo	"	2 00
Pork, salt	25 lbs. 7 oz.	48
Printing-presses		free.
Paper, writing	ream,	25
Rice	25 lbs. 7 oz.	24
Soap, common	"	72
Silk, raw	1.014 lb.	72
Shoes, calf-skin, for men	pair,	04
" patent-leather	"	57
Sheathing, metal	1.014 lb.	08
Spirit in casks	12 to 15 gallons,	3 44
Teas	1.014 lb.	18
Tobacco, unmanufactured	24 per cent. on the invoice value, with an addition of 20 per cent. on the aggregate amount.	
Tin, crude	101 lbs.	5 00
Wines in casks	12 to 15 gallons,	2 16
Wood, manufactured as furniture	40 per cent. ad val.	

IMPORTS AND EXPORTS.

The official statement of the imports into Guatemala for the year 1860 shows the amount to have been $1,495,191; exports, $1,870,631. Imports from Great Britain, $802,305; France, $295,651; Germany, $108,649; the United States, $50,235; Spain, $47,702; and small amounts from various other countries. Of the exports about two thirds were of cochineal, the remainder consisting of ores, sugar, coffee, sarsaparilla, dye-woods, and hides. The following comparative statement will show the increase of trade since the establishment of the Central American Steam-ship Line in 1856:

	Value.		Value.
Ores exported in 1855	$6,600;	in 1860	$92,575
Sarsaparilla exported in 1855	1,890;	"	13,800
Dye-woods " "	5,000;	"	27,672
Hides " "	26,000;	"	76,582
Sugar " "	none;	"	52,377
Coffee " "	none;	"	15,352

The coffee of Guatemala is of very fine quality, and promises soon to become a prominent article of export.

By a contract between the government of Guatemala and the Panama Railroad Company, a drawback of ten per cent. on tariff rates is allowed on all merchandise passing over the Panama Railroad en route for that state.

Rates of wages are much the same as in Costa Rica (p. 196). Laborers on estates receive from 1½ to 2 reals per day.

HONDURAS.

The Republic of Honduras has Nicaragua on the south, the Bay of Honduras and the Caribbean Sea on the north and east, Guatemala on the north and west, and San Salvador on the south and west. It lies between latitude 13° 10' and 16° north, and longitude 83° 11' and 89° 30' west, and contains an area of about 42,000 square miles, with an estimated population of 350,000. In its mineral resources Honduras ranks first among the Central American States; mines of gold, silver, lead, copper, and iron are abundant, but the inhabitants, mostly Indian, have done comparatively little toward developing their wealth. All the productions of the tropics flourish in Honduras, among which mahogany, dye-woods, sarsaparilla, and tobacco form the chief articles of export. Besides these, bullion, cattle,* hides, and tortoise-shell comprise the chief exports, the total estimated at $1,125,000 per annum, most of which formerly passed through its Atlantic ports Omoa and Truxillo. Since the establishment of the Panama Railroad line of Central American steamers, a large proportion of the trade has found its way out of the country through the port of La Union, State of Salvador, which is at the junction of three states on the Pacific. Its only sea-port on the Pacific is Amapala, on Tigre Island, a few miles distant from La Union. It is not, however, a port of entry for the Panama Railroad steamers.

The imports of Honduras, which consist chiefly of provisions, coarse cottons, and miscellaneous merchandise, may

* About 20,000 head of cattle are annually driven from Honduras to the great fair at San Miguel, Salvador.

be roughly estimated at $1,000,000 per annum, chiefly from Great Britain. The great obstacle to the development of Honduras is the want of roads, the interior transportation being wholly effected by means of mules.

The business returns of the Panama Railroad Steam-ship Company from Honduras are included in those of Salvador.

REPUBLICS OF SOUTH AMERICA

CONNECTED WITH THE PANAMA RAILROAD.

NEW GRANADA.

NEW GRANADA, the most northerly, as well as the most important of the South American republics, is situated mostly between the equator and 12° north latitude, and between 70° and 83° west longitude, containing an estimated area of 480,000 square miles. Its greatest length is about 800 miles, and its greatest breadth about 600. It is bounded on the north by the Caribbean Sea, on the east by the Republic of Venezuela, on the southeast by Brazilian Guiana, on the south by the Republic of Ecuador, and on the west by the Pacific Ocean. Along the western portion, the Andes, divided into three great chains, pass in a northeast and southwest direction through the republic. To the east of the most eastern chain the country is spread out into vast llanos or plains, about 300 feet above the ocean level, gradually descending to the River Orinoco, one of its eastern boundaries. These immense plains are said to be unfit for cultivation, but large herds of cattle and horses are raised upon them. The wet season on the llanos lasts from November till April, and the dry the remainder of the year. The average annual temperature is 80° Fahrenheit; the wet season averages about 8° hotter than the dry. This section is principally watered by the tributaries of the River Orinoco.

Upon the sides and summits of the Cordilleras are vast table-lands, varying in climate and productions with their elevation, and embracing every grade of temperature, from that of the torrid zone to the regions of perpetual snow and ice, and, with the exception of the snowy regions, these plains are said to be remarkably fertile, producing in great abundance.and perfection the fruits and agricultural staples of every zone. Between the mountain ranges are broad and beautiful valleys: that of Magdalena between the eastern and central ranges, and Cauca and Atrato between the central and western. These valleys are drained each by large navigable rivers of the same names. In the territories comprehended between the eastern and western Andes there are two wet and two dry seasons, the wet coming on at the approach of the equinoxes, and the dry at that of the solstices; each continues about ninety days.

The northeastern portion of the republic, bordering the Atlantic, is low and unhealthy, but of great fertility. At the northwestern portion the Cordilleras become depressed, and frequently disconnected, forming the low hill and valley country of the Isthmus, where, like the northeast portion, the climate is hot, and, in the lower lands, insalubrious, but richly productive. The seasons in these portions of the republic are divided into the dry and rainy, each occupying about six months of the year.

The population of New Granada, which has increased greatly during the past few years, is now estimated at 2,747,500, of whom 1,648,519 are said to be whites, mostly of Spanish descent; 188,166 pure Indian; 97,583 Negro; 366,332 Mulattoes and Samboes; 451,900 of different races mixed with Indian.

The Republic of New Granada is politically divided into eight states, viz.:

	Population.	Capitals.
Panama	168,500	Panama.
Cauca	404,000	Popayan.
Cundinamarca	635,000	Bogotá.
Boyaca	465,000	Tunja.
Santander	463,000	Bucaramanga.
Magdalena	89,900	Santa Martha.
Bolivar	222,100	Carthagena.
Antioquia	300,000	Medellin.

Agriculture holds the first place in the industrial interests of New Granada. Rice, cotton, coffee, tobacco, cocoa, sugar, and the tropical fruits are the principal cultivated productions of the low valleys and coast-lands, which also produce spontaneously caoutchouc, vanilla, anise, balsams, dye and cabinet woods, ivory-nuts, Peruvian bark, etc. The elevated valleys and plains yield wheat, maize, and almost all the other products of the temperate zone. The cultivation of the soil is, however, very rudely and indifferently managed, and the reclaimed lands bear a very small proportion to the whole.

The manufacturing interests of the republic are also in a very low condition, and consist of little more than coarse woolen and cotton cloths, earthen-ware, and cigars for the use of the lower classes, and the straw hats known in commerce as Panama hats.

The mineral productions of the republic are gold, silver, and platinum; it also possesses valuable mines of emeralds and of salt; but the mining interest is sadly neglected, being mostly left to the lower classes. Turtle-shell and pearls of fine quality are procured in considerable abundance. The entire annual exports are estimated as follows:

Gold	$5,000,000	Cacao	$200,000
Platinum, silver ore, and emeralds	1,000,000	Caoutchouc, maize, cotton, ivory-nuts, anise, rice, balsam, etc.	200,000
Pearls and turtle-shell	800,000		
Tobacco	3,500,000	Sugar, flour, preserves, rough woolen and cotton cloths, brandies, etc.	50,000
Straw hats	1,400,000		
Peruvian bark	600,000		
Coffee	600,000		
Hides	500,000		$14,350,000
Dye and building woods	500,000		

M

Education in New Granada is at a low ebb, though, nominally, liberal provisions for public instruction are made by the government. By law a free public school is established in every parish throughout the republic; in all there are said to be 800 public schools, and 60 high-schools and colleges, and 47 printing-offices.*

The capital of the republic is Bogotá, in the State of Cundinamarca, in lat. 4° 36' 6" north, and long. 74° 10' west, which is situated on a broad plateau 8655 feet above the level of the sea. It is regularly laid out, the houses mostly built of sun-dried bricks, and of two stories, and is amply supplied with water. It contains twenty-four churches, one fine cathedral, a national college, with a library of 33,000 volumes in fourteen different languages, mostly ancient, an observatory, eleven high-schools, besides a seminary, and two public schools in each ward (eight), fourteen hospitals, three lazarettos (both the schools and hospitals are very indifferent), seven printing-offices, three lithographic offices, a fine theatre, one manufactory of woolen cloths, and one of earthen-ware. It has a good market, supplied with fruits and vegetables of both the temperate and tropical zones. Population 60,000. The city of Bogotá is distant from the nearest sea-port on the Atlantic (Carthagena) about 700 miles, and from Buenaventura, on the Pacific, 800. From Carthagena the route is up the Magdalena River by steam-boats to Honda, 700 miles distant, and from thence 100 miles to Bogotá by mules: this is the usual route for merchandise and passengers from foreign ports to the capital. That from Buenaventura is long, difficult, and expensive, much of the distance over the Cordilleras having to be accomplished on mules or the backs of the natives. The roads throughout the republic are very bad.

* The foregoing statistics of population, exports, etc., were made out from official data kindly furnished by Señor Raphael Pombo, Secretary of New Granadian Legation.

The rivers of New Granada are numerous and important. The rivers Rio Negro, Caqueta, and Putumayo connect the eastern and southeastern portions of the republic with the Amazon. The Guaviare, the Meta, and their affluents, connect the east and southeast with the Orinoco. The Orinoco and the Amazon are connected at the boundary of New Granada with Venezuela by the Rio Cassequiare. Commercially, the most important rivers are the Magdalena and its tributary, the Cauca, each over 1000 miles in length, and crossing almost the whole of the most fertile and productive portion of the republic from south to north. The Magdalena empties by three mouths into the Atlantic, and is navigated by steam-boats for 700 miles of its length. It is through this river and the Cauca that the principal part of the interior commerce of the country is carried on. At its western mouth is the port of Sabanilla. It also communicates with the port of Carthagena by a dike or connected chain of lagoons 92 miles in length, and navigated by boats and small steamers.

The Rio Atrato, in the State of Antioquia, is about 300 miles in length, and is navigable for small vessels for about 150 miles. It empties into the Gulf of Darien. Besides these, emptying into the Atlantic, are the Chagres, in the State of Panama, and several other small rivers at present of little commercial importance. Emptying into the Pacific are the rivers Patia and San Juan, draining rich and extensive regions in the State of Cauca.

The principal sea-ports of the republic of New Granada are Rio Hacha and Santa Martha in the State of Magdalena, Sabanilla and Carthagena in Bolivar, and Aspinwall in the State of Panama, on the Atlantic coast; and Panama in Panama, and Buenaventura and Tumaco in the State of Cauca, on the Pacific.

Rio Hacha is an open roadstead. Vessels have to anchor one and a quarter miles from shore, at which distance large vessels can ride. Cargoes are landed by means of bongoes or canoes. This can only be done between 8 A.M. and 2 P.M., on account of northeast winds, which prevail almost all the year. The landing of cargoes is best effected during the summer season.

The aspect of the town is very pleasing, as most of it is of recent construction. Its business is principally with the interior, through the Indians of La Goajira. Its principal exports are divi divi, dye-woods, hides, skins, and mules. Population between 3000 and 4000.

Santa Martha, 90 miles southwest from Rio Hacha, has a good harbor, with the exception of being exposed to the northeast winds. Vessels are laden and unladen at the wharves. Merchandise is shipped from this port in large decked boats up the Magdalena River, from the mouth of which it is distant about 40 miles. Besides the staples of the country, from this place are exported considerable numbers of horses, mules, and cattle to Jamaica and other West India islands. It ranks as one of the first ports of New Granada.

The city of Santa Martha is the capital of the State of Magdalena. There is a good hospital, a college, and a printing-office here. Population 4340.

Sabanilla, at the western mouth of the Magdalena River, is a roadstead. On account of a bad bar at the mouth of the Magdalena, goods have to be transhipped for their transportation up the river. The town is low and unhealthy. The residences of the principal merchants are at Baranquilla, twelve miles interior.

Carthagena is the finest port and harbor and the chief naval arsenal of New Granada, and is connected with the Magdalena by the canal before mentioned, navigated by steamers of light draught. It is the principal depôt for the products of the provinces watered by the Magdalena and Cauca Rivers, and exports sugar, cotton, coffee, tobacco, hides, specie, bullion, Peruvian bark, anise, balsams, dye-woods, etc., etc. The port is defended by two forts, and is the only port of New Granada on the Atlantic which has facilities for the repair of vessels. Vessels are laden and unladen by means of flat-boats and bongoes. The town is well fortified and well laid out, the houses mostly of stone. It has a massive citadel, several churches, a college, various seminaries, and two hospitals. Population 10,000. There is a charity hospital at Carthagena, where sick American seamen are admitted at a charge of 40 cents per diem; accommodations very indifferent. The usual charge for storage of dry goods is about one per cent. on gross sales; drayage from wharf to store, 28 to 30 cents per ton; boat for landing, cartage to wharf, and storing at custom-house, about 11 cents per barrel. From the United States to this port are imported flour, codfish, hams, butter, cheese, glass-ware, earthen-ware, iron-mongery, pitch, tar, rosin, cordage, copper, and a great variety of articles from France, Spain, Italy, and Germany.

The ships of the Royal Mail Steam Packet Company, plying between Southampton, the West Indies, and the east coast of South and Central America, stop here monthly with mails, passengers, and freight. See Itinerary of said Company, p. 189, et seq.

Aspinwall, the Atlantic terminus of the Panama Railroad, in the harbor of Navy Bay, is a free port. The shelter here for shipping is extensive, and the anchorage good. Nothing obstructs the entrance to the harbor for vessels of the largest draught. No pilots are required. The wharf and storage accommodations are ample. Reference to connections of Panama Railroad, page 148, will give the principal maritime movements of this port. Harbor regulations, freight, wharfage, storage, light dues, etc., etc., will be found on page 143, et seq.

Panama is a free port. This port derives its importance

from being the Pacific terminus of the Panama Railroad. It is situated in the Bay of Panama, latitude 8° 56' north, longitude 79° 37' west. Its harbor is protected by a group of islands of considerable extent, distant about two and a half miles from the place of embarkation. The nearest secure anchorage for vessels of heavy draught is distant from shore one and three quarters of a mile, on account of coral reefs which extend for that distance out into the bay. The average tides at this point have a rise and fall of twelve feet,* and transportation between ship and shore is carried on at from one half to high tide by means of small steamers and large iron-decked launches, which discharge at the wharves of the Panama Railroad Company. Storms are unknown in the harbor of Panama, and the transportation between ship and shore is performed at every season with perfect ease and safety. The group of islands before mentioned furnishes the rendezvous for the vessels of the Pacific Mail and Panama Railroad Steam-ship Companies. About nine miles to the southeast of the harbor is the beautiful and productive island of Toboga, at which place is the rendezvous of the British Pacific Steam Navigation Company. At this place facilities are afforded for the repair of vessels

*	Table of the Tides on the		
	Pacific at Panama.		Atlantic at Aspinwall.
	May and June.	Nov. and Dec.	Aug. and Sept.
	Feet.	Feet.	Feet.
Greatest rise of tide.....................	17.72	21.30	1.60
Least " "	7.94	9.70	0.63
Average " "	12.08	14.10	1.16
Mean tide of Pacific above mean tide of Atlantic........................	0.759	0.140	
High spring tide of Pacific above high spring tide of Atlantic	9.40	10.12	
Low spring tide of Pacific below low spring tide of Atlantic........	6.55	9.40	
Mean high tide of Pacific above mean high tide of Atlantic.......	6.25	6.73	
Mean low tide of Pacific below mean low tide of Atlantic.........	4.73	5.26	
Average rise of spring tides..........	14.08	17.30	
" " neap tides	9.60	12.40	

of the heaviest draught by means of a "gridiron," which is rented at reasonable rates to vessels of all nations. There is also at Toboga a large machine-shop, where repairs for the largest varieties of machinery are effected at moderate charges. No pilots are required in the harbor of Panama. Fresh provisions and water are furnished to shipping in abundance, and at moderate rates.

Labor is cheap and easily procured; wages from eight to ten reals per day.

The city of Panama is a place of considerable commercial importance. Several mercantile houses of large capital are established here, which collect from the interior and the North and South Pacific coasts the various staple productions of South and Central America for exportation over the Panama Railroad to the United States and Europe, and receive from thence large quantities of merchandise for the use of the interior towns and different ports in the Pacific. For the maritime commercial movements of this port, see connections of Panama Railroad, page 148. Population of the city of Panama, 10,000.

About sixty miles southeast from the port of Panama is the group of islands called "Islas de las Perlas," or Islands of Pearls, where a pearl-fishery is carried on, producing about $100,000 worth of a fine quality of pearls per annum.

Besides Panama, on the Pacific coast of New Granada, are the ports of Buenaventura and Tumaco, in the State of Cauca, from which are exported Peruvian bark, cocoa, tobacco, hides, etc., to Panama, principally by the vessels of the Pacific Steam Navigation Company, which touch at each bi-monthly. The trade of these ports is chiefly with Panama, receiving from thence merchandise from the United States and Europe suitable to the demands of the country.

PORT REGULATIONS.

The port regulations of the Republic of New Granada are such as are deemed necessary, as well in view of the general convenience and safety of vessels as to answer proper police and harbor discipline.

There are no quarantine regulations at any of the ports of New Granada, and, consequently, no bills of health are required. Tonnage dues, port dues, pilotage, and visit fees are the same in all the ports of the republic, with the exception of the free ports of Aspinwall and Panama. Every vessel pays $6 40 for the visit of the captain of the port, and $11 pilotage in and out, besides $1 60 for an interpreter.

Every vessel pays 40 cents per New Granadian ton for her capacity for the first 100 tons, and 20 cents for every ton over the same. There are no light dues, except at the port of Aspinwall, where light fees are charged by the Panama Railroad Company (see p. 145). The river navigation of New Granada is free to flags of all nations, with the exception of vessels propelled by steam, the monopoly of which last is granted to certain individuals under contract with the government.

Tariff of New Granada on Articles received from the United States—1855.

Under this tariff weights and measures are, 1 pound = 1.014 pound; 100 pounds = 4 arrobas; 100 pounds = 101¼ pounds avoirdupois; 1 vara = 33½ English inches; 1 quintal = 101.44 pounds; 1 kilogramme = 2⅕ pounds; 1 miriagramme = 26 lbs. 9 oz. 10 pwt.

Money.—1 peso = 8 reals = 100 cents = $1.*

Denomination of Merchandise.	Number, Weight, or Measure.	Rate of Duty.
Beef..		free.
Beer, ale, porter, in bottles.............	1.014 lb.	$0 00¾
" " " in casks.............	"	0 00¾
Brandy in bottles............................	1 kilogramme, or 2⅕ lbs.	0 16
" in casks.............................	"	0 16
Candles, wax..................................	2⅕ lbs.	0 40

* The French decimal system of weights, measures, and currency has been recently adopted by the New Granadian government.

NEW GRANADA.

Denomination of Merchandise.	Number, Weight, or Measure.	Rate of Duty.
Candles, spermaceti	2½ lbs.	$0 20
Cheese of all kinds	"	0 02
Cider in bottles	same as beer.	
" in casks	"	
Codfish		free.
Copper, manufactures of	2½ lbs.	0 15
" in bars		free.
Cotton, raw	no importation.	
" manufactures of	2½ lbs.	0 40
Flour, wheat		free.
Glass, window	box of from 100 to 125 lbs.	2 40
Hams and bacon		free.
Hats, straw	dozen,	0 60
Household furniture	chairs, dozen,	6 00
" "	1 lounge,	12 50
" "	1 table,	5 00
Indian corn		free.
Lard		"
Lead in bars and sheets	1 miriagram. 26 lbs. 9 oz.	0 32
" manufactures of	2½ lbs.	0 05
Nails, iron	26 lbs. 9 oz.	0 48
Oils, whale and other fish	1.014 lb.	0 06¼
Pitch	"	0 00½
Paper, writing	ream,	0 40
" printing		free.
Paints	2½ lbs.	0 12
Pork		free.
Rice		"
Rosin	"	0 00½
Soap, common	26 lbs. 9 oz.	0 72
" perfumed	2½ lbs.	0 50
Shoes and boots, leather	10 per cent. additional to the duty on leather.	
Sugar, refined	1.014 lb.	0 02¾
Tallow	101 lbs.	2 00
Tar	26 lbs. 9 oz.	0 08
Teas	2½ lbs.	0 20
Tobacco, unmanufactured	"	0 20
" cigars, Havana	"	0 80
" " others	"	0 80
Umbrellas, silk	each,	0 60
" cotton	dozen,	2 00
Wax, raw, white	2½ lbs.	0 20
" " yellow	"	0 20
Wood, boards, pine		free.
" shingles		"
Wines, red	2½ lbs.	0 06
" white	"	0 10

Goods imported into the Isthmus of Panama, although a part of the New Granadian Republic, are exempt from duty; but if imported from the Isthmus into New Granada, they are charged the regular duties as if coming from foreign countries.

FREE LIST.

Animals for breed; beaver and other skins; bee-hives and bees; books, printed; carts; casks; coal; gold, silver, and platina, in dust; implements for agriculture and mining; scientific and surgical instruments; medals; mills; paintings and engravings; paper for printing; plants; seeds; statues and busts; steam-engines; wool; effects of embassadors, and equipage of travelers.

PROHIBITED LIST.

Arms; obscene books and prints; coin, defaced or clipped; rum; tobacco, raw.

Coasting trade free to foreign vessels.

By virtue of the tariff act which came into force in New Granada, June 25, 1856, an increase of duty from 25 to 100 per cent. was imposed on nearly every article of import, presenting an exception to the tariff modifications of almost every other commercial country for years past. The percentage increase of rates on the principal articles of merchandise, by virtue of this act, on the rates previously levied, has been noted as follows, fractions being disregarded:

On the following articles the increase is 25 per cent.: steel, not manufactured; needles and fish-hooks of certain descriptions; indigo; sugar-candy; phials; cocoa, manufactured; cocoanuts; padlocks of iron or brass; candlesticks of glass or crystal; brushes for the teeth, nails, etc.; locks; beer; copper in sheets; glasses, small, for liquors, cut or not; knives for shoemakers, etc.; spurs, cast iron; chisels; bottles; large forge bellows; carbine hooks; buckles of metal; watchmakers' tools; common lead-pencils; china-ware, small articles; mirrors of certain sizes; hammers of all kinds; mills, small, and coffee-mills, etc.; razors; brown paper; Jamaica pepper; pipes of clay, for smoking; dishes of glass or crystal; lead in pigs, plates, balls, and shot; metallic pens; reins for bridles; castors for tables, etc.; tallow or stearine; ink in powder, paste, or liquid; glasses, watch, magnifying, etc.

On the following articles the increase is 26 per cent.: spirits from cane and its compounds, in those provinces in which this article is not a monopoly; spirits of turpentine; scented waters of all kinds; iron wire; white lead in powder or oil; raw cotton in bulk and in seed; trunks with merchandise; bottles and demijohns; brooches for clasps, etc.; shoe-brushes, etc.; copper in bars or cakes; compasses; fine penknives; spoons of tin, iron, copper, etc.; large knives, and knives of ivory, etc., and balance-handle knives with forks; thimbles; snuffers; screw-drivers; fowling-pieces; mirrors with gilt frames; tin, pewter, etc., in bars or cakes; felts for hats; nails, brads, etc.; liquor cases; saddle-trees; toilet soap; sealing-wax; files;

linen manufactures, common; mustard; mainsprings for clocks and watches; paper, writing, hanging, etc.; umbrellas of silk of all sizes; pincers of all sorts; pistols, common; earthen pitchers, jars, etc.; salt-cellars of glass or crystal; saws, pit and frame; scissors, small, etc.; turpentine; zinc, manufactures of.

On the following articles the increase is 27 per cent.: cruet-stands; needles of wire, bone, etc.; silver, brass, and piano wire; door-bolts, small; carpeting in pieces; cotton manufactures; curry-combs of iron; plate-holders; pin-cases; chandeliers of glass or metal; harness for two beasts; trunks without merchandise; scales; bridle-bits; copper pumps for engines; silk brocade; wax candles; bedsteads; sofas; sieves of wire, silk, etc.; clothes-brushes, etc.; cranks of iron; clothes-presses; watch-guards; swords; small looking-glasses; iron pickaxes; stirrups; pianos; flasks; decanters; small buckles for braces, etc.; whips; lawn; lace; fringes, etc., of linen; porcelain; manufactures of German silver; saddles; dial-plates; razors in cases; organs; gilt paper-hangings; cotton umbrellas; pistols; powder-flasks; bottle-stands; watches; manufactures of silk of all kinds; fine scissors; gold braid; window-glass.

On a certain description of needles, packing, sailmakers', etc., the increase is 100 per cent.; on irons for carpenters' planes, etc., and small hand-bellows, 150; on fine gold wire, 154; and on sperm-oil, manufactured, 160 per cent.

There is a decrease of duty on buttons of from 40 to 80 per cent.; on chairs, of 68; augers, 36; common glass bottles, 40; gloves of buckskin, etc., 54 and 52; stirrup-leathers, 37; and on a few other unimportant articles.

ECUADOR.

THE Republic of Ecuador, joining that of New Granada on the south, is situated between latitude 1° 35' north and 5° 50' south, and has its name from its position under the equator. Its eastern boundary is formed by a portion of New Granada, Brazil, and Peru; its southern by Peru, and its western by the Pacific Ocean. Estimated area 250,000 square miles.

The three ranges of the Andes pass through the extent of the western part of the republic from north to south. As in New Granada, they abound in high fertile valleys and elevated plains of great productiveness and salubrity; they also shoot up into frequent lofty volcanic peaks, many of which are in active eruption: 17 of these have an average height of over 16,000 feet each, while several others range from 17,000 to 21,000 feet, their summits covered with perpetual snow. The lower valleys and plains yield all the staples and fruits of the tropics, while the higher produce the grains and fruits of the temperate zone, and afford the finest pasturage for numerous herds of cattle, horses, sheep, lamas, guanacos, and vicunas. Here the Peruvian bark, sarsaparilla, balsam of tolu, vanilla, canella, copaiva, gentian, and many other medicinal productions, are indigenous. There are also vast tracts of wooded lands, producing the finest timber for ship-building and cabinet-work, besides many excellent varieties of dye-woods, and numerous fibrous plants suitable for the manufacture of hats, cordage, cloth, paper, etc.

The mineral productions of Ecuador are gold, silver, mercury, iron, tin, lead, copper, antimony, manganese, sulphur, and salt.

Gold is abundant in the sands of almost all the rivers. From not being properly or efficiently worked, the produce from the mining interest of Ecuador is inconsiderable.

The navigable rivers of Ecuador are numerous. Flowing into the Pacific are the Esmeralda, the Rio Guayaquil and its tributary the Daule (emptying into a gulf of the same name), and the Tumbez, forming a part of the southern boundary, all of considerable importance, draining rich and productive districts, and affording for a considerable portion of their extent an easy passage for the productions of the Pacific slope to the coast. Flowing westward into the valley of the Amazon and uniting with that river are the Putumayo, navigable for the greater part of its extent; the Napo, navigable for steam-boats for 550 miles; the Tigre for 230 miles; and the Santiago, 400 for steam-boats, and

120 more for smaller vessels. The Amazon, which forms a large portion of the southern boundary of the republic, is navigable for large vessels as far as the River Tigre (about midway of the southern boundary), making the navigable portion of that river in Ecuador about 350 miles for steamboats, and nearly 300 farther for rafts or balsas.

The climate of Ecuador varies with the situation of different portions; that along the Pacific coast is decidedly tropical and insalubrious; but as the slopes of the Andes are ascended, the temperature is decreased, until, reaching the valleys and plains at a height of nine or ten thousand feet, a perpetual spring prevails. The valley of Quito, in which the capital is located, is said to possess the most equable and delightful climate in the world, having a temperature varying from 56° to 62° Fahrenheit.

The year is divided into two seasons. In the elevated lands the winter commences in December and lasts until May, and is a season of clear skies, with a delightful temperature; the summer begins in June and ends in November: during this season high winds prevail. In the low land the temperature is hot and moist, and in the winter incessant rains prevail.

The population of Ecuador is estimated at about 800,000, composed of

Whites of European descent	351,672
Indians, descendants of the "Quiches"	274,440
Indians of the Orient	135,000
Negroes	7,831
Mixed races	31,057
	800,000

The whites are the principal landholders, traders, etc. The Quiches are mostly mechanics and agriculturists.

The Indians of the Orient are wild, and warlike, and uncivilized.

The prevailing religion is Roman Catholic, and the open profession of no other is tolerated, but foreigners are not molested on account of their religious faith. Education is at a low ebb.

The chief city and capital is Quito, and is situated 9453 feet above the level of the sea, in a valley of the same name, 150 miles from Guayaquil, the chief sea-port. It is well built, and has several handsome squares, in one of which are the cathedral, the town hall, and palaces of the archbishop, etc. There are also in this city many churches and convents, a work-house, an orphan asylum, a university, and a large hospital. It has manufactories of coarse cotton and woolen goods, lace, hosiery, jewelry, etc., and a large trade in corn and other agricultural produce, which, with some of its manufactured goods, are sent by way of Guayaquil to Central America in return for indigo, iron, steel, and to Peru in return for brandy, wine, oil, and precious metals, etc. There is said to be much wealth among its inhabitants. The markets are well supplied. Population 50,000.

The chief sea-ports and harbors of Ecuador are Guayaquil, Manta, and Esmeralda.

Guayaquil, the principal port, is situated at the head of a bay of the same name, and at the mouth of the River Guayaquil, 50 miles from the sea. The harbor is excellent, and affords great facilities for ship-building, excellent timber being found within a few rods of the river, where building-yards of capacity for the largest ships have been constructed. The city consists of the old and the new town, and is intersected by five small creeks which are crossed by wooden bridges. The houses are mostly of wood. The principal edifices are a cathedral, several churches, two hospitals, and two colleges. The city is defended by three forts. It is unhealthy, with a mild, humid climate: mean annual temperature 88° Fahr. Population 22,000. Guayaquil is an important entrepôt for the trade between Lima and Quito.

The ports of Manta and Esmeralda are chiefly ports of export for silver ore and the produce of the country surrounding. The towns are of small size and of but little importance. The regular ships of the Pacific Steam Navigation Company touch at Guayaquil on the 13th and 28th of each month, and a special steamer plies monthly between Guayaquil and Panama, touching at the ports of Manta and Guayaquil (see Itinerary, page 215). In 1856 the foreign exports by the ports of Manta and Guayaquil were $2,833,141 50, of which $67,562 12 was silver and silver ore. The exports across the country to New Granada were about $300,000, and to Peru $100,000. The imports for the same year were, through the port of Guayaquil, $2,874,439 38; through Manta, $112,267 39; from New Granada, $40,000; and from Peru, 100,000.

The chief exports consist of silver and silver ore, cacao, sombreros (or Panama hats), tobacco, cascarilla, sarsaparilla, agave fibre, tamarinds, caoutchouc, canes, coffee, hammocks, etc.; the imports, textiles of cotton, wool, flax, and silk, wine, spirits, flour, hardware, paper, furniture, musical instruments, etc., etc.

Port Regulations at Guayaquil.—There are no quarantine regulations. Tonnage dues, 25 cts.; light money, $6\frac{1}{4}$ cts.; hospital, 50 cts. per day. Vessels lie in the stream, and are loaded or discharged by means of rafts, $4 to $5 per load.

The commercial charge for storage is 1 per cent. Merchandise is carried on by porters, who charge from 10 to 50 cents, according to bulk.

Passengers, on landing, are obliged to present themselves at the police-office, where their passports are examined. Their baggage is examined at the custom-house, and no fees are exacted with the exception of those for a new passport on leaving the country.

The currency is the same as in Mexico.

Coin.—1 peso=100 cents=$1 00.
Weights.—1 quintal=4 arrobas of 25 lb. 7 oz.
Measures.—1 vara=$33\frac{1}{2}$ inches English.

Tariff on Articles received in Ecuador from the United States—1856.

FREE LIST.

Printed books and music, maps, ships' materials, fresh fruits, vegetables, fire-engines, surgical and mathematical instruments, agricultural implements, tools of emigrants, useful machines, inventions, etc.

Denomination of Merchandise.	Number, Weight, or Measure.	Rate of Duty.
Alcohol	gallon,	$1 50
Beef	quintal (101 lbs.),	2 00
Beer, ale, porter, in bottles	dozen,	75
" " " in casks	gallon,	25
Brandy in bottles	dozen,	2 00
" in casks	gallon,	50
Cables and cordage	101 lbs.	37½
Candles, wax	1.014 lb.	18¾
" tallow	"	03
" spermaceti	"	06¼
Cheese of all kinds	101 lbs.	2 00
Cider in bottles	dozen,	1 00
" in casks	gallon,	25
Codfish	101 lbs.	3 00
Copper, manufactures of	1.014 lb.	06¼
" in bars	101 lbs.	2 50
Cotton, raw	"	50
" manufactures of	yard,	(drills) 02¼
Flour, wheat	barrel, about 200 lbs.	6 00
Glass, window	box of 100 feet square,	1 00
Hams and bacon	101 lbs.	50
Hats, straw	each, for ladies,	2 00
Household furniture	1 table,	4 50
Indian corn	101 lbs.	1 00
Lard	"	4 50
Lead in bars and sheets	"	1 00
" manufactures of	"	1 50
Nails, iron	"	1 00
Oil, whale and other fish	gallon,	05
Paper, writing	ream,	25
" printing	"	75
Paints	101 lbs.	2 00
Pitch	"	30
Pork	"	2 00
Rice	"	3 00
Rosin	"	20
Shoes, boots, leather	1 pair,	1 50
Soap, common	101 lbs.	1 50
" perfumed	dozen cakes,	12½ cts. to 25
Sugar, refined	101 lbs.	4 00
Tallow	"	2 00
Tar	"	25
Teas*	1.014 lb.	18¾
Tobacco, unmanufactured	101 lbs.	10 00
" cigars, Havana	1000,	5 00

* Teas, when imported direct from the place of production in American or equalized vessels, are *free*.

Denomination of Merchandise.	Number, Weight, or Measure.	Rate of Duty.
Umbrellas, silk........................	one,	$1 00
" cotton......................	dozen,	2 00
Wax, raw, white.......................	101 lbs.	9 00
" yellow...........................	"	9 00
Wines, red.............................	gallon,	15
" white............................	"	15
Wood, boards, pine..................	1 foot,	02
" shingles	1000,	3 86

The duties are to be paid within 10 days when they amount to $100; within 30 when from $100 to $500; within 45 from $500 to $2000; within 75 from $2000 to $6000; 100 from $6000 to $12,000; over $12,000, 150 days. Besides the duties small sums are levied as toll tax.

Export duties: gold, $\frac{1}{2}$ per cent. ad valorem; silver, 1 per cent.; manglewurzel, 50 cents per 100 lbs.; straw for hats, 10 per cent. ad valorem.

PERU.

THE Republic of Peru, between latitude 3° 25' and 21° 48' south, and longitude 68° and 81° 20' west, embraces an area of 520,000 square miles, and had, by the census of 1852, a population of 2,106,492. Peru is bounded on the north by Ecuador, on the east by Brazil and Bolivia, on the south by Bolivia and the Pacific, and on the west by the Pacific Ocean, and has a coast-line on the Pacific of 1240 miles.

The double cordillera of the Andes traverses Peru from northeast to southwest, separating it into three regions. The central has an elevation of about 12,000 feet; the eastern forms a part of the great plain of South America; and the western, between the Andes and the Pacific, has a breadth of from 60 to 70 miles. The Andes and their branches are estimated to occupy about 200,000 square miles of the surface of Peru. The whole of the coast region is arid and barren; the upland or central region abounds in fertile valleys and plains. To the east of the mountains the country is covered with vast forests, which have as yet been but imperfectly explored. Between the coast regions and the mountains are numerous valleys and plains of great fertility, where tobacco, sugar, maize, cotton, indigo, cocoa, cochineal, and various tropical fruits are produced, besides the copaiva, vanilla, balsams, etc., and valuable cabinet woods, which are indigenous. Here rain rarely falls, but fogs and dews are frequent. In the central region the grains of Europe are successfully cultivated, and the finest pasturage for sheep and cattle is abundant. The lama, alpaca, guanaco, and vicuna are natives of this region, where they abound in great numbers; their wool, especially that of the alpaca, is said to be the finest in the world except the Cashmere, and forms an important article of export. Here also are found the cinchona-trees, from which the Peruvian barks of commerce are obtained.

The mineral wealth of Peru is very great: gold, silver, copper, tin, iron, and saltpetre are found in abundance; the region between the mountain ranges is especially rich in mineral products.

A very great source of wealth to Peru is its deposits of guano, which occur on the islands of Chincha and Lobos along its coast. These were estimated in 1842 to contain no less than 46,632,000 tons, valued at $20 per ton; the annual consumption was then assumed to be about 300,000 tons.

Peru is politically divided into eleven departments and two littoral provinces, as follows, from north to south:

Departments.	Population.	Capitals.
Amazonas	43,074	Chachapoyas.
Libertad	266,553	Truxillo.
Ancach	219,145	Huaras.
Junin	222,949	Cerro de Pasco.
Lima	259,801	Lima.
Huancavelica	70,117	Huancavelica.

Departments.	Population.	Capitals.
Ayacucho	132,921	Huamanga.
Cuzco	349,718	Cuzco.
Puno	285,661	Puno.
Arequipa	119,336	Arequipa.
Moquega	61,432	Tacna.
Province littoral de Callao	8,453	
" " " Piura	76,332	
Total	2,106,492	

The population consists of Spaniards, native Indians, Negroes, and the mixed races resulting therefrom: whites about 400,000; Indians, 1,000,000; the remainder Negroes and mixed bloods.

Education in Peru is in a very low condition, though there are many Lancastrian schools in the republic, where the elemental branches are taught. At Lima, the capital, there is a University and several colleges, but they are poor and thinly attended. "Superior education is confined to a very few among the whites, and the ornamental almost universally takes the precedence of useful instruction. There are at the capital some good libraries and a medical college."

"The established religion is Roman Catholic, though other denominations are now tolerated. The clergy are said to be careless of their duty and lax in their morals."

Agriculture is in a very primitive state. Manufactures are also in a backward condition, principally confined to ponchos, or loose cloaks (some of which are of great fineness and beauty), coarse blankets, mats, hats, cordage, and the beautiful filigree silver-work for which the interior of Peru is celebrated.

Lima, the capital of Peru, is situated on a beautiful and extensive plain 560 feet above the ocean, and from Callao, its sea-port, distant about eight and a half miles. It is about two miles in length, about the same in breadth, and is surrounded by massive brick walls. The River Rimac flows through the city, and is crossed by a fine stone bridge 530 feet in length. The streets are regularly laid out, the houses low, and built of sun-dried bricks. The grand plaza is about 500 feet square, in the centre of which is a handsome stone fountain, surmounted by a bronze statue; besides this there are about thirty other open squares in the city. There are two foundling asylums and eleven public hospitals, one of which has 600 beds. The city contains fifty-seven churches, sixteen nunneries, and twenty-five chapels, many of which are rich in decorations of gold and jewels. The church of the Dominican convent is 300 feet in length by 80 in breadth, and has a steeple 180 feet in height. The convent of St. Francis covers two whole squares, and has magnificent cloisters. Lima has a University, numerous primary and two high schools, also three Latin schools, and four colleges. There are two theatres, an amphitheatre for cock-fighting, and another for bull-fights capable of accommodating 12,000 spectators. The manufactures, which are very limited, consist of gold lace and fringes, glass, cotton cloth, cigars, chocolate, and paper. Its population is about 100,000, one fourth of whom are white, one fourth Negroes, and the remainder Indians and mixed races. The climate of Lima is delightfully mild and equable, ranging from 60°. to 80° Fahrenheit. Rain is extremely rare. The communication between Lima and Callao, its sea-port, is by a railway eight and a half miles in length, built in 1850–51 by English engineers, with materials brought from England. There is another railway running from Lima to Chorillas, a favorite bathing-place on the coast, nine miles distant. The country in the vicinity of Lima is exceedingly pleasing and fertile, producing all the fruits and vegetables of the temperate zone in abundance. Earthquakes occasionally occur, but are usually so slight that they rarely create alarm.

The chief sea-ports of Peru are Payta, San José, Huanchaco, Callao, Islay, Arica, and Iquique. These are the ports of entry for foreign commerce, and are called "*los pu-*

erto mayores," or major ports. There are, besides these, open to the coasting trade and for the exportation of the products of the country, the minor ports of Ylo, Chala, Pisco, Huacho, Casma, Pacasmayo, and Tumbez, and the small harbors of Sechura, Samano, Santo, Supe, Huarmes, Echinique, Chancay, Ancon, Cerro Azul, Chincha, Cancato, Nasca, Quilca, Cototea, Morro de Sama, and Pisaque.

The steam-ships of the Pacific Steam Navigation Company touch at all the principal and at most of the minor ports of Peru (see Itinerary, p. 215, et seq.).

The chief staple of export from Peru is guano; crude wools, bar silver, copper, and tin, Peruvian bark, nitrate of soda, are exported in considerable quantities. The average annual value of exports, in round numbers, is $12,000,000. The chief imports are textiles of silk, linen, cotton, wool, gold and silver ornaments, fruits, provisions, timber, furniture, wines, and liquors. The average annual value of imports, in round numbers, is $9,500,000. Of this the United States imports to Peru about $500,000 per annum, and exports about $2,000,000.

The chief trade of Peru is with Great Britain.

PORTS.

The principal sea-port of Peru is Callao. The town is badly built, and contains about 7000 inhabitants. It is connected with Lima, the capital, by a good carriage-road and a single-track railway, which last is used almost exclusively for passengers. Callao possesses good shelter for shipping. Vessels lie at anchor in the harbor and discharge their cargoes by lighters and launches. There is a circular mole into which the launches go to be unloaded by cranes and winches upon a railroad track, which takes all goods to the custom-house, where they are deposited in the public stores for an indefinite time, under fixed rates of storage, from three to twelve cents a package per month.

The general features of commercial transactions at Callao, and at the ports of Peru generally, are set forth in a communication of a late date from the consul of the United States at that port as follows: "The most valuable articles imported into this consulate are assorted merchandise from England, France, Italy, and the United States, Chili, Spain, and Ecuador, viz., cottons, linens, silks, wines, hardware, etc.; from the United States, domestic cottons, furniture, lumber, provisions, etc. The export trade of Peru consists chiefly of guano, which is sent to England, the United States, France, and Spain, and in smaller quantities to Italy, India, and the West Indies. Crude wools are largely exported, but the high duty on them in the United States throws nearly all that trade into Europe, mostly to England, where wool is duty free. The same remark also applies to the barks of Peru and to copper. The bar silver all goes to England, because there is no *direct* steam navigation with the United States. Nitrate of soda is largely exported—at least 600,000 quintals annually, valued at $2 per 100 pounds; much of this goes to the United States. Dry and salted hides and straw hats are exported in small quantities."

Pisco, a port for exportation, about 100 miles south of Callao. A railway has been projected to connect this port with "Yca," a city in the interior, distant about 40 miles; this, when completed, will bring to the sea the products of a very rich agricultural district.

Arica, a major port, through which a large business for Bolivia is transacted, and the outlet of a large mining district. A railway was constructed in 1854–5 for an English company from Arica to Tacna, a distance of 40 miles, by Walton W. Evans, Esq., an American engineer. Six and a half per cent. on $2,000,000 was guaranteed by the government of Peru. This road overcomes an elevation of 1800 feet in its course. Over it large quantities of goods are carried to Bolivia. From the interior of Bolivia, coffee, tin, and copper barilla are brought over it to Arica for exportation; besides this, all of the calisaya bark and alpaca wool known to trade finds its way to the sea through the same channel.

Iquique.—From this port immense quantities of nitrate of soda (saltpetre) are shipped to the United States and England, said in amount to exceed 30,000 tons annually. Out of a population of 15,000, more than four fifths are engaged in this trade. A railroad is projected from this port to "Terrapaca," the centre of the saltpetre region, distant from the sea-coast about fifty miles: this road, when completed, will greatly increase the trade.

There are no navigable rivers in Peru; the interior transportation is effected principally by means of mules.

There are no pilots (the nature of the ports rendering them unnecessary), no quarantine system, no light-houses, no hospital fees in Peru. There are no facilities for the repair of ships in Peru.

Tonnage dues in the ports of Peru are 25 cents per ton. Port charges, exclusive of tonnage, amount to about $25 at Callao, and $40 at Payta.

Passengers are allowed to land at all the ports of Peru as soon as the captain of the port has made his visit on board. No passports are required on arriving, but they are usually required on leaving Peru, and cost $3 at the offices of the local authorities. Passengers take their baggage on shore with them, or on board of vessels in the port; the inspector examines the luggage on the wharf. No fees are exacted.

CURRENCY.

The circulating currency, representing silver, and now the only money in common use in Peru, is below the nominal standard about 52 per cent. The rate of exchange fluctuates from five to fifteen per cent. on the dollar. The dollar of Peru in invoices of export to the United States is usually valued at from 80 to 85 cents of United States currency. The Peruvian dollar of pure silver (not in circulation) is worth about 87½ cents United States currency. Gold coins of Peru are not now in common use. Patriot doubloons pass current at $17, and of late are worth three per cent. premium, and but few to be obtained.

TARIFF REGULATIONS.

The tariff is that of November 25th, 1854, modified by a decree of May 1st, 1855.

Money.—1 peso = 100 cents = $1.

Weights and Measures.—1 quintal = 4 arrobas of 25 lbs. 7 oz. each = 100 libras = 101.45 lbs.; 1 pound = 1.014 lb. English.

FREE LIST.

Principal articles: tar; live animals; quicksilver; iron chains and cables; salted pork and beef in barrels; stone coal; geographical charts; lumber for house-building; cooking apparatus for vessels; scientific collections and objects of curiosity; staves and heading of all kinds; oakum; fresh fruits; printing-presses; scientific instruments of all kinds; cordage and tow; bricks; iron bars; timber for ship-building; hops; machines for agricultural and mining purposes; printed music; sheathing copper in sheets; seeds of all sorts.

If imported through the ports of Iquique, Arica, or Islay: fresh or salted meat; barley; beans; lard; lentils; and Indian corn.

In the port of Iquique, foreign goods in national vessels, if consisting of iron nails, steel, wood, tallow, and articles of food (flour excepted), pay only one half the ordinary duty. Empty sacks, gunny cloth, yarn for making bags, wood and stone coals, are free under all flags.

PROHIBITED LIST.

Gunpowder; all kinds of fire-arms and munitions of war; books offending public morals, and eatables of bad quality.

All merchandise imported direct from Europe, Asia, or North America, through the larger ports of the republic, are permitted to pay 10 per cent. of the total amount of duties levied in government bonds. Gold and silver in bullion or coin are exempt from export duty.

Tariff on Articles imported into Peru from the United States.

Denomination of Merchandise.	Number, Weight, or Measure.	Fixed Value on.	Percentage on fixed Value.
Beef	101 lbs.	$6 50	$0 03
Beer, ale, and porter, in bottles	dozen,	specific duty,	1 50
" " " in casks..	gallon,	"	0 25
Brandy in bottles	dozen, over 30°,	"	1 50
" in casks	gallon, "	"	1 50
" "	gallon, under 30°,	"	1 00
Cables and cordage		free.	
Candles, tallow	1.014 lb.	specific duty,	0 12½
" spermaceti	"	"	0 12½
Cheese of all kinds	101 lbs.	"	4 00
Cider in bottles	dozen,	"	1 50
" in casks	gallon,	"	0 25
Codfish	101 lbs.	$5 00	0 10
Copper, manufactures of	1.014 lb.	0 37	0 15
" in sheets		free.	
Cotton, raw	101 lbs.	$4 00	0 01
" manufactures of	fustian, dozen,	6 00	0 15
Flour, wheat	101 lbs.	specific duty,	2 00
Glass, window		valuation,	0 25
Hams and bacon	1.014 lb.	20 cts.	0 03
Hats, straw		free.	
" other kinds		valuation,	0 30
Household furniture		"	0 30
Indian corn	101 lbs.	$1 50	0 20
Lard	"	specific duty,	1 00
Lead in bars and sheets	"	free.	
" manufactures of	"	$7 00	0 20
Nails, iron	"	5 50	0 06
Oil, whale and other fish	gallon,	0 35	0 20
Paints, common	101 lbs.	7 00	0 20
" fine, in pots	dozen,	0 75	0 20
Paper, writing		valuation,	0 20
" printing	for music,	"	0 10
Pitch		free.	
Pork, salted		"	
Rice		specific duty,	2 00
Rosin	barrel,	$4 00	free.
Shoes and boots, leather	dozen,	8 00	0 30
Soap, perfumed	101 lbs.	25 00	0 20
Sugar, refined	arroba 25 lbs. 7 oz.	specific duty,	0 30
Tallow	101 lbs.	"	1 50
Tar	barrel,	$4 00	free.
Teas*	1.014 lb.	specific duty,	0 18¾
Tobacco, unmanufactured	101 lbs.	"	20 00
" cigars, Havana	1.014 lb.	"	0 62½
" " others	"	"	0 62½
Umbrellas, silk	dozen,	$40 00	0 20
" cotton	"	10 00	0 20
Wax, raw, white	101 lbs.	50 00	0 20
" " yellow	"	30 00	0 20

* Teas of all kinds, when imported direct from the place of production in American or equalized vessels, are free of duty.

Denomination of Merchandise.	Number, Weight, or Measure.	Fixed Value on.	Percentage on fixed Value.
Wines, red............................	dozen bottles,	specific duty,	$1 50
" white........................	"	"	1 50
Wood, boards, pine................		free.	
" shingles......................		"	

BOLIVIA.

This republic extends from 10° 30' to 25° south latitude, and from 57° 50' to 71° 30' west longitude, with an area of 473,298 square miles. Its greatest length is estimated at about 1000 miles, and its greatest breadth at 800. It has about 250 miles of sea-coast. Population, according to latest authorities, 1,425,758. Bolivia, in the general characteristics of its topography, soil, climate, productions, and inhabitants, does not differ materially from Peru, already described. Its facilities for internal navigation on the east of the Cordilleras are very great through the River Marmore and its affluents, whose waters flow into the Amazon, and the Pilcomayo, whose waters empty into the Paraguay, thereby affording communication with the Atlantic Ocean. The very liberal inducement offered to foreigners by the government of Bolivia for navigating these rivers and settling her rich and extensive eastern plains promise, at no distant day, to aid in developing her vast resources. By a decree promulgated by President Belzu in January, 1853, navigation through the above-named rivers was declared free and their ports free to all nations; a bounty of $10,000 to be awarded to the first steamer reaching any of her river ports from the Atlantic, and from one to twelve leagues square of Bolivian territory to the individuals or companies who, sailing from the Atlantic, shall arrive at any of the river ports and desire to found near them agricultural or industrial establishments. The commerce of Bolivia is carried on through its only available sea-port, Cobija, and through the port of Arica in Peru. All of the alpaca wool and calisaya bark known to commerce is produced in Bolivia, and finds its way to the market across the narrow strip of Peruvian territory which separates Bolivia from the Pacific at Arica. Deposits of guano exist along the coast, and form a considerable article of export. The mineral productions of Bolivia are similar to those of Peru. Its silver mines are world-famed, though from inefficient working their produce has of late years greatly declined; at present the export of silver and gold amounts only to about $1,400,000 per annum. The entire exports are estimated at $4,000,000 per annum. The imports by Cobija amount to about $500,000 per annum, and the internal traffic with Peru and Chili to about $1,500,000. Manufactures are carried on on a small scale: woolen and cotton cloths, hats made from the vicuna wool, tin-ware, and fire-arms, are the chief.

Agriculture is in low condition. Cocoa, cotton, rice, indigo, coffee, sugar, ginger, and tobacco, all of excellent quality, are cultivated.

Cobija, or "*Puerto del Mar*," the only legal sea-port of Bolivia, is a small town with a population of 2000. The harbor is bad, and the transportation of merchandise from this place to the interior, performed by means of mules, is difficult and expensive, from which cause most of the trade of Bolivia is carried on through the Peruvian port Arica. The steam-ships of the British Pacific Steam Navigation Company touch at Cobija four times a month on their upward and downward voyages (see Itinerary, page 215).

PORT CHARGES.

There are no pilots or wharves, but it is necessary to pay mole and tonnage dues—rates not ascertained. Passengers, before entering Bolivia, are required to have passports.

Money, weights, and measures, the same as in Peru.

TARIFF ON IMPORTS INTRODUCED INTO BOLIVIA

By way of Arica. Ad val.
- Clothing, and men's boots and shoes.................................30 pr. ct.
- Perfumery, clocks, playing-cards, cigars, women's shoes, caps, and bonnets, iron and brass bedsteads, sofas, mirrors, lamps, candlesticks, and all other articles not enumerated in this class....20 pr. ct.
- Woolens, silks, and linens.....15 "
- All cotton goods except tucuyas or cotton shirtings ......12 "
- Tucuyas ....40 "
- Earthen-ware, glass-ware, and writing-paper.................. 8 "
- Silver and gold plate, jewelry, and watches....................16 "
- Books..........................12 "
- Quicksilver, musical instruments (except guitars), agricultural implements, and for the arts and trades, free.
- Liquors and wines pay duty to Peru, as if intended for consumption there.

By way of Cobija. Ad val.
- Clothing, and men's boots and shoes, saddles, hats, tucuyas.20 pr. ct.
- All kinds of wines, liquors, etc. 18 "
- Perfumery, clocks, playing-cards, cigars, women's shoes, caps, and bonnets, iron and brass bedsteads, sofas, mirrors, lamps, candlesticks, chandeliers, gold and silver lace, all kinds of haberdashery, and all other articles not enumerated in this class.10 pr. ct.
- Cotton goods, except tucuyas. 5 "
- Earthen-ware, glass-ware, writing-paper, silver or gold plate, jewelry, and watches.. 3 "
- Quicksilver, iron not manufactured or wrought for manufactures, musical instruments (except guitars), implements of agriculture, the arts, and trades, carriages and printing-presses, types, etc., printed books (except the 2 per cent. on the library), free.

Specific Duties on Imports both by Arica and Cobija.

Description of Goods.	Quantities.	Rates.	Description of Goods.	Quantities.	Rates.
Alforgas (saddle-bags)...............	pair,	$2 50	Galloons............	ounce,	$0 50
Sugar................	arroba,	50	Caps of fur.........	each,	1 00
Boots................	dozen,	6 00	Caps of silk or straw	"	1 50
Bootees for men.....	"	4 00	Caps for children..	"	50
" " women.	"	1 50	Horseshoes	dozen,	4 00
Trunks..............	pair,	5 00	Toys of all kinds...	box,	15 00
Nails................	pound,	12½	Picklocks	dozen,	1 50
Locks and keys.....	dozen,	1 50	Trunks of hide.....	pair,	2 00
Cigars	1000,	2 00	Gunpowder.........	pound,	50
Wax.................	arroba,	1 00	Saddles	each,	6 00
Sperm candles......	dozen,	2 00	Hats................	"	2 50
Bridles or bits......	"	1 50	Hat-bodies	"	2 00
Matches	gross,	2 00	Shoes for women...	dozen,	1 50
Saddle-frames	each,	2 00	" men......	"	3 00

There is no transit duty through Peru. The custom-house charges amount to about two per cent. The higher duties by Arica are for the purpose of encouraging commerce through the port of Cobija. All the foregoing duties took effect in November, 1849. On the 26th of June,

1854, five per cent. ad valorem was added to the rates by Cobija. All the ad valorem duties are on the value of goods at Pacific ports. Duties on all goods by Cobija are adjusted and paid there, for which bonds are received, payable one half in 30 and the other in 120 days. Payment may be made two thirds in the small coin and the other third in government scrip, issued for a contingent reserve from salaries, worth from 25 to 50 per cent. The duties on all goods by Arica for La Paz are adjusted and paid at La Paz, and those for all other points at Oruro.

CHILI.

This republic extends along the Pacific coast from latitude 24° to 56° south, varying in breadth from 80 to 130 miles. The Pacific Ocean forms its western and southern boundaries, Bolivia its northern, and the Andes its eastern, embracing (according to Lieut. Gilliss, U. S. N.) an area of 146,300 square miles. Population, by the census of 1857, 1,468,448, besides the tribes of independent Indians, estimated at 25,000 or 30,000.

Chili is divided into thirteen provinces and three colonies, named in the order of their situation from north to south, as follows:

Atacama...............Pop.	55,567	Nuble.....................Pop.	110,219
Coquimbo............... "	119,991	Concepcion............... "	122,281
Aconcagua............... "	121,654	Araucania............... "	48,995
Santiago............... "	203,113	Valdivia............... "	31,983
Valparaiso............... "	124,600	Chiloe............... "	65,743
Colchagua............... "	206,919	Juan Fernandez Colony. "	136
Talca............... "	84,461	Llanquihue " "	3,826
Maule............... "	168,807	Magellanic " "	153
			1,468,448

The great Andean chain (which attains its maximum elevation in Chili) occupies quite two thirds of the surface of the republic. The two most northern provinces, Atacama and Coquimbo, are occupied by mountain ranges rich in mineral deposits, but mostly barren in their agricultural productions, and do not supply the necessities of one half of their limited population. But the remaining eleven provinces of the republic possess much fertile and cultivated land; besides raising enough for their own wants and supplying the northern deficiency, they export agricultural produce to the amount of over $2,250,000 annually. Santiago, Valparaiso, Colchagua, Nuble, Concepcion, and Chiloe comprise the chief agricultural districts. The principal grains raised are wheat, barley, oats, and maize; excellent potatoes are also produced. In the provinces of Aconcagua, Santiago, and Valparaiso fruits of both the temperate and tropical climates are abundant. Nuble, Concepcion, Valdivia, and Chiloe produce large quantities of valuable timber. In Aconcagua, Santiago, Colchagua, Maule, Nuble, Concepcion, and Araucania cattle-raising is extensively carried on.

Almost the whole extent of the Republic of Chili is rich in mineral productions, but the chief mining districts are in the provinces of Atacama and Coquimbo. The exports of gold, silver, and copper are estimated at over $15,000,000 per annum.

Coal of fair quality is abundant and extensively mined in the province of Concepcion. These mines were opened in 1840, at a heavy expense, by the Pacific Steam Navigation Company, and now produce over 300,000 tons annually.

The entire exports of the republic for the year 1857, which may be considered as the annual average, were as follows:

Bars of gold and gold coin...	$497,736	Butter and cheese...........	$36,055
Silver and silver ore.........	4,725,655	Tallow and lard..............	2,729
Copper and copper ore.....	10,760,589	Hides, horns, and hoofs....	501,104
Wheat........................	1,050,718	Goat, sheep, and chinchilla skins....................	40,861
Flour.........................	798,112		
Biscuit, bread, and frangolio.............................	108,223	Wool	397,643
		Assorted provisions	27,189
Barley.......................	257,970	Dried fodder.................	41,790
Beans	24,904	Cords, rope, and rigging..	18,464
Potatoes.....................	35,506	Planks and lumber..........	265,287
Wine and chicha.............	1,612	Coal	176,765
Nuts, dried and fresh fruits	89,052	Guano..:.....................	5,600
Salt beef.....................	10,880	Miscellaneous................	143,009
Jerked beef..................	104,178	Making a total of....	$20,121,626

The climate is equable and healthy. The interior is hotter than the coast. In the former, at the northern portion of the republic, the thermometer often rises to 90° and 95° in the shade during the summer months of January and February; on the latter, at the same season, it is seldom higher than 85°. North of the parallel of 27° it seldom or never rains, but heavy dews are frequent. In the central portion of the republic, during June, July, and August (the winter months of the southern hemisphere), occasional rains occur, and the thermometer falls as low as 49° Fahrenheit; and in December, January, and February it rises to about 90°. During these months no rain falls, but the night breezes from the sea render the temperature refreshing. The mean annual temperature at Santiago is 70°. From thence southward the mean temperature declines, and the humidity of the atmosphere increases, until, at the extreme southern portions, rains are frequent and severe at almost every season. Earthquakes are common.

The inhabitants of Chili are mostly descendants of the Spaniards, the aboriginal tribes, and admixtures of these. It is estimated that not more than one fourth are of pure Spanish blood. There is a small proportion of Negroes and Mulattoes. The foreign population was estimated in 1854 at 19,699, viz.: 11,324 natives of the Argentine Republic, 1934 English, 1929 Germans, 1650 French, 680 Americans, 915 Spaniards, 399 Italians, 168 Portuguese, 599 Peruvians, and 71 Chinese.

Agriculture and mining are the chief employments of the Chilenos. Manufactures of cotton, wool, glass, silk laces, fringes, gold and silver embroidery (wrought by hand), utensils and ornaments of gold and silver, copper utensils, leather, etc., are carried on to some extent, but do not form an important item in the resources of the country.

The Chilenos are more enterprising than the inhabitants of most of the South American states, and the haciendados, or planters, and merchants often accumulate large amounts of property. With the exception of those destined for the learned professions, they have generally but little education. Their educational system is, however, more efficient than any of the other South American states. There are in the republic 562 schools for males and 295 for females. The books are furnished by the government. There are two normal schools in a flourishing condition; a government university and theological seminary, a school of agriculture, a naval school under the direction of the minister of marine, and a military school under the care of the minister of war: these last are all at Santiago, the capital, where is also a government library of 22,000 volumes, founded by the Jesuits.

The established religion is Roman Catholic. While the public services of other denominations are not permitted, their private exercise is not interfered with.

The city of Santiago, situated 100 miles in the interior, southeast from Valparaiso, is the capital of the republic and seat of government. It occupies nearly seven square miles. It is regularly laid out into squares of 420 feet each way. Most of the houses are of one story, and built of sun-dried brick, plastered and whitewashed. Santiago possesses quite a number of fine public edifices, among which the Mint is the most extensive and imposing. Its architecture is of the Doric style, and covers about 400 square feet. It was built by the Spanish government at the close of the last century, and cost nearly a million of dollars. It has numerous churches, several extensive hospitals and alms-houses, and several institutes of learning, which have been already referred to. Connected by railway with the chief sea-port, Valparaiso, it is the chief mart for the interior commerce of the republic. Population about 90,000. An astronomical observatory was established at the city of Santiago by Lieut. Gilliss, U. S. N., under orders from the United States government, in 1851.

The ports of chief importance in Chili from north to south are as follows, viz.:

Caldera.—Here is a fine bay of nearly square form, about a mile across, with neither internal nor external dangers, and deep water. At the southeast quarter is a long pier, which serves for loading and discharging vessels. The exports are silver and copper. The Copiapo Railway, which was commenced in 1850 and completed in 1852, under the direction of Mr. William Wheelwright, connects Caldera with the city of Copiapo, fifty miles in the interior, since which time it has been run with great success, developing the wonderful mineral wealth of that region, and paying 16 per cent. dividends on its capital, which is equal to 20 per cent. on its cost. It overcomes 1300 feet elevation. Its chief business is bringing copper and silver ore to the coast, and carrying to the interior coal for smelting purposes, also provisions and building materials. In 1854 this railroad was extended to a point 24 miles in the interior, and 2195 feet above the sea. This extension, as well as the original line, was built and is still owned by a Chileno Company. In 1858 Walton W. Evans, Esq., of New York, constructed for an English company a branch line to this railway, 26 miles in length, terminating at Chanarcilla, one of the richest silver mining districts known. The summit is more than 1300 feet higher than any other summit in the world over which a locomotive has climbed, its elevation above the sea being 4467 English feet. Another branch to the Copiapo Railway is contemplated and has been surveyed; it is to connect Copiapo with the rich silver mining district of Tres-Puntas, in the desert of Atacama, and, if built, will give great activity to rich copper and gold mines in that region. It will be 54 miles in length, and terminate at a point 6400 feet above the level of the ocean.

Huasco is a port of entry, though scarcely more than an open roadstead. It exports copper and copper ore, and imports supplies for the mining population of this portion of the province of Atacama.

Coquimbo.—The business of this port is the same as Huasco. There is good shelter for vessels. A railway is in course of construction from the port to Serena, 8 or 9 miles in length; it is intended to extend this to a rich copper district, and terminate it at 30 or 40 miles from Coquimbo. Large quantities of rich copper ores are found in this region.

Tongoy, a small port for coasting trade, 30 miles south of Coquimbo. A railway has been surveyed from this port to the rich copper mines of Tamaya, and thence to Ovalle, a town in the interior, about 40 miles from the sea-coast. If built, this road will assist in developing one of the richest copper districts in the world. Señor Don Jose V. de Urmenita, of Chili, has a mine in this region which yields a net revenue of over $500,000 annually. The copper vein in this mine is about 15 feet thick, and yields ores from 30 to 70 percentum of pure metal.

Valparaiso.—This is the greatest port and city of the whole South Pacific coast. It is situated in latitude 33° 2'. The port is a semicircular bay about two miles in breadth, and open to the westward. Shelter is secure except in the winter months.

The great depth of water near the shore has thus far prevented the establishment of wharves for loading and discharging cargoes, and these operations are safely accomplished by means of launches, to and from which all packages are carried through the surf on men's shoulders. The harbor is well defended by several forts.

The city stands upon a steep declivity and in the ravines along its bay to the northward. It is mostly constructed of adobe or sun-dried bricks. It is well paved, but has few remarkable edifices. There is an English church, where the Episcopal service is performed every Sabbath; also a free Protestant chapel has been permitted. The hotels are numerous, but indifferent. There are two clubs, conducted after the English fashion. There is also one large theatre. The city is lighted with gas, and is supplied with good water from basins built on the eminences back of the town, and conveyed throughout the city in iron pipes; both these improvements are due to Mr. William Wheelwright, an American gentleman, whose name is identified with almost every important internal improvement which has been established in Chili for the last twenty years. Valparaiso monopolizes most of the foreign trade of Chili. Its direct imports in 1850 were $11,110,844, against the entire imports of the republic for that year, amounting to $11,500,968, or over $\frac{23}{24}$ths of its entire importing trade. There is a magnetic telegraph line connecting Valparaiso with Santiago, the capital and seat of government of the republic, 100 miles in the interior. There is also a railway in process of construction from Valparaiso to Santiago. Forty miles of this road (with the exception of one tunnel) has been completed and opened for travel; the remainder has progressed but slowly of late, on account of the difficulties attending its construction and the disturbed political state of the country. It is now in the hands of the government, and they propose to complete the whole line in three years, but this is very doubtful. The population of Valparaiso is about 45,000.

Constitucion, at the mouth of the River Maule, is the outlet of a rich and productive agricultural district. Population of the city between 4000 and 5000.

Tomé, a small port, with a business similar to Constitucion.

Talcahuano possesses a fine harbor, and is the entrepôt for the trade of a large and fertile surrounding district. The town is well built and flourishing. Population 5000. Extensive coal deposits exist in the vicinity of Talcahuano. It is proposed to connect Talcahuano with Concepcion, a city of considerable importance about 12 miles in the interior. Its business will be in passengers and general merchandise.

Coronel and *Lota*.—At these ports extensive deposits of coal exist, and form a large item of export. At Lota is a coaling depôt for the steam-ships of the Pacific Steam Navigation Company.

Valdivia is a secure harbor, formed by the estuary at the mouth of the river of the same name. The export trade here is in the agricultural products of the rich surrounding country. Lumber is largely exported. The city of Valdivia is 8 miles from the mouth of the river, which is navigable for large vessels to this point, and navigable for boats for 12 leagues farther. A colony of Germans have settled in this vicinity.

Ancud and Albuco, ports of the island and province of Chiloe, and Puerto Montt—these three are all small ports of export for lumber and provisions.

The ships of the Pacific Steam Navigation Company touch at all the above-mentioned ports (see Itinerary, page 215, et seq.).

The imports of Chili consist chiefly of distilled spirits, ale and porter, alpaca goods, baizes, bedsteads, books, buttons, cabinet-ware, calicoes, candles, canvas, carpets, carriages, cassimeres, cigars, clothing, cotton and woolen goods, crape shawls, drugs, earthen and glass ware, gloves, gold in bars and coin, gunpowder, horned cattle and horses, household furniture, indigo, iron and iron goods, jewelry and cutlery, leather, linen goods, machinery, matches, maté, merino cloths, muslins, molasses, oils, paints, paper, perfumery, pianos, quicksilver, raisins, rice, rigging, salt, satin goods, shoes and boots, silks, silver coin and bars, soap, steel, straw goods, sugar, tea, tobacco, umbrellas and parasols, velvets, watches, wax, wines, and wool shawls. Among the countries furnishing these goods, England holds commercially the first rank, France the second, United States the third. Germany, Switzerland, Belgium, Spain, Central America, Peru, and Bolivia also export to Chili certain of their manufactures and productions. Previous to the establishment of the Panama Railway the European trade with Peru was all carried on around Cape Horn, but since the completion of that road in 1855 large amounts of the most valuable goods have been sent by the direct route to the port of Aspinwall, and across the Isthmus by the Panama Railway, and from thence, by the steamers of the Pacific Steam Navigation Company, to the ports of Peru. The transportation by this route to South America for European goods, as well as American, is steadily and rapidly increasing.

Tariff of Chili on Articles received from the United States.

Denomination of Merchandise.	Number, Weight, or Measure.	Rate of Duty.	Percentage, Duty on fixed Value.
Beef...........................	quintal (101 lbs.)	$7 00	free.
Beer, ale, porter, in bottles	dozen, specific duty,	1 00	
" " in casks..	gallon, "	0 25	
Brandy in bottles...........	dozen, "	3 00	
" in casks............	gallon, "	1 00	
Cables and cordage.........		valuation,	$0 25
Candles, wax...............	1.014 lb.	$0 50	0 25
" tallow............	101 lbs.	16 00	0 25
" spermaceti.......	1.014 lb.	0 40	0 25
Cheese of all kinds.........	"	0 18¾	0 25
Cider in bottles.............	same as beer.		
" in casks...............	"		
Codfish.......................	101 lbs.	6 00	0 25
Copper, manufactures of..	1.014 lb.	0 40	0 25
" in bars.............	101 lbs.	13 00	0 25
Cotton, raw.................	101 lbs., picked,	8 00	0 25
" manufactures of...	1 lb.	0 37½	0 25
Flour, wheat................	quintal, if price is under $4,		0 25

Denomination of Merchandise.	Number, Weight, or Measure.	Rate of Duty.	Percentage, Duty on fixed Value.
Glass, window	100 superficial feet,	$3 00	$0 25
Hams and bacon	1.014 lb.	0 14	0 25
Hats, straw		valuation,	0 25
Household furniture		"	0 25
Indian corn	fanega, if price is under $3,		0 25
" "	" " over $3,		free.
Lard	1.014 lb.	$0 12½	0 25
Lead in bars and sheets			free.
" manufactures of	101 lbs.	6 00	
Nails, iron	1.014 lb.	8 to 12½c.	
Paints	101 lbs.	$6 00	0 25
Paper, writing		valuation,	0 25
" printing		"	0 25
Pitch	101 lbs.	$2 00	free.
Pork	"	8 00	"
Rice	Carolina, 101 lbs.	5 50	0 25
Rosin	101 lbs.	2 00	free.
Shoes, boots, and leather.	dozen, for men, calf-skin,	18 00	0 15
Soap, common	101 lbs.	6 00	0 25
" perfumed	1.014 lb.	0 40	0 25
Sugar, refined	arroba of 25 lbs. 7 oz.	2 00	0 25
Tallow	101 lbs. (raw)	7 00	0 06
Tar	"	2 00	free.
Teas	pound, specific duty,	0 25	
Tobacco, unmanufactured	monopoly.		
" cigars	per pound,	0 75	
Umbrellas, silk	each,	2 50	0 25
" cotton	dozen,	6 50	0 25
Wax, raw, white	101 lbs.	0 50	0 25
" yellow	"	0 50	0 25
Wines, red	gallon, specific duty,	0 25	
" white	" "	0 37½	
Wood, boards, pine	1000 feet,	35 00	free.

PORT CHARGES.

The port charges of Chili are as follows: Tonnage dues, 25 cents per ton; light dues (where light-houses exist), 3⅛ cents per ton; captain of the port's fees, $4; harbor-master's fees, $8. National or foreign vessels of war, national or foreign steamers, whale-ships, vessels in distress or in ballast, or discharging under twenty packages, are exempt from tonnage and light dues. When tonnage dues have been paid at one port, they are not levied in another.

MEXICO.

THE chief and almost the sole communication between the Pacific coast of this country and the Panama Railroad is by the vessels of the Pacific Mail Steam-ship Company and the steamers of Flint and Holliday's Oregon and California Line.* Occasional British men-of-war, however, bring shipments of silver from the Mexican Pacific coast to Panama for transportation over the railroad for English ports.

Acapulco, the first Mexican port of entry of the Pacific Mail Steam-ship Company's steamers on their upward voyage, is situated in latitude 16° 55' north, 1440 miles from Panama. Its harbor is one of the finest on the whole Pacific coast. The Pacific Mail Steam-ship Company have established an agency there, and a depôt for coals, from which their vessels are supplied on their upward and downward voyages; they also take in occasional supplies of fresh provisions at that port.

Although the State of Guerrero, in which the port of Acapulco is situated, is rich in mineral resources, possessing extensive deposits of silver, gold, and copper, and a soil and climate capable of raising the tropical staples in abundance, its commerce has for many years been very small. Its exports of silver for the year 1860, by the Pacific Mail Steam-ship Company's steamers, amounted to a little more than $200,000, chiefly the returns from foreign

---

* The offices of this Company are at No. 35 William St., New York, and 407 Washington Street, San Francisco.

goods for Acapulco and the interior. In 1856 the legal returns of specie exported from the port of Acapulco amounted only to $32,485. Recently, however, the government roads from Acapulco to the city of Mexico have been reopened, and regular weekly communication established with the city of Mexico, which has given a fresh impetus to trade at this port. Population of Acapulco about 4000.

About 325 miles to the northeast from Acapulco is the port of Manzanilla, situated in the State of Colima, and is the port of export and import for a wide extent of rich mining country in the interior. The city of Colima, the capital of the state, 28 leagues in the interior, is a flourishing city, containing about 32,000 inhabitants. The exportation of silver from Manzanilla previous to the year 1860, according to the custom-house records of that port, amounted to about $500,000 per annum; but recently, on account of the difficulty and danger attending transportation of goods and treasure to the Gulf ports, *via* the capital, from the adjoining states Jalisco and Michoacan, a large portion of their trade has been carried on through the port of Manzanilla, and the exports of silver have increased to over four millions of dollars for the year 1860, with a prospect of much greater increase for the present year, 1861. Silver, the chief export of the Pacific ports of Mexico, is the only export at Manzanilla; this is shipped on the vessels of the Pacific Mail Steam-ship Company, which touch there on their downward voyages, for Panama. From Panama it goes to Aspinwall by the Panama Railroad, and from thence to England by the British West India Mail Line.

The remaining Pacific ports of Mexico—San Blas, in the State of Jalisco, 228 miles northeast from Manzanilla; Mazatlan, in the State of Sinaloa, 140 miles northeast from San Blas; Guaymas, in the State of Sonora, 400 miles northeast of Mazatlan; and Cape St. Lucas, 220 miles southwest from Guaymas, and 1066 miles from San Francisco, are touched at by the steamers of the San Francisco and Oregon Line, and will connect with the Pacific Mail Company's steamers at Manzanilla. Correct commercial data of these ports are not at present attainable. The British government keeps constantly on the coast of Mexico a ship of war, which receives from mercantile houses at the various ports above mentioned (brought from the mining districts of the interior) silver in coin and bars, varying in amount from three to six millions of dollars per annum, which is taken to the port of Panama for transportation over the Panama Railroad to Aspinwall, and from thence to England by the ships of the British West India Mail Line. All this treasure is consigned to the Bank of England. So soon as the recently organized line from San Francisco to these Mexican ports shall have become thoroughly established, it is expected that a large portion, if not the entire amount, of this treasure will find its way to the port of Manzanilla for reshipment to Panama by the Pacific Mail Steam-ship Company's steamers.

The merchandise for the Pacific Mexican ports has, until very recently, reached them chiefly from England *via* Cape Horn; but large amounts of goods have, during the past year, been received at the port of Aspinwall by the Panama Railroad's line of sailing vessels from New York, and by Holt's propeller line from England, and transported over the road for shipment by the Pacific Mail Steam-ship Company's steamers, and this trade is rapidly increasing.

Through bills of lading are now issued at the office of the Panama Railroad Company in New York for goods from thence to the Mexican ports of Acapulco and Manzanilla at rates varying from $50 to $60 per ton of forty feet.

The Pacific Mail Steam-ship Company's steamers now stop at the port of Manzanilla monthly, on their upward and downward voyages, leaving New York and San Francisco on the 11th, and arriving at Manzanilla about the 28th of each month.

PASSENGER REGULATIONS AT THE MEXICAN PORTS.

"Every passenger arriving at the ports of the republic shall be free to land without passport or letter of security, and shall be at liberty to take ashore a small bundle of wearing apparel.

"Every passenger can enter free of duty ten pounds of cigars or cigarettes, one bottle of snuff, two bottles of wine or liqueur, two watches, with their chains and seals, one pair of pistols, one sword, one rifle, musket, or carbine, and a pair of musical instruments, except pianos or organs.

"Passengers are prohibited the introduction with their luggage of goods by the piece, jewelry, gold or silver wrought, unless of personal wear, or of any other commercial commodity specified in this ordinance; but should they, through ignorance or as presents, bring in small quantities of any of these articles, by making, before the commencement of the examination, a declaration on oath of the fact, the officer of the customs shall appraise the articles, and collect corresponding duties.

"The dispatch of private apparel and jewelry is at the discrimination of the custom-house officers, with due regard for the character and personality of travelers.

"Operatic or comic artists shall be permitted, besides the exemptions already conceded to passengers, to introduce free of duty their scenic costumes and ornaments, provided the same make a part of their luggage and be not excessive. Should the officers consider the amount in excess, they shall collect 30 per cent. ad valorem, or by appraisement, to be practiced in the manner prescribed for goods entered under appraisement. The supreme government will ordain what is convenient as regards the privileges and exemptions to be extended to emigrants or colonists."

MEXICO.

Currency of Mexico.

1 onza........gold.........	=	$16 00
1 peso.........silver........	=	1 00
1 real.......... "	=	0 12½
1 medio real. "	=	0 06¼
1 quartillo....copper.......	=	0 03⅛
1 tlaco........ "	=	0 01 2/16

Weights.

1 onza....................	=	1 ounce.
1 marco..................	=	½ lb.
1 libra.....................	=	1 lb.
1 arroba..................	=	25 lbs.
1 quintal................	=	100 lbs.
1 carga...................	=	300 lbs.
1 fanega.................	=	2 bushels.

Measures.

1 foot....,..=0.928 feet English.
1 vara...=2.784 "
1 legua=5000 varas ....=2.636 miles.

CALIFORNIA, OREGON, VANCOUVER, WASHINGTON TERRITORY, ETC.

The port of San Francisco, California, the great commercial entrepôt of the United States possessions on the Pacific, is situated in the Bay of San Francisco, in latitude 37° 47′ 35″ north, and 122° 26′ 15″ west longitude. Its harbor is one of the best of the Pacific Ocean. Through the port of San Francisco nearly all the foreign trade of California, Oregon, Washington Territory, and the British possessions is carried on.

The city of San Francisco, situated on the eastern slope of the ridge which divides the Bay of San Francisco from the Pacific Ocean, is handsomely laid out and well built, containing many fine public edifices and private dwellings of brick and stone, and is the centre of the wealth and commerce of the Northern Pacific coast. Population 80,000.

The great mineral resources of the State of California, the fertility and productiveness of its soil, its varied and delightful climate, are so familiar to the world that it is not thought worth while to give in this place more than such a brief summary of its commercial transactions as will enable the reader to form an estimate of their influence upon the great channels of steam communication between the Pacific coast and the United States, the resources of which it is the particular object of this volume to set forth.

EXPORTS.*

The great staple product of California is gold; but the recent discoveries of vast deposits of silver on the eastern slope of the Sierra Nevada Mountains at Washoe it is thought will, in time, make the exports of this metal rival the gold in commercial importance.

Quicksilver is also largely exported.

Next in importance among the exportable commodities of the state are hides, wool, and grain. The entire product of hides and wool go to the New York market. The grain, consisting of wheat, barley, and oats, have for the last five years found a market in New York, the west coast of South America, the East Indies, China, Australia, and the Pacific Islands.

Wool is a large and growing article of export. The exports of this article in 1856 amounted to 600,000 pounds; in 1860 the amount was 2,981,000 pounds.

The exports of gold from the port of San Francisco since its discovery in 1848, according to Custom-house manifests, were as follows:

Year.	Shipments to all Quarters.	Shipments to New York.	Rec'ts at U. S. Mint and its Branches.	Estimated Yield of California Mines.
1848	....	....	....	$ 60,000
1849	$ 4,921,250	....	$ 5,232,249	8,000,000
1850	27,676,346	....	28,206,226	33,000,000
1851	45,582,695	....	57,138,980	55,000,000
1852	46,586,134	....	51,470,675	57,000,000
1853	57,331,024	$47,916,448	62,838,395	69,000,000
1854	51,328,653	46,289,649	46,719,083	64,000,000
1855	43,080,211	38,730,564	47,419,945	65,000,000
1856	48,887,543	39,765,294	56,379,901	70,000,000
1857	48,592,743	35,287,778	55,217,843	70,000,000
1858	47,548,025	35,578,236	51,494,311	70,000,000
1859	47,640,463	39,831,937	52,000,000	70,000,000
1860	42,325,916	35,661,500	27,037,919	70,000,000

* The commercial statistics of California are taken, by permission, from advance sheets of the Annual Report of the New York Chamber of Commerce for 1861.

Statement of Amounts and Destination of Treasure exported from San Francisco during the Year 1860.

To New York.		Exported to	
In January	$3,360,296 25	New York	$35,661,500 37
" February	3,126,183 77	New Orleans	57,795 93
" March	2,177,395 67	England	2,672,936 20
" April	2,692,728 88	China	3,374,680 27
" May	2,905,028 40	Japan	94,200 00
" June	3,709,755 01	Manilla	75,659 94
" July	1,969,435 05	Panama	300,819 00
" August	2,502,070 47	Sandwich Islands	40,679 57
" September	3,157,303 59	Mexico	19,400 00
" October	2,958,784 19	Costa Rica	3,145 00
" November	2,982,704 78	Vancouver Island	25,100 00
" December	4,119,814 31	Total	$42,325,916 28
	$35,661,500 37		

Exports of Silver.—The exports of silver ore during the year 1860, according to the San Francisco Custom-house records, were of the value of $416,613. This is, however, no guide as to what the ores yielded. In addition to the ores exported, several hundred tons were smelted at two establishments in San Francisco, yielding about $150,000. When it is considered that the Washoe mining district was a howling wilderness at the commencement of 1860, and that every necessary of life, even the material for habitations, had to be transported across the Sierra Nevada on the backs of mules, it must be conceded that vast progress has been made in opening the mines, and, without doubt, their product this year (1861) will ascend to millions.

Exports of Quicksilver.

Years.	To New York. Flasks.	To other Countries. Flasks.	Years.	To New York. Flasks.	To other Countries. Flasks.
1853	......	18,800	1857	8,374	18,888
1854	......	20,963	1858	3,559	20,573
1855	......	27,165	1859	250	3,149
1856	1,500	22,240	1860	400	8,948
Total				14,083	140,726

From the above it appears that the total amount of quicksilver exported from the state during the past eight years was 154,809 flasks; there was consumed within the state, during the same period, 16,000 flasks, making a total production (almost entirely from the New Almaden mine) of 170,809 flasks of 75 pounds each. The price ranged from 1853 to 1860 from 75 to 50 cents per pound.

Table of Exports of leading Articles of California Produce to New York for the last five Years.

Articles.	1856.	1857.	1858.	1859.	1860.
Barley, 84-lb. sacks.......	....	97,675	51,103	97,947	16,510
Hides, number	132,032	170,447	142,399	151,364	200,116
Quicksilver, flasks	2,414	8,374	3,559	250	400
Skins, bales................	1,506	798	876	975	939
" number..........	9,313	26,363	8,812	....	2,874
Salmon, barrels............	256	212	906	250	1,112
Tallow, packages	3	826	194	888	518
Wool, lbs..................	600,000	1,100,000	1,428,351	2,378,250	2,981,000
Wheat, 100-lb. sacks	....	....	....	12,054	203,528

Exhibit of the Exports of a few leading Articles of California Produce to all Countries in 1860.

Barley, 84-lb. sacks	136,916	Oats, 55-lb. bags..............	76,590
Beans, 50-lb. "	1,397	Potatoes, 110-lb. bags........	34,161
Flour, barrels	121,688	Skins, packages...............	580
Hides, number..................	200,116	Tallow, packages	2,181
Hay, bales......................	9,637	Wheat, 100-lb. sacks.........	1,135,098
Lumber, M. feet................	3,976	Wool, lbs......................	3,060,000

The value of the exports of California, other than treasure, during the last five years, has been as follows:

1856....................	$4,270,260	1859...........................	$5,533,411
1857....................	4,369,758	1860...........................	8,532,489
1858....................	4,770,163		

IMPORTS.

The following statement of the tonnage arriving at San Francisco from Atlantic ports, from 1856 to 1861, will show the extent of the imports from that quarter for a series of years. The statement exhibits, 1st, the number of vessels; 2d, the aggregate registered tonnage; 3d, estimated tons of cargo at sixty per cent. over register; 4th, total amount of freight moneys paid in each year:

Where from.	No. of Vessels.	Registered Tonnage.	Tons of Cargo.	Amount of Freight paid.
1856: New York	79	103,532	165,652	$2,167,045
Boston	37	42,200	64,320	924,957
Other ports	7	5,602	8,963	144,867
Total for 1856	123	151,334	238,935	$3,236,869
1857: New York	61	74,402	119,043	$1,309,244
Boston	28	33,802	54,083	469,798
Philadelphia	1	1,219	1,950	22,390
Total for 1857	90	109,423	175,076	$1,801,432
1858: New York	66	77,882	124,611	$1,503,955
Boston	34	32,166	51,370	607,329
Other ports	5	4,345	6,952	68,919
Total for 1858	105	114,393	182,933	$2,180,203
1859: New York	90	107,276	171,641	$2,107,924
Boston	43	44,799	71,678	892,704
Other ports	8	5,001	8,002	92,582
Total for 1859	141	157,076	251,321	$3,093,210
1860: New York	76	93,240	149,184	$1,777,802
Boston	30	30,661	49,057	624,396
Other ports	9	6,341	10,145	82,988
Total for 1860	115	130,242	208,386	$2,485,186

The bulk of the imports of California come from the United States in sailing vessels *via* Cape Horn, but large quantities of light goods and provisions are sent *via* the Isthmus of Panama. The total value of shipments per steamers, and *via* the Panama Railroad, in 1860, according to Custom-house records, was but little short of eight millions of dollars.

The following figures exhibit the passenger movement of the port of San Francisco since 1856:

Arrivals.	1857.	1858.	1859.	1860.
From Panama	17,637	....	26,907	20,092
" other countries	6,963	40,739	11,276	10,619
Total arrivals	24,600	40,739	38,183	30,711
Departures.				
For Panama	12,367	27,994	19,030	10,084
" other countries	4,584	....	5,751	4,492
Total departures	16,951	27,994	24,781	14,576

On the 5th of March, 1860, the rates of fare were reduced, and a tri-monthly communication *via* Panama was established, instead of the previous semi-monthly trips, which accounts for the great increase of the inward passenger traffic for the year 1860.

OREGON, WASHINGTON TERRITORY, VANCOUVER ISLAND, AND BRITISH COLUMBIA.

THE commerce of this region, which is almost entirely carried on through the port of San Francisco, California, is yet in its infancy. Oregon, with an area of about 80,000 square miles, and possessing on its Pacific coast broad and fertile valley-lands, rich in agricultural resources, has as yet but about 50,000 inhabitants; the tide of emigration from the Western United States is, however, going on with vigor, and the time is probably not far distant when its population will be sufficient to develop an important exporting trade. Already large quantities of grain, lumber, etc., are exported to California. Cattle, fresh and dried fruits, salmon, eggs, butter, lard, hams, etc., are also becoming noticeable articles of export. Deposits of coal, iron, copper, and gold have been found in Oregon. Washington Territory, joining Oregon on the north, has an area of 113,821 square miles. Its white population in 1854 was only about 5000. Since that time it has been slowly but steadily increasing. It possesses much land well adapted to agriculture and grazing. It abounds with fine timber, and its rivers with excellent fish, which at present form its chief exports. Joining it on the north, at the parallel of 49°, is British Columbia, covering an area of about 200,000 square miles. This is also a country of great agricultural promise, and possesses a vast wealth in its salmon fisheries, its forests of fine timber, and its rich deposits of coal and gold; the latter, mined from the vicinity of Frazer River, has been exported to a considerable extent since its discovery in 1856.

SEA-PORTS.

The sea-ports of Oregon, Washington Territory, and the British possessions which have direct communication with San Francisco by the California and Oregon Line of Steamships are as follows, viz.: in Oregon,

Eureka, the most southern port of entry in Oregon, distant 238 miles northeast from San Francisco, is situated in Humboldt Bay, a deep and narrow indentation of the coast, with a dangerous shifting sand-bar at its entrance. The town of Eureka is about four miles to the north side of the entrance of the bay. There is a United States government fortification here, and an Indian reservation in the vicinity. It is a thriving town, and has a large lumber-trade with San Francisco.

Trinidad, 28 miles north from Eureka, is situated in a small bay protected only from the northeast winds. The town contains but few inhabitants. The chief export is lumber. The land in this vicinity is rich, and well adapted to agriculture. There is gold in the neighborhood.

Crescent City, 43 miles northward from Trinidad, on Crescent City Bay, is one of the most dangerous roadsteads on the whole coast. The town of Crescent City is the depôt for the supplies of miners working the gold diggings on the Kalmath, Trinity, and Salmon Rivers, in the interior; it is also the centre of a large and rich agricultural district. It contains about 1500 inhabitants.

Port Orford, 70 miles from Crescent City, is a good roadstead. A large lumber-trade is carried on here. A much-esteemed variety of the white cedar abounds in this vicinity, and is exported in considerable quantities under the name of the Port Orford cedar.

Gardiner City, 75 miles to the northward from Port Orford, is on the Umpqua River, five miles from its mouth.

A United States custom-house is located here, besides which there is only a small wharf and one house. A steam-boat runs from Gardiner City to Scottsburg, a town of 1000 inhabitants, fifteen miles farther up the river.

Astoria, 88 miles from Gardiner City, is the most northern port of Oregon. It is situated on the Columbia River (which separates Oregon from Washington Territory), nine miles from its mouth. The river at Astoria is between three and four miles in width. Population of Astoria 800. There is a dangerous bar at the mouth of the Columbia River which interferes greatly with its commercial growth.

Portland, the chief sea-port and chief town of Oregon, is situated on the Willamette River, a branch of the Columbia, 100 miles from Astoria. Population 2700. It is the centre of a rich and well-cultivated agricultural region. Large numbers of cattle are exported from Portland to Vancouver's Island. About forty miles south of Portland, on the Willamette, is Salem, the capital of Oregon. Population 1500.

The next port of entry northward is *Esquimault*, on the British island of Vancouver, 270 miles from Portland. Here is said to be one of the finest harbors on the Pacific coast. The neighboring country is very fertile. The fisheries in this section are extensive. Lumber is of excellent quality and abundant. There is a British naval station at Esquimault, and it is the rendezvous for the small steamers running on Frazer River.

Port Townsend, 85 miles from Esquimault, the most southern port of entry in Washington Territory, is favorably situated at the termination of the Straits of Fuca, at the outlet of the waters of Admiralty Inlet, Puget's Sound. The town contains about 500 inhabitants. A military post has been established two and a half miles from this place. In the vicinity of the town are some good farms. The principal export is lumber.

Olympia, 80 miles from Port Townsend, is situated at the head of a deep inlet six miles long by three quarters of a mile wide. It is a thriving town, and the capital of Washington Territory. Its principal business is in agricultural products and lumber. The total distance made by the vessels of the California and Oregon Steam-ship Company on their route from San Francisco to Olympia, the northern terminus of the route, is 1022 miles.

THE END.

www.ingramcontent.com/pod-product-compliance
Lightning Source LLC
Chambersburg PA
CBHW022021240426
43667CB00042B/1039